Medusa's Mirrors

Medusa's Mirrors

Spenser, Shakespeare, Milton,
and the Metamorphosis
of the Female Self

Julia M. Walker

DELAWARE

Newark: University of Delaware Press
London: Associated University Presses

Associated University Presses
440 Forsgate Drive
Cranbury, NJ 08512

Associated University Presses
16 Barter Street
London WC1A 2AH, England

Associated University Presses
P.O. Box 338, Port Credit
Mississauga, Ontario
Canada L5G 4L8

The paper used in this publication meets the requirements
of the American National Standard for Permanence of Paper
for Printed Library Materials Z39.48–1984.

Library of Congress Cataloging-in-Publication Data

Walker, Julia M., 1951–
    Medusa's mirrors : Spenser, Shakespeare, Milton, and the
metamorphosis of the female self / Julia M. Walker.
        p.   cm.
    Includes bibliographical references and index.
    ISBN 0-87413-625-3 (alk. paper)
    1. English literature—Early modern, 1500–1700—History and
criticism.   2. Women and literature—England—History—16th century
3. Women and literature—England—History—17th century.
4. Spenser, Edmund, 1552?–1599—Characters   Women.   5. Shakespeare,
William, 1564–1616—Characters—Women.   6. Milton, John, 1608–1674—
Characters—Women.   7. Femininity (Psychology) in literature.
8. Metamorphosis in literature.   9. Renaissance—England.   10. Women
in literature.   11. Self in literature.   I. Title.
PR429.W64W35   1998
820.9′352042—dc21
                                                                97-35455
                                                                CIP

PRINTED IN THE UNITED STATES OF AMERICA

for TPR
"no good deed . . . ."

Contents

Acknowledgments

Oɴᴇ of the great things about our profession is that, as time goes by, teachers become friends and friends become teachers. My first thanks must go to four wonderful friends who have taught me widely and variously: D. Allen Carroll, Michael Lieb, Carol Thomas Neely, and Thomas P. Roche Jr.

Since I got the idea for this book a decade ago—while sharing a summer on the back porch of a two-hundred-year-old house in Princeton with two other women (we styled ourselves as the Three Fates: I was Atropos) and a vast number of visitors—many people have helped me bring the disparate pieces of Medusa's mirrors into a well-reflected whole. I am both lucky and grateful to have the help and support of Bill Cook, Laura Doan, Celia Easton, Sheila ffolliott, Marshall Grossman, Achsah Guibbory, Ron Herzman, Tom Hester, Anne D. Lutkus, Mary Ann Radzinowicz, John Shawcross, Anne Shaver, Susanne Woods, and Mary Ellen Zuckerman. Anne Clark Bartlett—who has moved much faster than this project has—was my undergraduate research assistant for the Milton chapter and is now an esteemed and scholarly colleague. Lauren Silberman spent a big chunk of her over-scheduled time reading the manuscript and making very enlightening, valuable, and stringent suggestions. Stella Perse Revard offered both depression-averting tales of publishing, as well as some Latin and more Greek. And right from the beginning, Anne Lake Prescott, who truly and frighteningly may know *everything*, generously showered me with mirror references in primary and secondary texts. Gail English and Marie Henry have gone far beyond the call of secretaries at all stages of this project; the SUNY Geneseo English Department could not exist (let alone function) without Marie Henry, and I would not exist without the *esprit de corps* of that department.

While working on this project, I have received grants from SUNY Geneseo, New York State UUP, Brown University, the Newberry Library, the American Council of Learned Societies, NEH, and the British Academy. Thanking places is an activity too often neglected; so in addition to the Village of Geneseo and the underpaid Utopia of SUNY Geneseo,

I want to acknowledge the cosmic debts I owe to the late, beloved Crosby Hall, to London House of the London Goodenough Trust, and to Via delle Donzelle 12, Siena.

Here in Geneseo, so much depends upon the devotion of my springer spaniel, Rosemond Tuve. And goodnight Freddie, wherever you are.

introduction:
the metamorphosis of terminology

THE question of selfhood in Renaissance texts presently constitutes a scholarly and critical debate of almost unmanageable proportions. Because the grounds for discussion are so broad, I want to carefully define the corner of the field in which I will be working. Whether a writer's sense of self in the 1590s was significantly different from a writer's sense of self in 1300 or how different either might be from the self conceptualized by a writer in 1990 is an argument impossible to settle definitively, although the debate over this issue has generated much heat and some light. The same might be said of all of these writers' attempts at constructing selfhood in and for their characters. Gender—the writer and the character's gender—adds yet another layer of complexity to the issue. The scholar who argues for a sense of interior selfhood in male Renaissance writers, however, can also advance the premise that a male writer cannot perceive and construct the selfhood of a female character with the same assurance that he crafts male interiority. It is this element of the constructed self that interests me, not the face and figure and scripted speech of an imagined woman, but the mind and emotions and perceptions behind those surfaces—mind and emotions and perceptions that constitute a selfhood constructed as interior, as private, as both conscious and subconscious. I will argue that male Renaissance writers—specifically Spenser, Shakespeare, and Milton—did attempt to construct interior selfhood, to construct the rough equivalents of our concepts of conscious and subconscious thoughts and actions for the powerful women in their texts. That is not to say that I find their attempts entirely successful or convincing, but I do believe that the evidence of the imaginative struggle we find in the representations of Britomart, Cleopatra, and Eve can tell us much about both the concept of selfhood and the issue of gender identity in the Renaissance.

Is it possible to argue for the existence of a constructed subconscious interior self in Renaissance texts? Certainly not if the argument depends upon finding that vocabulary in the texts of Renaissance writers. But

11

when Hamlet, as he glosses the Mousetrap for the court, slips and says that the newly entered murderer is a "nephew to the king" not a "brother" as the parallel plot demands, surely we are being shown the triumph of an interior, unarticulated struggle to confront Claudius with Hamlet's own plans for regicide. Shakespeare would not have used the terms *selfhood* or *interiority* or *subconscious*, but they can be useful tools for us, if we don't make too many easy equations between the metapsy-chological context of contemporary scholarship and the concept of crea-tive imagination in the Renaissance. Within the same play we are given glimpses of the inner devices and desires of Claudius and of Polonius, but the surfaces only of Gertrude and Ophelia. For all the pathos of the latter's mad scene, we are given no chance to hear or to see what was in her mind when that branch broke. Any argument for interiority in Ophelia in relation to her death would be the product of the scholar's inference only, rather than a reading of her scripted lines or her re-ported actions. Hamlet, as Katharine Eisaman Maus has pointed out, calls our attention to the interior self when he claims "I have that within which passes show, / These but the trappings and the suits of woe."[1] That he handles his actions with such singularly disastrous effects sup-ports the argument that he fails to fully understand whatever it is that "passes show" within. Instead, Shakespeare shows us a character whose unacknowledged emotions are in conflict with his consciously articulated goals, a conflict so severe that it poisons his own life and the lives of an astounding number of other characters.

Whatever terminology Shakespeare might have used had he penned critical theory, what he constructs is the conflict between the conscious and subconscious in a complex interior self. The use of the verb "con-struct" implies a mode of representation that is both deliberate and complex. In critical discourse, "construct" is also used as a noun, again implying an identifiable mode of representation, while *representation* it-self has come to be the late twentieth-century critic's favored term for that which Philip Sidney called a figuring forth by the poet maker. The danger of using words such as "deliberate" and "complex construction," "conscious and subconscious interiority," "selfhood," and "representa-tion" resides chiefly in the fine line between acknowledging that a poetic imagination is at work and attributing to that imagination either the sort of intentionality that is unrecoverable or the sort of canonical status that the word "imagination" acquires in the Romantic period. Today, merely acknowledging that poetic imagination functions in imaginative literature of the Renaissance is ironically made difficult by both the ambitious assumptions of an earlier generation of critics and the poetic concerns of another period in English poetry. Maus addresses this problem forcefully:

> Some critics apparently minimize or underestimate the significance of conceptions of psychological interiority for the English Renaissance because they imagine that admitting such significance would necessitate embracing a naive essentialism about "human nature." This is not the case. Surely nineteenth- and twentieth-century convictions about subjectivity are indeed culturally specific phenomena, and we risk misconstruing the Renaissance *mentalité* if our criticism fails to take into account the immense cultural changes of the last four centuries.[2]

Acknowledging both the cultural changes of the last four centuries and ceding the further complexity of addressing an interiority that is imaginatively constructed (Maus very astutely grounds her argument in English legal practice before moving onto a discussion of *Othello*), I want to examine three major texts in which the writers construct elements of psychological interiority for their major female figures.

The premise upon which this study rests is that for a male Renaissance writer, the construct of an interior self was neither unnatural nor uncommon in his male characters. While this statement calls forth armies of critics, I have set those forces on the field of my first chapter. For the moment, however, the premise can be broadened to consider the construction of an interior female self by a male writer. This, I will argue, is a much more difficult task. As the three canonical writers included in this study work to construct complex female interiority, they all face a basic failure of cognition. *Imagination,* no matter how it is defined, must have some relationship to cognition. In Plato's divided line, the relationship is an inferior one, while poets and the scholars who study them have long elevated the term, sometimes to divine status. When the male poetic imagination attempts to represent female interiority, there is a basic failure of cognition. The male writer knows something of the male self insofar as he recognizes his own interiority. As he constructs his male characters, there is thus a sense of recognition. Today, with our hypersensitivity to gender identity, a writer's failure of cognition may be less great than it must have been in the Renaissance, a time when the shadows of Aristotle's and Galen's definitions of the differences between male and female were only beginning to fade. Current scholarship shows us that Renaissance thinking on gender identity was more sophisticated than we have easily supposed, but still, the suggestion that the genders were generally viewed as inherently and deeply different is not an argument that requires much ink in a study of the early modern

period. As Renaissance writers tried to construct complex but essentially
different interior selves for the powerful women in their texts, the element of recognition could not exist. Instead, we find each writer falling
back on a canonical construct of female identity and power. Actually,
falling back is probably the wrong term, implying as it does a conscious
decision or at least a failure to acknowledge that a decision needs to be
made. What we find in these male writers' constructions of powerful
women's selfhood is a very old paradigm of gender and power and
transformation. The pattern of reflected identity and power found in the
Medusa story is at the heart of Spenser's representation of Britomart, of
Shakespeare's character Cleopatra, and of Milton's construction of Eve.
The story itself is not the key issue here, rather it is the intellectual
equivalent of a genetic fingerprint that so clearly marks Ovid's tale of a
woman who seems to have power, but who actually has none except as
a result of the reflected vision of a man. In the second chapter of this
study, I tease out the relationships between the Medusa story and Ovid's
other great mirror narrative, the Narcissus story. Again, the stories
themselves are secondary to the patterns of knowing they evince. Knowing by reflection is not the same as recognition. In the chapter entitled
"The Chiasmus of Perception" I use those two Ovidian mirror stories
to illustrate the distinction between knowing by recognition and knowing
by reflection. This distinction is the key to my readings of the three
Renaissance texts and of the constructions of female interiority we find
within them.

That Spenser, Shakespeare, and Milton consciously incorporate mirrors and mirroring into their representations of powerful female interiority is very telling. But, while reading the texts in light of the paradigms
of those Ovidian mirror stories is useful, we find no simple answers to
a complex set of questions. After isolating the common topos of the
mirror as central to the representation of powerful women's sense of
self in three major texts, I not unnaturally hoped to offer this paradigm
as a sort of key to reading a cultural and poetic pattern of perception
and representation of empowerment, gender, and selfhood in early
modern English texts. But the representations of the female self in
Spenser's Britomart, in Shakespeare's Cleopatra, and in Milton's Eve are
so at odds with each other that any generalizations about female power,
female selfhood, and Renaissance writers would have to be so broad as
to be meaningless. On the other hand, although these three disparate
representations of powerful women figure selfhood very differently and
to very different ends, they do have two significant elements in common:
mirrors and transformations that diminish the power of the female self.

The mirror topos does not reveal a consciously articulated theory of representation; its significance resides in the fact that three authors with three very different views of women's identity and power, writing in three significantly different cultural and historical sets of circumstances, have turned to the construct of the mirror as a means of complexly representing both the power and the interior identity of their female figures' sense of self. This is what I mean when I speak of an intellectual fingerprint. These texts and the powerful women represented within them are marked by the cultural and intellectual changes of the Renaissance; but they are also marked with the fingerprint of a habit of thought more powerful than the changes of a mere century.

The power of Britomart, of Cleopatra, and of Eve—each is different, but each figure's power is linked to her sense of self, and both the power and the self are initially represented and ultimately diminished through strategies of mirroring. The common ground turns out to be not the Medusa story itself, but the paradigm of reflection as a strategy of containment rather than a consistent definition and representation of female selfhood. After examining the imaginative constructs implanted in minds formed by the various mutations of Ovid's two great mirror stories, those of Medusa and Narcissus, I devote a chapter to each of the powerful women in the texts of these three Renaissance writers. Unlike a number of recent studies of Renaissance representations of women, I have pushed this study on to include Milton's Eve, for while I believe that the figure of Elizabeth I was of central importance in forcing writers to come to terms with female power and identity, I do not believe that her historical immediacy explains everything about the problems of a male writer representing a powerful woman in early modern England. Both both Shakespeare's Cleopatra and Milton's Eve were constructed after Elizabeth's death, and yet it is in the *Faerie Queene* that the possibility of a powerful female self is most clearly set forth, only to be most openly challenged. Cleopatra's sense of self, multivalent throughout the play, is neither fully represented nor materially challenged until after her death, while Eve's sense of self is defined initially by its relation to Adam and the cosmos and ultimately by its absence—a sense of self constructed as at once possible and inaccessible even in an unfallen world. A further reason for including Milton in this study is the evidence that Eve gives that whatever social, political, religious, and imaginative upheavals may have been caused by the English Civil War or Revolution, the way in which a male writer strives to capture and represent the construct of female interiority was altered very little, if at all, in the early modern period. Gender construction in imaginative literature, when

viewed from this perspective, may be less socially mobile and more culturally absolute than many recent scholars have argued.

What I offer here, then, is neither a neat paradigm of gendered selfhood nor a chronologically ordered argument for the development of
the female self in Renaissance texts. Instead, I examine three attempts
both to construct and to control the female self; the common ground
of the transformative mirror will tell us something about the poetic
imaginations of the three authors, but the variations and discontinuities
we find can tell us even more about the problems of gender and power
and representation in the period we call the English Renaissance. That
female power was perceived as a problem is evident from both the history and the literature of the period. That three writers who claim to
be representing variously powerful women in their imaginative texts
should qualify or revoke those powers through the common paradigm
or metaphor of the mirror suggests a pattern of gendered representation that transcends canonical periodization. In the final pages of this
study, I turn to the insights of contemporary criticism on pornography
to make this point. Here the goal is not to apply necessarily anachronistic
perspectives to Renaissance texts, but rather to suggest that the historical
development of a strongly voiced and nearly canonical woman's cognition can itself be read as a reflection—a reversal, if you will—of the male
imagination evinced in these canonical texts. These twentieth-century
feminist critics cannot answer our questions about selfhood and gender
and power in Renaissance texts; indeed, they do not even mention the
topic. What their analyses of male constructs of female identity have to
offer us is the realization that the questions we ask about Renaissance
poetics have answers that reach beyond the walls of the academy and
beyond the historical limits of the English Renaissance.

Medusa's Mirrors

1

the construction and recognition
of a female self

RENAISSANCE PSYCHOHISTORICISM

W HEN John Milton has Adam say that as he sees Eve, he sees "my Self / Before me," what does Milton mean by "Self"? Certainly not the same thing he means when he has God speak to Eve of her reflection, saying "What there thou seest fair Creature is thyself" nor yet when he has God promise Adam that he will be given one who is "thy other self." When Antony tells Octavia "If I lose mine honor, / I lose myself," when after Actium he says "I have fled myself," and when he says of Cleopatra's supposed suicide that she "by her death our Caesar tells, / 'I am conqueror of myself,'" does Shakespeare use the term *self* to mean always the same thing? Spenser makes some clear distinction between meanings of selfhood as he describes Britomart looking into her father's magic mirror: "Where when she had espyde that mirrhour fayre, / Her selfe a while therein she vewd in vaine; . . . she gan again / Her to bethink of, that mot to her selfe pertaine." The self for which Britomart initially gazes in vain is merely a physical reflection. The self for which she then seeks information is a nonphysical identity. Her resulting vision is an attempt on the part of the poet to represent what we would now call the conflict of the conscious mind with the subconscious desire. But how did Spenser conceive of this interior struggle for self-knowledge? In this passage, as well as in the passages from Milton and Shakespeare, we are confronted with the problem of gauging and defining the interiority of self in Renaissance texts. Our own definitions of interiority are unhelpful, to say the least, in a discussion of Renaissance texts. As historicist critics rightly point out, our psycho-jargon must and cannot simply be anteriorized. Nevertheless, the line from Spenser shows us a Renaissance writer trying to make a distinction between modes of selfhood. It is an awkward attempt in book III, and although it becomes more controlled

19

in book V, it can in no way be taken as a pattern for such strategies of representation.

Can we say there is a pattern? Even a paradigm? Probably not, but there are significant instances of poetic representations of interiority. Katharine Eisaman Maus sets forth a strong argument for a sense of interiority in this period, tracing it first through discussions of evidence and the jury's knowledge in the legal system. Maus states: "Inwardness in the English Renaissance is almost always formulated in terms of a double spectatorship."[1] If no other form of spectatorship is possible, then God is the presumed observer.

> The difference between the inner and the outer man is a function of the difference between the limited, fallible human observer and the unlimited divine observer. . . . The work of interpretation is thus imagined as a process by which limited human spectatorship might approach divine omniscience.[2]

That the poet has long usurped the paradigm of the divine observer makes the transition to a discussion of imaginative literature a natural one. Indeed, the idea of interiority formulated through spectatorship is doubled when a writer constructs a character's interior self, for the spectatorship of the poet is a necessary prelude to spectatorship of the reader. Using three of the major works of three major Renaissance writers, I wish to explore these instances, and while making the argument that—as slippery as a definition of self may be in all Renaissance texts—there is a profound and significant difference between the interior self that male writers construct for male figures and the interior self that those same poets and playwrights construct for female figures.[3]

By locating my argument around the concept of selfhood in the Renaissance, I place myself in danger of being sucked into what has become—given the acceleration of time—virtually a Hundred Years War between factions of scholars and critics. As with all wars, the first cause of the pitched battle between historicist and psychoanalytic critics is as debatable as any other aspect of the dispute. Did it began with Stephen Greenblatt's pronouncement that "psychoanalysis is, in more than one sense, the end of the Renaissance"[4] or with Lisa Jardine's paper at the 1986 International Shakespeare Congress in West Berlin? Regardless of first causes, the conflict was soon defined—both historically and psychoanalytically—by Carol Thomas Neely's 1987 talk at the CUNY Graduate Center Conference (a talk in which she analyzed both her presence and presentation on the program—the only major woman speaker and the only major speaker to be given a moderator),[5] and escalated from MLA to MLA. As the Hundred Years War began over the inheritance of power, the place of women in paradigms of power, and the possession of turf, so has the current state of the academic marketplace flavored this supposedly literary dispute with baser considerations. That it has become an industry in its own right and that its discourse is now seen less as textual analysis than as the text itself is evinced by the clusters of essays in the spring 1990 issue of *New Literary History*[6] and in the March 1993 issue of *Modern Language Quarterly*.[7] Anyone wishing to study the debate from the perspective of ideology, gender, geography (the East coast/West coast split is a tempting topic for satire, if nothing else), or nationalism has more than enough material in these essays and their footnotes for a busy career as either a war correspondent or a diplomat. As for the combatants, they have come to sound less and less like people who might have sung on St. Crispin's Day and more often like people trying to justify My Lai. This study, however, is in no way a version of "once more into the breach. . . ."

I want to talk about texts, Renaissance texts which I believe will benefit from the insights provided by many of these critics, for strategists in both camps—when they turn their attention from each other to the texts themselves—have said much to illuminate our study of Renaissance literature.[8] In *Paradise Lost,* Adam smugly tells Raphael of his own creation, opening his narrative with the obviously rhetorical disclaimer "to tell how [it] began is hard." He then pours forth over three hundred facile lines of confident observation. While I would prefer to view my efforts to discuss the psychohistoricism debate as entirely dissimilar, I fear that the nature of the topic invites the level of criticism Raphael ultimately brings to bear on Adam. Perhaps I can save myself by making clear my limitations in the larger field of critical methodological conflict: I don't want to explain it, I don't want to take part in it, and I certainly don't think I can resolve it. I want to get past it. To argue for a constructed interior self in Renaissance texts is certainly to argue for a sense of an interior self in Renaissance writers. What sets me at some distance from the warring camps I mention above and list in my footnotes is that I would like, insofar as is possible, to step outside of the battle over terminology that generates so much sound, if relatively little light. In her chapter entitled "Psychoanalyzing Epic History," Elizabeth J. Bellamy argues that "psychoanalysis can serve as a useful interpretive tool for Renaissance studies, but only if, ironically, we *de*-contextualize it from unfair generalizations that it is . . . merely a bourgeois praxis that is of little value in elucidating the role of the subject in history."[9] Speaking of Stephen Greenblatt's much-cited essay, she suggests that his argument

"constitutes the paradigmatic new historicist move whereby psychic experience disappears in the gaps of the subject's dispersal in the discursive
formations of ideology."[10] Bellamy continues:

> Greenblatt's charge that psychoanalysis is "marginal"—and that it "can re-
> deem its belatedness only when it historicizes its own procedures"—can per-
> haps best be viewed as a microlevel reenactment of some of the current
> (non)receptions of psychoanalysis within the larger spectrum of post-Marxist
> cultural critique. Here, psychoanalysis (in either its clinical or its hermeneutic
> form) has for some time now been dismissed as a bourgeois praxis—perhaps,
> indeed, the last gasp of bourgeois, or even ironically Renaissance (or Burk-
> hardtian), humanism—perpetuating obsolete emphases on the importance of
> psychic history of the ego as an "object" of study.[11]

While I agree with the heart of Bellamy's argument, I would further
argue that her insistence on incorporating as much psychoanalytic and
poststructuralist jargon as a sentence will hold works against her own
goal; more to the point, such rhetorical strategies militate against Bellamy's own dismissal of Shoshana Felman's argument that "literature is
effaced by psychoanalysis and its ambitious 'desire for mastery.'"[12] Bellamy defends literature from Felman's "allegories of desire and mastery," only to subordinate it to her own display of extraliterary erudition.
If literature is in danger of being effaced in any of these theory-
enhanced discussions, I would suggest that the greater danger comes
from the political display of metacritical buzzwords. While sophisticated
ideology does of course require some specialized vocabulary, we cannot
suggest on the one hand that early modern notions of the self are variously and often awkwardly articulated while on the other hand feud
over which set of technical terminology best makes that point. Insofar
as it is possible, we must move beyond rhetoric to substance, move from
turf wars to ground our argument in the texts we wish to discuss.

Having implied that some sort of synthesis is not only possible, but
desirable, I might feel called upon to introduce one, had not Meredith
Anne Skura already so eloquently begun that task in her 1993 essay.
Skura insists that the heart of the issue lies not in "whether Freud's (or
Klein's or Lacan's or my) psychoanalysis is the product of a historically
determined culture (they all are)," but whether the general vocabulary
and principles of inquiry we have rather carelessly come to call psychoanalytic criticism is "useful in talking about early modern texts and subjects."[13] New Historians, of course, have long countered the implied
answer (yes, it is useful) with arguments about the concept of the self as
it had or—more to the point—had not developed in the Renaissance.

Skura skirts this deadlock with an admirable refusal to employ the jargon of either side: "historians should pay attention to inner reality, to the feelings and fantasies that distort judgment and perception, and to the irrational motives that complicated our expectation that people act out of rational self-interest."[14] As I will argue in my chapter on the *Faerie Queene*, however Spenser may have conceived of his own sense of self, he was obviously expecting his reader to pay close attention to the inner reality of a female figure who is told that she will marry a great knight but who searches for that future husband by telling people she wishes to find and punish him as a rapist. As Skura observes: "The biggest difficulty in transposing psychoanalysis through time, in fact, is not so much the historicity of its assumptions about the individual as its failure to theorize the individual's relation to his or her culture in any period, including our own."[15] The solution to this problem lies within texts—the literary texts we study and the varied texts of history. But which individual do we mean? The creator of Britomart or Britomart herself as a figure within a text written against the historical reality of the unmarried Elizabeth? Skura, too, raises this question, only to back away from it.

> The psychoanalyst's question, like the historian's, is precisely what past subjects were like. The way to collect material for an answer is not simply to look at everything that helped produce them—individual childhood experience along with pervasive social constructions—but to listen to patterns of repetition and inconsistency in their talk, in the texts. . . . For sixteenth-century subjects, no less than for ours or for Freud's, the royal road to subjectivity in any context is texts.[16]

Pushing Skura's observations into the context of a more specific question—can we speak of the author's experience only or of the textual persona's experience or use one to read the other—I must dislocate the focus of her argument into my own. Skura does acknowledge the problems inherent in this issue: "To psychoanalyze James I or the author of *Macbeth* (Macbeth himself, of course, presents additional problems), we would have to come as close as possible to that shared world; we would need the broadest and thickest descriptions of cultural context."[17] But she moves away from the definition of the individual toward the definition of the text as a source for the necessary cultural context: "The claim that 'history is a text' needs to be amended to 'history is texts'—many texts, of different kinds, nonnarrative floor plans along with narrative histories, and nondiscursive practices along with discursive materials."[18]

So what do we mean when we speak of self in Renaissance texts, in

Renaissance history? Definition is both the heart and the black hole of this argument, and making that point is as close as I intend to move toward any neat definition. We would all do well to heed Catherine Belsey's admonition: "the readiness with which we reach for categories can be worrying: classification is dangerous to the degree that it creates an illusion of clarity, and seems at a stroke to do away with the fumbling and the puzzles."[19] So we should resist seeing the problem as simply one of etymological limits. Greenblatt and his followers regularly cite Leo Spitzer's 1946 essay, "Notes on the Empirical and Poetic 'I' in Medieval Authors,"[20] as proof positive that a medieval writer had no sense of or "respect for the integrity or property of the first-person pronoun" and would thus "incorporate without any apparent concern the experiences of another into his own first-person account."[21] While Spitzer's argument is important to consider in a discussion of medieval concepts of invention of personal narratives (the context from which it is lifted and paraphrased), it is hardly the last word in an analysis of imaginative texts of the Renaissance. For example, Maus sets up her discussion of *Othello* with an analysis of English treason trials, where "according to medieval statute, treason is the crime of 'compassing or imagining the death of the king.'"[22] She quotes the words of the legal commentator Fernando Pulton as recorded in William Vaughan's *Golden-Grove, Moralized in Three Books* (London, 1600): "Seeing compassing and imagination is a secret thing hidden in the breast of man, and cannot be known but by an open fact or deed." Maus observes that this makes treason "a crime which occurs in the imagination, before and even in the absence of any manifestly treasonous activity."[23] The self must therefore exist in this imagination, for while treason may be a collective crime, it is a charge brought against the individual for actions both preformed and intended. Here, in the legal context, the concept of the spectator—God seeing that which is invisible within the person or the jury attempting to infer the same— is a key element in recognizing an internal self. In her discussion of *Othello*, Maus argues that in this play "the capacity, or incapacity to know another is as pertinent to the relation between spectator and character as it is between character and character."[24] This play provides such an effective example of the relation between the spectator and the selfhood of a character because "there is a minimal epistemological boundary between characters and audience."[25] Maus concludes, countering the arguments of Belsey and others who claim that the element of display in drama is itself evidence "that the Renaissance lacked a conception of inwardness or privacy."[26]

Truth exceeds public methods of representation, whether that truth be Cordelia's love, Desdemona's fidelity, or Hamlet's "that which passeth show." What
can be seen on the stage is only part of the truth, an evidence of things not
seen, or not entirely seen. The English Renaissance theatre, and the Shakespearean theatre perhaps most self-consciously, struggles like the English Renaissance courtroom with the limitations and potential falsifications involved
in the process of making visible an invisible truth.[27]

This is what a writer tries to do when he represents interiority. He
constructs an internal self to make the invisible accessible to his audience
or his reader.

As Skura implies, if the study of an historical self—that of Shakespeare or James I—is difficult to articulate in the differing discourses
of the psychoanalytic and the historicist, the study of a constructed self
is that much more elusive. Even more problematic, I would suggest, is
the study of a constructed self that is based on an historical figure.
Macbeth, Skura's example, falls partly into this third category, since the
existence of an historical Macbeth—however lost in the mists of time—
is one of the foundations upon which Shakespeare's Scots play for a Scots
king rests. The question of gender identity, however, adds yet another
dimension to the problem. A male writer presenting the construct of a
female self has at once made the problem of interpretation more simple
and more difficult. With the crossing of gender boundaries, the imaginative female self is now further dislocated from the self of the writer, but
the nature of that dislocation raises other complex problems of reading.
Then there is the question of what difference, if any, lies between a
constructed female self that is entirely the imaginative product of the
male writer and the constructed female self that has its source in history.
In other words, is there a difference in the definition of self when we
talk of the constructed self of the Queen in *Richard II*[28] or of Isabella in
Measure for Measure—both completely imaginary characters—and when
we speak of the constructed self of Cleopatra, the Egyptian queen made
famous by legend and by Plutarch's history and re-created as an imaginative construct in Shakespeare's drama?

Yes, there is an important difference. It is this construct of the female
self that I wish to examine in the following chapters. Eve, the biblical
identity of the first woman, is constructed by Milton into a female figure
with a problematic sense of self, and much of the drama of Milton's epic
arises from perceptions of Eve's interior identity; Cleopatra's historical
identity is usurped by Shakespeare as he creates an imaginative self that
develops before the eyes of his audience in the context of action, and

that is ultimately taken from her as a commentary on the lately deceased English queen, Elizabeth I; Spenser creates the figure of Britomart so that he may construct an imaginative self for the living Elizabeth. The closer the writer works to an historical female identity, the more difficult his task becomes.

Before I address the major constructs of Britomart/Elizabeth, Cleopatra, and Eve, however, I want to offer a less complex example of what I will demonstrate in the chapters devoted to each of these major female figures. In this introductory example, I have chosen a male-constructed female who has some relation to an historical woman, John Donne's representation of Anne More Donne in "A Valediction of my name, in the window." This example is less complex for two reasons: the woman herself is not famous and the degree of development of a female identity that could in any way be called a self is very slight. By setting up my argument for the problems of reading a male-constructed interior female self within the confines of this relatively simple lyric, I hope to clear some ground for my discussions of the vastly more complex figures in the epics of Spenser and Milton and in Shakespeare's play.

THE EVAPORATION OF THE FEMALE SELF IN DONNE'S POETRY

John Donne's distinction between the self as a marker for the physical and the self as a concept of interiority is loosely modeled on the distinction between the body and the soul. Significantly, his few complex representations of selfhood occur in poems that concern death and in verse letters written to contemporaries. In "The Legacie"[29] the speaking persona declares himself to be dead, but speaks of his dying words to his lover: "Tell her anon, / That my selfe, that is you, not I, / Did kill me" (2.9–11.) Here the self is clearly something separate from the body, but—much like Adam's statement in *Paradise Lost*—Donne's speaker identifies this self as being the beloved woman. Unlike Milton, however, Donne is playing with hyperbole in a poem that contains conceits of separation as living death and images that parallel the self/body split to the physical and emotional heart. In the verse letter "To Mr. R.W." we see a similar distinction:

> As this my letter is like me, for it
> Hath my name, words, hand, feet, heart, minde and wit;
> It is my Will, my selfe the Legacie.

> (2.5–8)

The physical name, words, hand, feet, and heart along with the intellectual mind and wit are grouped together as something different from the self. The letter is the Will; the letter "is like me"; the self is that which the letter bequeaths as a legacy. Similarly, in the "Elegie to the Lady Bedford," probably written on the occasion of the death of her cousin Lady Markham,[30] Donne elides the concepts of self and soul: "You that are she and you, that's double shee, / In her dead face, halfe of your selfe shall see; / Shee was the other part. . . . She like the Soule is gone, and you here stay / Not a live friend; but th'other half of clay" (1–3, 13–14). To say that Donne sees the self only as an analogue of the soul in the soul/body split is far too simple. Indeed, it would be impossible to say that Donne's poetry offers us any clearly definable construct of the self. But in the passages just quoted and in the following example, we see a keen Renaissance mind playing with the concept of a constructed interior self.

The most complex conceit Donne develops about the self comes at the end of another verse letter, "To Mr. Rowland Woodward."

> Seeke wee then our selves in our selves; for as
> Men force the Sunne with much more force to passe,
> By gathering his beames with a christall galsse;
>
> So see, If wee into our selves will turne,
> Blowing our sparkes of vertue, may out burne
> The straw, which doth about our hearts sojorne. . . .
>
> We are but farmers of our selves, yet may,
> If we can stocke our selves, and thrive, uplay
> Much, much deare treasure for the great rent day.
>
> Manure thy selfe then, to thy selfe be'approv'd,
> And with vaine outward things be no more mov'd,
> But to know, that I love thee'and would be lov'd.
>
> (19–24, 31–36)

Arguing that men should "Seeke wee then our selves in our selves," Donne holds up separate concepts of the self—the physical and the interior. Here the interior self is something to be nurtured by the exterior person, something to be loved, something that is apart from "vaine outward things." Donne's interior self is separate from Woodward's self and both are held up as powerful, like the magnifying glass that can concentrate light to burn straw. But, although Donne speaks of both his own and Woodward's selves, he makes no attempt to represent either.

He speaks *of* the self, but even the analogy of the magnifying glass is the comparison of two sets of actions, not a definition. But because Donne so seldom concerns himself with the interior existence of others, his few attempts to do so are all the more noticeable. The oft-touted dramatic quality of Donne's verses is not in itself a factor that would prevent the representation of interiority. A fairer statement would be that Donne's concept of the dramatic is active rather than psychological. Even in so subtle a poem as "The Extasie," the emphasis is on action as observed by a passive third party, a paradigm he repeats often, most notably in "The Canonization." In both of these poems Donne constructs a speaking persona who has a beloved; the beloved is not described outside of first-person plural pronouns; the speaker explains the relationship to an observer, a silent persona within the poem. By creating what becomes essentially a cast of characters within a lyric poem, Donne chooses a poetic strategy that evinces little concern for the exploration of the self—the self of the speaker or the self of the beloved woman or the self of the observer.[31] Similarly, he rarely offers us a fully developed figure other than the speaker, who is developed only within the dramatic confines of the problem or situation presented in the lyric. In "The Relique," the speaker may claim to strive for the explanation of "what a miracle" his beloved is, but what we find in the poem is rather the representation of how to speak about the unusual, not of an unusual woman.

If Donne seldom represents the self in his poetry, he represents women even less often. But no, you say; this is absurd; we find women in almost all of Donne's poems. Yes, we find Donne writing about what men think about women; this is not the same thing as representing women. In "The Flea," we are given the woman's speech and actions by implication, but the woman remains a construct whose reactions are both anticipated and controlled by the speaker. In "The Break of Day" the speaker is a woman, but her focus is so entirely upon the actions of the man that she never uses "I" to speak of herself. Certainly there is a woman in Elegy 19, but her objectification by the speaking subject is too obvious to require argument. In the poems written to real women— Lucy, countess of Bedford and Magdalen Herbert, to name the most frequently addressed—Donne does focus more upon the woman as subject. The poem I want to examine, however, is written not to these famous women, but to/about a woman who is at once less public and yet better known to the poet: Anne More Donne.

An exceedingly rich example of the problems of defining the subject of a psychohistorical study is the case of the representation of Anne

More Donne by John Donne in a poem in which he identifies the speaking persona as himself.[32] I have elsewhere argued[33] that we make a great error when we give in to the temptation to read Donne's personable speakers as the historical Donne. A number of other critics have argued otherwise.[34] If reading John Donne's lyric poetry as biography is the dangerous act I believe it to be, then reading the poetry for information about Anne More is at yet one more remove from any pretense of reality. And yet, probably because of the impact of his secret marriage on Donne's career, we are aware of Anne More, so aware that we construct an historical persona for her on little more evidence than Virginia Woolf provides for her fiction, Shakespeare's sister. Dennis Flynn's essay "Donne and a *Female* Coterie"[35] is an excellent example of such bio-fictions, conflating as it does the historical subject and the literary subject. In an argument built around a seductively interesting reading of "Woman's Constancy," Flynn suggests that "many, perhaps most, of the Songs and Sonets and the Elegies are plausibly understood as written for a female audience."[36] Better-researched than John Carey's[37] remarks on Anne More and responding to the blind spots in Arthur Marotti's study,[38] Flynn's thesis is still a tissue of speculation held together by the honest (if too frequent) use of "may" and "perhaps"; his very syntax reveals the heart of the problem: "we can reason that Donne's wife is not likely to have been uneducated."[39] Indeed, Flynn's most solid conclusions about learned women in Donne's home life concern not Anne More, but the poet's mother:

> Born into a family in the line and social circle of Sir Thomas More, this daughter of John Heywood was raised at court under the same (in some ways gender-neutral) humanist educational program in which Heywood himself had long been employed as a music teacher, poet, and entertainer. Elizabeth Heywood's older brothers Ellis and Jasper became Jesuit priests and were well known for their humanist writings and eloquence. Herself a less conspicuous humanist, Elizabeth inculcated the values of her own education while preparing her children for the world.[40]

The intellectual and historical realities of the time, however, militate against even this left-handedly positive a statement, since as Joan Kelly points out, any woman's relationship with the early humanist movement must of necessity be problematic, at best. For women, there was nothing golden about the classical past:

> No sooner had a humanistic outlook started to form among the upper reaches of lay society, in short, and among its authors and teachers, than a fateful

dialectic began between its female and male proponents. Imbued with rena-
scent ideas of civic virtue, humanism was far more narrow in its views of
women than traditional Christian culture. The religious conception of women,
although misogynist in its own way, did regard women as equally capable
of the highest states "man" could attain: salvation and sainthood. Classical
republican thought, rooted in a society that confined women to a *gynecaeum*
and reserved political life for men, threw in doubt this sense of single human
destiny—or even a single human nature. . . . Only as viragos, as exceptions to
their sex, could women aspire to the Renaissance ideal of man.[41]

Speaking of Elizabeth Heywood as a daughter and as a sister of human-
ists (and including Anne More's education only by implication) Flynn
relies too heavily on the weight of the phrase "in the line and social
circle of Sir Thomas More." Yes, Thomas More believed in the education
of women—Margaret More Roper is proof of this—but Thomas More
did not supervise the education of Elizabeth Heywood, much less that
of Anne More Donne. Using the decline in Latin training for women,
even in nunneries, in the late Middle Ages and early Renaissance as a
concrete example of the reality of women's education, Susan Groag Bell
points out that, though it may not have been the intention of individual
humanist scholars, the result was a society in which women were even
less educationally empowered than in most centuries of the Middle Ages.

> Exceptional male humanists, men like Leonardo Bruni, Vittorino de Feltre,
> Erasmus, Vives, Ascham, and Thomas More, all wanted girls to be as proficient
> in Latin as boys and advocated teaching Latin to girls as a new departure from
> the medieval norm. It is clear that the first rank of humanists did not have
> their way, however. Walter Ong suggested that the grammar schools and insti-
> tutions that proliferated from the sixteenth century onward used the study
> of Latin as a kind of male puberty rite that would make boys independent of
> women. . . . Thus the aim of Renaissance teachers and humanists to revolu-
> tionize primary education by taking boys into institutions and by teaching
> girls Latin at home was frustrated.[42]

Contemporary social conditions, of course, as well as the place of women
in the classical world, played a major part in the failure of the humanist
ideals to spread equally to both halves of humankind and may go far to
explain why Elizabeth Heywood was "a less conspicuous humanist" than
her brothers. Of course there were exceptions, but exceptions such as
Elizabeth Tudor rather than Elizabeth Heywood. In *From Humanism to
the Humanities,* Anthony Grafton and Lisa Jardine nail the issue with
devastating clarity: "Only if mythologised can the woman humanist be
celebrated without causing the male humanist professional embarrass-

ment."[43] Flynn makes Elizabeth Heywood an honorary humanist by virtue of her male relatives; Anne More, then, becomes the beneficiary of humanist learning only by marriage, so to speak. Even Flynn can offer none but the lone voice of Izaak Walton crying that Anne More Donne "had been curiously and plentifully educated."[44]

In her essay "Textual Intercourse: Anne Donne, John Donne, and the Sexual Poetics of Textual Exchange,"[45] Janet E. Halley sets forth this convoluted case of an historical presence that must be read largely through its absence, asking if it is possible to read silence. Halley positions herself not so much between as away from R. C. Bald's biographical work,[46] which "suggests a willingness to abandon the problem of Anne Donne's historical presence for the satisfactions of representing an entirely masculine history" and the theories of Arthur Marotti, who "purports to recover Anne Donne without acknowledging that the object of his rescue is her representation in masculine exchange."[47] In either approach, Halley argues, "Anne Donne herself is either lost completely or rendered falsely present."[48] Using John Donne's letters, Halley sets out to read Anne Donne's absence, observing:

> Anne Donne is absent from these texts, but their strategies depend on her passionate presence outside of them. These letters insist, again and again, that the material and literary traffic in women in which Donne engages requires not only women's absence from the exchange itself, but their presence somewhere else.[49]

Halley points out that we cannot know for sure the extent to which Anne More Donne was educated, cannot know for SURE if she was even literate. Yes, we can cite the statistics for female literacy (although it is essential to resist equating being literate with being learned) in that period, the social position of Anne More's family, and we can assume much. All the more important, then, to recognize the fact that we can prove virtually nothing. Halley's scorn in dismissing scholars who claim a literate Anne More—but one whose intellect was not so great that it would have made her discontent with the sphere of loom and womb— is well justified. Critics who construct an Anne More Donne as a selective reader of John Donne's work are telling us more about their own idealization of a woman married to a poet than about Anne More Donne's education and intellect. Interestingly and unusually, this is an idealized vision generally shared by biographical critics of both genders: the women evincing a desire to absolve John Donne of what Dorothy L. Sayers calls the tendency of great men to marry women of no sort of greatness at all, and the men offering an intellectually acceptable excuse for all those ultimately fatal pregnancies . . . he couldn't resist her mind. On the other hand, I would not accept Halley's contention—based almost entirely on one ambiguous phrase in one letter—and go so far as to class Anne More Donne as "functionally illiterate."[50] The essential point Halley makes about Anne More Donne, however, and it is a point that sorely needs to be made after generations of keyhole portraits of the woman, is that many of Donne's letters in prose and verse "directly refer to Anne Donne's presence outside the circuits of epistolary exchange,"[51] figuring her as a part of his own life rather than presenting her as a figure with a life of her own. This is hardly a surprising conclusion to reach about a seventeenth-century wife, but in the canon of Donne scholarship the judgment has a certain freshness. For decades of Donne critics, Donne's wife has been first cousin to Shakespeare's sister, but those critics have failed to retain Woolf's grasp of the distinction between fact and fiction. And what is true of the letters, I would argue, is also true of the lyrics. We can theorize Anne More Donne in the margins of various poems or as the "she" next to whom "nothing else is," as part of that unified soul in "The Extasie," but we cannot point with confidence, even in "St. Lucies Day," to any specific reference to Anne More Donne in her husband's poetry. We may, however, find her name. Although I will argue for the representation of the name of Anne More in one poem, I would not equate that name with the representation of the real woman.

All this may seem a very long windup for a relatively short pitch. What I hope to establish by providing this reading of Donne's poem is that much of what has been condemned as sloppy critical thinking about selfhood in criticicism of Renaissance texts is actually biographical criticisim poured into new bottles. Flynn and his supporters do not concern themselves with the concept of selfhood as discussed in the first part of this chapter; they speak of literal selves: Anne More and John Donne. Having declared biographical readings of Donne's lyrics to be suspect at best and critical wish fulfillment at worst, I now must clarify my definition of biographical reading. Using what sparse facts we have about Donne's early life to illuminate aspects of the poems that we can date in relation to those facts—as some critics have with the travel poems—is a worthy scholarly undertaking; not so, but far otherwise is the practice of using the poems themselves to construct a biography— in the manner of those Shakespeare critics who play with the fair young man and the dark lady in order to populate the playwright's social life— for such readings (in addition to requiring more than a fair share of critical imagination) of necessity deny the poet's imaginative ability to write from any perspective other than that of a rigidly chronological diary. Flynn's reading of "Woman's Constancy" in light of his knowledge of the Egerton women at York House falls mainly into the first category of scholarship, although his desire to make that argument specific to Anne More and to generalize one poem to all of the *Songs and Sonets* and the *Elegies* edges toward the second, the dangers and discontents of which are admirably set forth in Halley's essay. As I discuss Donne's use of his wife's name, I obviously see my argument also falling on the side of the divide that puts verifiable fact before hopeful fiction. The poem I want to discuss in this essay is, as far as I can tell, unique among the *Songs and Sonets.* "A Valediction of My Name, in the Window" is a poem to which Donne signs his name internally, in the text of the verse itself, a poem that therefore requires no multiple choice matching of jigsaw bits from imagery and biography and speaking persona and auditor (although the chronology is still up for grabs). In this poem no one need theorize an autobiographical speaking persona (thus constructing that poetic keyhole giving on Donne's life) because the poet himself has identified the personae by name and has thrown open the door—or the window, to be more accurate. And behind that window we find Anne More. But before I present such a reading of the poem, let me first establish the existence of what I call Donne's internal signature.[52]

In John Skelton's "Garland of Laurel," a poem with which Donne's hydroptique and immoderate desire for learning would surely have acquainted him, we find employed—and probably invented by Skelton[53]— a system of English gematria. Gematria, the identification of each letter of the alphabet with a different number, is a system of encoding and decoding meaning employed by the Cabalists and other mystics with the Hebrew alphabet and by some Latin poets who capitalized on the fact that Roman numbers *were* letters. As I have argued elsewhere,[54] Donne's love of systems of knowledge that he could appropriate as subtexts led him to incorporate both alchemy and numerology in his lyrics. "The Extasie," "Loves growth," and "Elegie XI: The Bracelet" are but three poems in which Donne constructs elaborate numerological conceits. Gematria, of course, has the added charm of allowing letters to take on the properties of numbers, with values that are at once constant and capable of being regrouped according to the rules of playful language.

In Skelton's system the vowels are numbered 1–5, and the consonants are numbered as though the vowels were in place. Therefore *B* and *E* are both numbered 2, *D* and *O* are both 4, and so on. *J* and *I* are counted as the same letter, which is numbered 3.[55]

```
1   2   3   4   5
A   E   I   O   U


2   3   4   6   7   8   3  10  11  12  13  15  16  17  18  19  21  22  23  24  25

B   C   D   F   G   H   J   K   L   M   N   P   Q   R   S   T   V   W   X   Y   Z

3 4 8 13        4  4 13 13 2
J O H N         D O N N E
```

The total by this system is 64. John T. Shawcross, in his edition of Donne's poetry, also argues that Donne is playing with gematria in this poem, but believes that Donne would have used his signature, Jo. Donne, thus making the total of 7 and 36.[56] I believe that Donne did not content himself with this ornamental esoteric flourish, but instead jumped into number play with both feet. The poem itself yields three types of evidence supporting the more extended use of gematria. First, in the third stanza, we find the lines "As no one point, nor dash, / Which are but accessaries to this name" and the words "this intireness." Here we are being told that the speaker has engraved his name with *no* point nor dash, but in it entirety. Furthermore, 7 and 36 must be arrived at by totaling the Jo. and the Donne separately, and this poem speaks of "my name," not "names," in the window.

Secondly, we have the significance of the total numbers themselves. Shawcross points out that both 7 and 36 are very important numbers in any of the systems of Renaissance number theory. This is certainly true, but the meanings attached to these numbers have no particular significance in the context of this poem. That is not true of the number 64. Sixty-four (64) is the square of 8, which is the number of regeneration, of resurrection (and therefore a good number for a promise of return), the first cube, and a marriage number. In the Renaissance sonnet sequences of Sidney, Drayton, and others, 63 is the climacteric number, being the product of $3 \times 3 \times 7$, explained by Henry Constable as the order of a sequence in which the sonnets are "divided into 3 parts, each part containing 3 several arguments, and every argument 7 sonnets."[57] From the Renaissance to the present 64 has been the number that "overgoes" the perfection of 63.[58]

I do not believe, however, that it was the significance of 64 or of any other number that initially attracted Donne to this numerological conceit, for I suggest that in this case his imagination would have progressed more naturally from letters to numbers, rather than the other way around. Who, when confronted with an intriguing puzzle such as Skelton's system, would not try to count out his own name? And then other names or words that are personal importance? As he did this, Donne would have uncovered a coincidence that I believe would have proved impossible for him to ignore and that very probably gave birth to this poem—although this element of intentionality is itself dangerously close to the biographical criticism I reject and, in any case, is not central to a reading of the poem. The heart of my argument is that JOHN DONNE equals 64. So does ANNE MORE. And we move far beyond the realm of coincidence when we add up the numbers for MY NAME, finding 64 again. JOHN DONNE and MY NAME thus become the same in a double sense, as does the identity of—indeed, the essence of—ANNE MORE. Having these lovely sets of correspondences before him, Donne could have placed the oneness of his and Anne More's names at the heart of a poem. That Donne chose to privilege the duality of JOHN DONNE and MY NAME over the equal value of JOHN DONNE and ANNE MORE suggests that he was more concerned with working out a clever conceit, one participating in what Halley so rightly defines as a masculine economy, than with inscribing the identity of this woman in the text of his poem.

Whether Donne moved from the number generated by the names to that number's significance or whether he began with 64 and set out to find words to fit it, is a question to which we have no sure answer, although the former does seem far more likely. I agree with A. Kent Hieatt that the symbolic numerological structures matter more as poetic symbolism within a poet's own system than as objective data, and—especially in relation to this poem—I also agree with his warning that "the problem must be historical before it can become aesthetic, because . . . we must be particularly sure of what we are looking at before we decide what we think of it."[59] I say "especially in relation to this poem," because caution is needed when assessing the weight we can place on the numbers we find. If Donne used Skelton's gematria in all of the *Songs and Sonets* or if he confined himself to any one system of numerological symbolism,[60] we could generalize beyond the confines of these sixty-six lines. Similarly, if Donne worked some reference to Anne More into all of—or many of or even ANY of—his other poems, we could more safely extract what we find here and treat it as more closely related to reality than is possible for us to regard one conceit in one poem.

While it is possible to follow with pleasure the phantoms of numerological nuances down endless garden paths or, as Donne himself said, for a mystical rabbi to find that "the hairs on the tail of his Dog are numbered, and from their various backward twists and intertwinings letters are formed which yield wonderful words,"[61] I do not wish to make more of this than Donne himself did—a combination of intellectual/poetic fun-with-numbers and what I spoke of earlier as an internal signature. The existence of this signature, of a speaking persona who says "my name equals John Donne," allows us to view the poem as a literary/biographical artifact, an artifact which, moreover, calls into question both assumptions about the dating of this poem and others like it and many of the general critical assumptions about the correspondence between Donne's poetic tone, style, and content and his relationship with Anne More. The number games that give us the signature are interesting; the signature itself is important. His use of the name of Anne More may be unique, as is his attempt to represent her within the poem—to represent her external physical self and her interior psychological self.

The conceit of a name engraved in the glass of a window provides the imaginative field of action for the two major images of the poem. The first image pattern springs from the JOHN DONNE equals MY NAME equals ANNE MORE equation and depends upon the qualities of window glass: that which may be seen through, that which may be written upon, and that which will reflect back. When Anne looks at the window she sees through it to the world beyond, but she also sees John's name superimposed upon this world—for even one who could be called functionally illiterate could recognize a well-known name. Furthermore, she sees that world of action as belonging to him and to other men, for her place is clearly inside the window. At the same time she may perceive her own reflection in the glass, a reflection now inscribed with Donne's name, thus the line "Here you see mee, and I am you" (1.12). Here we see the paradigm of identity that Milton will construct half a century later when he has Eve look into the pool, fail to recognize herself, and yield to the voices of God and Adam that tell her that Adam's image IS her self.

The second major image pattern is more extensively developed and has more influence upon the tone of the poem. In the first two lines Donne sets up a pun on "engrave," which he develops into the second major metaphor of the poem. "Engrav'd herein" is both "written" and "entombed"—written on the glass and entombed in that which the glass reflects, Anne. MY NAME, which is John Donne, thus contributes "firmness" to both the glass and to Anne. The "which" of line 3 is deliberately ambiguous. If it refers to the glass, we have "that which grav'd it" as the diamond used for writing. If it refers to "my firmness," we see a graphic image of "hard" Donne "grav'd" in an Anne who had once resisted him. She looks in the glass, sees herself reflected in this mirror held up to nature, and also sees Donne's "ragged bony name" (1.23), which is his "ruinious Anatomie" (1.24); Anne and John are thus joined in this image just as they are joined in the sex act. (The Renaissance pun on "die," implicit here, and Donne's association of death and sex in this and other poems provide the context of wit for the second reading.) And what he has done once, he promises to do again: "So shall all times finde mee the same; / You this intireness better may fulfill, / Who have the pattern with you still" (11.16–18). Other lines and phrases that figure forth this punning image are found in stanza 5, especially "Emparadis'd in you" (1.26); similarly, "will come againe" (1.30) and "this name flow / Into thy fancy, from the pane? (11.57–58) develop the sexual word play. These lines, which can apply themselves to Donne's name in the window or to Donne himself in Anne, establish a wittily bawdy tone that biographical critics have consistently classed as Donne-pre-Anne. But from the evidence of this poem we see that Donne could write witty evaporations to/about Anne More with the same facility that he produced about those anonymous "ladies" and in the same spirit as the more serious poems, such as "The Extasie"—although even that very serious poem can be read wittily.[62]

This poem in which we can acknowledge an autobiographical Donne ironically calls into question the standard assumptions about the correlation between Donne's life and his art and thereby stresses how necessary it is that critics avoid building their arguments on blocks of biography. I can only conclude that this case of biographical poem that casts the shadow of doubt on biographical interpretation constitutes a paradox that would be worthy of and that would have delighted Donne himself.

Finally, having "found" Anne More's presence in a poem by John Donne, what are we to make of it? As I suggested earlier, there's a sort of negative evidence of priority in Donne's choice of JOHN DONNE/ MY NAME as the inscribed equivalents. Surely here is Donne's golden opportunity to build a poem around this specific woman, to inscribe her name in the text of one of his poems. ANNE DONNE equals 65, and since the poem has 66 lines, we could stretch the inclusiveness of overgoing to make something of this. I would be more inclined, however, to impute this significance to 65/66 if the number of lines in each stanza and the total number of stanzas had no other or no consistent meaning. On the other hand, the shift to a plural pronoun in the last stanza (of which I will say more later), could be linked to ANNE DONNE having "overgone" ANNE MORE by becoming one with the speaker. But this reading, too, fails to privilege Anne More Donne as an individual. Fur-

thermore, when we realize that ANNE MORE DONNE equals 100 we
must acknowledge that John Donne allowed a number of massive power
to go unused.

Given Anne's family name, we should certainly expect a pun on
"more," and here we do find not *one* but three: "'Tis *more*, that it shews
thee to thee" (l.9) and "As much *more* loving, as *more* sad" (l.40, emphasis
mine). In line 9, it is the "Glasse" of line 7 that is at once "more" than
window glass, being also a looking glass, and therefore also More, when
Anne More looks into the glass. In line 40 the sight of Donne's name is
said to make More "more" loving as his absence will make her "more
sad." But all three puns fall in lines speaking directly about the effect
of the dual subject (JOHN DONNE/MY NAME) upon the object "thee."
And this, overtly at least, is the paradigm of power and identity we
find within the poem as a whole. It's John Donne's name, John Donne's
signature, and the point of the name engraved in the window is to keep
Anne More's mental and physical eye focused on both within the context
of John Donne's poem. Nor does the speaker stop at focusing her attention on him and his name, for she is identified with both, as we see in
the key line "Here you see mee, and I am you" (l.12). There may be
three puns on "more" in the poem, but there is none on "done." The
speaker may play with or upon the identity of the auditor, but his own
name is writ large, beyond the subtle discourse of puns, beyond even the
need for its own letters as, godlike, MY NAME gives us JOHN DONNE;
and the words "my name" also appear three times—four if we count
the title. By writing his name across the window (not HER window, ever,
but "the" or "this" window), Donne constructs a barrier across an opening into the space that contains Anne More. She is figured as having
possession of an eye (2.5 and 10), a hand (1.43), a heart (1.46), a maid
(1.49), a lover (1.50), a pillow (1.51), rage (1.52), and fancy (1.58). The
speaker claims direct possession of his name (title and 2.1, 46, 54), firmness (1.2) a ruinous Anatomie (1.24), souls (1.25), a body (2.28 and 32),
a return (1.31), Genius (1.48), and sleep (1.64). In addition to the relative
frequency of these possessive pronouns, the things that the two personae
possess differ significantly. Much like the woman described in the first
sonnet of Spenser's *Amoretti,* this woman exists only in separate pieces
of a person: an eye, a hand, a heart. She can claim that tradition of the
sonnets, a lover who rivals the speaker, and she has the services of her
maid and the comfort of her pillow, in addition to possessing both rage
and fancy. By contrast, the speaker has both body and soul, both firmness and genius, and—most importantly—he has a name, "my name."

And yet Donne never applies that possessive pronoun directly to the woman his speaking persona addresses. Nor do the almost generically inevitable words "my love" appear within the poem. The one time a possessive pronoun is articulated in relation to "love" it is plural, "our firme substantiall love" (1.62), although I would argue the tone of the whole poem suggests at least a tenuous mutuality. Moreover, this note of mutuality—*equality* would be too strong a term, I think—is sounded much earlier in the poem, in the astonishing syntax of line 12. When the auditor looks into the glass of the window and sees the name writ large across her own reflection, she is told: "Here you see mee, and I am you." She recognizes her own image; she recognizes the name; and she realizes that her identity is conflated with that of the owner of the name. This is not exactly the same thing as figuring an interior self, but the operations of cognition and recognition, followed by revised identity, are more interior than exterior.

I must stop for a moment to point out how brilliantly structured this line is; it at once encapsulates both the metaphysical conceit of the poem and the heart of the argument. As Anne More sees John Donne's name both across her own reflected face and between herself and the outside world, so does the line itself enact the properties of reflection. The pronouns form a chiasmus, a crossing, that turn that is enacted by a mirrors' reversal: you . . . me . . . I . . . you: second-person subject, first-person object, first-person subject, second-person object. At the heart of the chiasmus, on the tain of the reflecting glass is both the object (the name inscribed) and the subject pronoun of the writer; at either end of the reflected gaze is the multivalent "you," without whom the entire exercise would be meaningless. The writer is in control, but in control of a process that would not be possible without the "you" who gazes. Here we see that rare paradigm in Renaissance poetry, the male representing himself as object of the female gaze. Ah, but that may be going too far. The male in question is absent, and we have instead the NAME as object of the female gaze. Still, I find it fascinating that Donne chooses this figuration over one that presents the woman as being the man's image—"you are me" or even more traditionally, "you are mine." I would also distinguish this figuration of identity from the meaninglessly clichéd phrase "I am yours." The line is free of the element of possession and becomes a statement of conflated identity. Of course it is only a partial statement of dual identity, for the female subject is allowed to see the male as object, but the male subject identifies himself with the female object. And, I would argue, it is because her gaze falls upon the name, not, Eve-like, upon the man himself, that this degree of mutual identification is possible, as the numerological equivalency of JOHN DONNE,

MY NAME, and ANNE MORE brings these various images together in a textbook example of a metaphysical conceit. Although stanza 4 suggests that the name should be identified with the speaker's body, this metaphor soon goes the way of all flesh as he moves into—variously into—stanza 5, 5 the number of physical union between man and woman.

Since the main conceit of the poem involves Anne More reading John Donne's name, this alone would seem to militate against Halley's argument that the woman was functionally illiterate, although (in addition to the fact that mere recognition of the shape of the name would be sufficient to sustain the conceit, a contention strengthened by the line-18 reference to the signature as a "patterne") we could argue that in the universe of this poem, Anne More's literacy is a convenient fiction. The metaphor of reading is developed, however, in stanza 9; and in stanza 10 it is joined by the related metaphor of writing—Anne's writing, not that of John or of her other lover. Without transferring the identity of the Anne More of the lyric whole cloth over to the biography of Anne More the real person, let us examine the image of this poetic female fiction who is represented as both a reader of various texts and as a writer of sorts.

In stanza 4 we find two lines that speak to the difficulty of reading: "Or if too hard and deepe / This learning be, for a scratch'd name to teach" (2.19–20). The limits being discussed here, however, are not those of the auditor/reader, but of the medium—can a single name scratched in a windowpane bear the weight of this elaborate argument, stand part-for-whole for an entire relationship? Indeed, the speaker evidently considers the woman to whom he is speaking to be capable of multiple levels of reading, as he adjures her to read the name as a representation of his body, which (he continues in stanza 5) houses his soul; thus, he offers his name lodged in her eye and understanding as a metaphor for the body and soul he would have "Emparadis'd in" (1.26) her. Interestingly, however, the word "read" never occurs within the poem, although the entire conceit depends upon an act of reading. To speak of reading is to speak of interiorizing knowledge, and the interior identity of this woman is exactly what is not being represented here. The speaker knows the woman to be a reader of more than his signature, as we see in stanza 9 with the reference to the letter from a rival lover. When her maid, "melted" by the rival's servant in the best tradition of romantic intrigue, places a letter from the rival on the woman's pillow, the woman—so the speaker suggests—will, after her initial rage, calm down enough to soften toward the rival lovers, presumably after having read his letter.

The speaker anthropomorphizes his name at this point, willing it to "step in" (1.54) and hide or displace that of the rival lover.

And after having read, the woman may write, or—more to the point—rewrite. Only in stanza 10 does any form of the word "write" appear within the poem, and here the act of writing is the act of the woman. The name of the speaker/poet is "engrav'd" (1.1), "scratch'd" (1.20), and "cut" (1.37), but the verb "to write" is never used. What the speaker has, by implication, written is the poem itself. The writing of which the woman is said to be capable in stanza 10 is quite a different sort of writing. Here, to borrow a phrase from another poem, the body is the book. Just as he has linked his name engraved in glass with his body engraved in the woman, so the speaker realizes he might be erased, or at least overwritten. Rather than investing the rival lover with the power to do this, however, Donne sets up the more unusual paradigm of the woman having the power to write with these men upon her own page, the page of her body. "And if this treason goe / To'an overt act, and that thou write againe" (if you progress from merely liking his letter to having sex with him and thus write his name on/in the text of your body as mine was once written); "In superscribing, this name flow / Into thy fancy, from the pane" (as this physical rewriting is happening, my name, my image, will flow into your imagination / desire from the pane of glass or the pain of the act); "So, in forgetting thou rememberest right, / And unaware to me shalt write" (as you forget the new name of the new lover's body, you will remember me—both recall and re-embody—thus, unconsciously, writing my name again). This is a complex image, all the more so for the unusual figuration of the woman as writer. But the woman is not a writer in the literary sense, as is the speaker; she writes in her mind and, metaphorically or literally, upon her body; but she does not, as Shawcross's note suggests, write letters.

Nevertheless, even with the emphasis on the physical, this stanza gives us the closest thing to a representation of a female self that we can find in the poem. If the woman writes to or sleeps with another man or even thinks about doing either, she is assured that "this name [will] flow / Into thy fancy from the pane. / So, in forgetting thou remembrest right, / And unaware to mee shalt write" (2.57–60). Here, I would argue, we find a representation of not only the self, but a rudimentary representation of the subconscious self. Any of the "overt act[s]" of "treason" that the woman might enact would trigger the remembrance of that identity with which she has already been stamped. The pane/pain will cause her fancy to substitute the lover from whom she takes her identity; she will re-member, re-cover, re-cognize who she is, and in doing so will right/ write herself, even "unaware" to the "mee" who is the speaker.

COGNITION AND RECOGNITION

The problematic last stanza, of course, calls the entire argument of the poem into question. After developing this elaborate and complex conceit, the speaker declares it to be inadequate: "But glass, and lines must be, / No meanes our firme substantiall love to keepe" (2.61–62). This, followed by the next four lines, sounds a bit too much like Gilda Radnor's famous "never mind." In his notes, Shawcross explains the last four lines in reference to the illness that has necessitated the lover's absence. I would suggest an alternate reading, that of the whole poem— like "The Sun Rising" or "The good-morrow"—being spoken in bed. The "Neere death" that "inflicts this lethargie" in line 63 would then become postcoital exhaustion; 63 is, after all, the climacteric number. If she were in bed with him, the woman would be able to hear "this I murmure in my sleepe" and could "Impute this idle talke" to loving pillow talk between fond lovers; she would know from experience that "dying men"—or at any rate, this dying man—would "talk often so." If we read this stanza as I suggest, we not only banish the arguably insulting suggestion that the woman would actually take multiple lovers (an empowering idea for the twentieth-century reader, but unlikely to be read as such in the seventeenth century), but we strengthen the power of the main conceit JOHN DONNE equals MY NAME equals ANNE MORE equals OUR LOVE, and we find that the two personae have been joined literally as well as by the manipulations of metaphor and gematria. The witty argument of the first ten stanzas—now complete in themselves— is thus over-gone by the reality of the last stanza.

We also, of course, lose the concept of the female self. So where does this leave the figure of Anne More? Just that: she is an imaginative figuration of woman in a witty love poem. That this poem acknowledges the existence of Anne More is, I believe, beyond debate. In the chiasmic line "Here you see mee, and I am you" Donne acknowledges the existence of an interior female self, and does so by employing the topos of the transformative mirror. That stanza 10 constitutes a effort to represent the interior self of Anne More is arguable; that stanza 11 nullifies any importance invested in that self is less debatable. Whether or not she was its primary reader (or even one of a group of readers) is a question about which we can only speculate. The play upon her name within this poem allows us to conclude that Donne did use his wife as a persona within his poetry. We cannot, however, selectively generalize the Anne More of "A Valediction of my name, in the window" to other female pronouns within the lyrics. These are John Donne's poems, just as it is John Donne's name that is privileged in these lines. The name of Anne More remains a name not written, not even on glass.

But it is the glass that also claims our attention here. That Donne should have tried—however briefly and superficially—to represent the female self of Anne More in relation to her reflected image in a glass is, I believe, a crucial point in any discussion of constructed female self-hood in Renaissance texts. That the strategy appears in a minor lyric broadens the implications for my argument. For Donne, a poet who evinces little concern with representing women and who is not forced to do so by a preexisting narrative structure (as are Milton and Shake-speare and, to a lesser extent, Spenser), any attempt to figure female interiority is innovative, not prompted by a poetic tradition, the Renaissance love lyric being notoriously indifferent to representations of the female self; thus, his use of the topos of the transformative mirror constitutes a stronger argument for an imaginative, intellectual association between female identity and reflection. As I suggest in the introduction, the mimetic act of representation requires some degree of recognition. As problematic as we may find the representations of male selfhood by male writers, we can at least assume self-recognition—however articulated—to have some part in the process. For male writers to represent female selfhood in the same manner would require the fanciful finding of that "woman's part" of which Posthumous speaks, and even then the act of having to FIND a PART of oneself militates against the possibility of recognition. We cannot reknow what we have never acknowledged.

There lies the heart of the problem for a male writer trying to represent a female self with any sense of interiority. Cognition must come before recognition. The poetic response to this problem is often the solution employed by Donne in his lyric; the poet somehow incorporates a mirror—sometimes metaphoric but more often literal—into his representation of the female self. This allows the poet to construct immediate responses for his female creations, conflating knowing and recognition within some construct of selfhood. But, as I will argue in the next chapter, knowing by reflection is a false construct for interiority, for all that its roots lie deeply embedded in Western European representation of women. For so often—as we find in Donne's lyric—that mirrored act of recognition leads to a transformation that diminishes the power and selfhood of the woman. Although I want to defer the discussion of the three major Renaissance texts yet once more, I want to ponder the significance of the paradigm of reflection in two stories from Ovid with the representations of Britomart, Cleopatra, and Eve very much in mind. The Medusa narrative gives us a clear distinction between identity directly beheld and identity reflected in a mirror. And while the Narcissus narrative was originally about a man gaining self-knowledge, Ovid's tale has been elided by medieval misogyny into a paradigm of female identity. While the next chapter delays a full examination of the texts of Spenser, Shakespeare, and Milton, it serves as does the title of this study before the colon—as a frame of reference for the central analysis.

2

the chiasmus of perception

To look at a reflection in a mirror is an act significantly different from looking directly at a person or object. Most commonly we use mirrors to see ourselves, an act otherwise impossible in premodern culture, and even today without the intervention of technology, although, as John Donne observes in "The Good-morrow," the eye itself can serve as a mirror for another's eye. Additionally, we can gain this reflected vision by indirection if we wish, angling the mirror to gain access to an object outside of the line of our direct sight-lines. But any face or object that our eyes find upon the surface of a mirror is essentially altered by the process of reversal, which may be one reason why knowledge gained by looking in a mirror has always been marked off by Western European culture as special. We use the word "mirror" as both a noun and a verb in its literal sense, and we use it even more complexly in literary and artistic discourse. In this chapter I want to explore the properties of mirroring by picking apart two mirror stories from Ovid's *Metamorphoses*, the narratives of Medusa and of Narcissus. Because my main interest is the process or paradigm of mirroring itself, I organize my analysis around the properties of mirroring, using the traditional metaphor of the text as a mirror to present them in reversed order. The process begins with the mirror itself and the eye that turns to it; the surface of the mirror, called the tain, reverses the image that the eye beholds via the mirror; that which is returned to the eye is called the reflection. I take these elements—reflection, tain, and mirror—in reversed order because it is this hierarchy that is valued in both practical and imaginative usage. The mirror *qua* mirror is almost always secondary to its property of reflection, while the concept of the tain has become virtually elided onto the definition of mirror itself. In a study with so many subtle valences of the mirror existing both simultaneously and in flux within the texts under discussion, however, I clearly need to establish and call attention to the discrete elements of the process of mirroring.

Relationships between the mirror and the concepts of selfhood, iden-

45

tity, gender, and power saturate the pages of the Western canon. That Ovid's two stories allow me to examine the process of mirroring and its literal and imaginative implications is due largely to the complexity of these two narratives. Both stories are worn smooth with cultural usage, but I hope in this chapter to reconstruct some of the sharp edges that reside in the original narratives and the dislocations of those narratives into various social and artistic agendas. As I said in the introduction to this study, the patterns of knowing which reside in and have been extrapolated from these stories are more central to my argument about women in Renaissance texts than are the specifics of the two Ovidian narratives. But these narratives, bound up as they are with medieval and Renaissance notions about self-identity and gender and power, need to be teased out before I can turn to the figures of Britomart, Cleopatra, and Eve who are constructed with some key elements of the process of mirroring as it is represented in these two artifacts of the canonical imagination. If there is an element of circularity in this methodology, it derives from the process of mirroring itself, a process at once defined by the boundaries of the mirror and the eye and yet infinitely replicated by the addition of yet another mirror, another eye, literal or imaginative.

REFLECTION: THE IMAGE OF MEDUSA'S SECOND FACE

The thing in the mirror, the reversed image—is it stronger or weaker? Certainly it is DIFFERENT. In Ovid's story of Medusa we find a reflection of society's fear of the power of women, even as we find the paradigm poets have constructed to deflect that fear. First the object of male desire, then a monster, then a weapon, Medusa is the only mortal woman in the narrative. She is variously transformed by Neptune, by Minerva, and finally by Perseus, all of whom are concerned with differing manifestations of power. We know nothing of Medusa's desires, as she metaphorically reflects the desires of the other figures in the story. Because of those reflections, which culminate in the literal reflection on Perseus' shield, she is raped, transformed, killed. Those who gaze directly at the face of Medusa are vulnerable, rendered lifeless stone by the power of what they see. Medusa, when beheld in a mirror, becomes vulnerable herself, rendered lifeless by the hand of Perseus. But what Perseus sees in the mirror is a reversed image, not the face that causes death. Through this process of reflection, power is relocated from the face of Medusa to the eye of Perseus and the agency of that relocation is the surface of the mirror. Many of Western society's concerns with the representation of the relationship between gender and power are crystallized for us in the story of Medusa.

The violent power of Medusa's face can be contained, even negated, by the reflecting powers of the shield, but the powerful violence of her story escapes the containment of textual representation because the issues of power and gender and identity in Ovid's narrative are greater than the sum of the actions he presents.[1] Medusa's story becomes a paradigm of the power of representation: its violence in proportion to the fear of female power implicit in the tale, its disordered narrative and lacunae symptomatic of the indirection and manipulation by which representation can contain and displace power. And diminish it. Yes, of course the process of narrative representation can increase power through its reflection. As Ludovico Ariosto's Saint John suggests:

> Aeneas was not so pious, nor so strong
> Achilles was, as they are famed to be . . . but we see
> Their valour and their deeds enhanced in song.[2]

Francis Quarles makes a similar observation in an epigram in his 1635 *Emblemes:* "The glass of the world deceives, making a man look larger and fairer than he is. . . ."[3] But this process can also be reversed. In the same passage from Ariosto's *Orlando Furioso* in which Saint John credits poets with the power to create great reputations for their patrons, he also observes their power to diminish and denigrate:

> Consider Dido; she, whose heart was pure,
> Was faithful to Sichaeus to the end;
> But she is thought by all to be a whore,
>   Because Vergillius was not her friend.
>
> (35, 28, 1–4)

But Dido's story, terrible as it may seem, pales in comparison to Medusa's. Whatever Virgil may have done to Dido's reputation, in his story her power over Aeneas is limited by the Trojan's powerful knowledge of his fate—"It is not / my own free will that leads to Italy" he tells Dido in Book 4[4]—and mediated by the gods. Violence, in this representation of female power, is generated by Dido but is directed only toward herself and her own (alien) society. But in the story of Medusa as told by Ovid, we find a conjunction of violent acts that seems to challenge the power of representation. In what appears at first reading to be an afterthought, Ovid has Perseus, after he as killed the Gorgon and used her head to defeat others, tell her story:

quoniam scitaris digna relatu,
accipe quaesiti causam. clarissima forma
multorumque fuit spes invidiosa procorum
illa, nec in tota conspectior ulla capillis
pars fuit: invini, qui se vidisse referret.
hanc pelagi rector templo vitiasse Minervae
dicitur: aversa est et castos aegide vultus
nata Iovis texit, neve hoc impune fuisset,
Gorgoneum crinem turpes mutavit in hydros.
nunc quoque, ut attonitos formidine terreat hostes,
pectore in adverso, quos fecit, sustinet angues.

(4, 793–803)

(Since what you ask is a tale well worth the telling, hear then the cause. She
was once most beautiful in form, and the jealous hope of many suitors. Of all
her beauties, her hair was the most beautiful—for so I learned from one who
said he had seen her. 'Tis said that in Minerva's temple Neptune, lord of the
Ocean, ravished her. Jove's daughter turned away and hid her chaste eyes
behind her aegis. And that the deed might be punished as was due, she
changed the Gorgon's locks to ugly snakes. And now to frighten her fear-
numbed foes, she still wears upon her breast the snakes she has made.)[5]

There are so many aspects of this story that cry out to the modern
reader and that in turn force the reader to cry out, that one scarcely
knows where to begin.

She has no face. How hard this is to remember, how we rush to supply
her with one, with two, three. Ovid has Perseus speak of her beautiful
body and of her beautiful hair, but between these two beauties there is
nothing. We are not allowed to gaze upon even the most abstract of
descriptive images; the face of the beautiful virgin, of the horrific Gorgon, of the reflected power—none of these does the text offer to our
gaze. Instead of the face of the woman, it is the power of the act that
is described—both the act of rape and (more graphically) the act of
transubstantiation as this unspeakable face turns the power of the direct
gaze back upon the gazer. The once-mortal woman has no power to
keep herself safe; the power of Minerva makes her the locus of fear, a
monster. Those who gaze at her become monuments to the fear inspired
by the power of a female god. But this fear is named with the name of
Medusa, not Minerva who, as we see from the *Odyssey* onward, is the
goddess least threatening to men.[6] Her lack of sexuality and her own
motherless state may be the reasons for this, but however we explain it,
we find that any residual fear from the sexuality of a powerful woman
is displaced from Athena/Minerva onto Medusa by this story. The power

of Minerva is represented as being empowering to men as she punishes not Nepture but his victim, as she gives the power of the monster she creates to Perseus, who may look at the face of the goddess, but not at the face of the monster, the once-mortal Medusa.

In addition to the difficulty we have accepting the textual absence of the face that generates the narrative, we must also consider that the placement of Medusa's story itself serves as a sort of narrative mirror; at the very end of Book 4 after numerous unexplained references to the power located in her, the placement of the narrative forces the reader—modern or ancient—to reflect back over the text in the new light of this knowledge, to reread with a mediated gaze.

This reflective reading of the Perseus narrative of Medusa's story thus becomes a paradigm for the textual representation of images by reflection. It is important, I think, that we hear Medusa's history from Perseus, not from the poet-narrator. By having Perseus tell the story, tell it as an afterthought, Ovid further objectifies Medusa. We do not follow her metamorphosis in chronological order, seeing her as we first see Daphne or Arachne or Callisto. As an object of curiosity, as a history, the woman becomes inseparable from Minerva's act of transformation, for her actions are never the focus of the narrator's exclusive attention; she is presented instead as the object of the sight and speech of other characters in the narrative. Ovid's presents Medusa as a woman who *is* a monster, not as a woman who is transformed into a monster. Only after her final transformation into a dead body and head are we told of her rape and initial metamorphosis. Medusa before her metamorphosis was beautiful. There is no suggestion in Ovid's narrative that she invited Neptune's attention, in contrast to one of the Greek versions, where it is said that she "bedded" with him.[7] So what we have here is a rape story. Medusa is raped before the absent eyes of the statue of Minerva, as the goddess averts her gaze behind her shield. "And that the deed might be punished," Minerva transforms Medusa's beauty into a horror that will strike men stone-dead, turn them into statues that cannot avert their eyes. Insofar as the "deed" is the rape of Medusa by Neptune, the punishment is apt, even witty—a unisex, perpetual hard-on, although not for Neptune. But what of Medusa herself? Unlike Daphne or Syrinx, she does not ask for this metamorphoses. She says nothing. If she spoke, the narrative has deprived her of the power of that speech as Neptune deprived her of her virginity. Is her silence meant to imply submission? Or has she been subsumed by the deed done to her? Her identity annexed by the act of rape? Do her snaky locks thus perform an ocular rape of those who subsequently gaze upon her?[8] Neptune

gazes with admiration and rapes her; Minerva averts her gaze and transforms her; those who gaze at her transformed visage die of her; those
who gaze at the stone-dead gazers fear her; Perseus gazes at her reflection and kills her.

Medusa is both victim and monster and becomes both by being the
object of a gaze. After Neptune, only those who do not gaze at her—
Minerva and Perseus—have power over her. Nowhere does Ovid give
her any response of her own. She is the object of many responses, but
her power is generated only by the actions of others. *Her* gaze has no
power. Those she looks upon are unaffected, for only those who look
upon her will die. Her power to turn beings into stone is dependent
upon a gaze; the result of that gaze is death. But if distanced by a
mediating reflection—the surface of a shield—the image is powerless.

If the metamorphosis was supposed to punish those who gaze and
then act with uncontained desire, something has gone fundamentally
wrong, for in Ovid her victims gaze at the Gorgon only with fear or out
of ignorance.[9] In the second part of Medusa's story, desire inheres only
in Perseus, who desires the power of the Gorgon and who acquires that
power by *not* gazing directly at her. Ironically, Minerva's punishment
against the unbounded power of one man/god results in the empowerment of another man/warrior. Or is Minerva's punishment directed
against Neptune only?

As the embodiment of a violent act, Medusa becomes too terrible for
mortals to look upon, just as the act of rape was too terrible for Minerva
to look upon. Because of Minerva's vengeance, the violence of desire—
both of rape and of revenge—becomes so located in the snake-haired
woman that any desire to know her, even by looking, results in death.
Minerva puts snakes on her own shield, but only to frighten her foes,
not to kill them. Medusa's passive power is ultimate, irrevocable. Do the
stone-dead *see* Medusa before they die? Do they desire or love her? In
Ovid's narrative we do not know. What knowledge does their gaze convey
to them along with death? We cannot be told. What is Medusa's reaction
to her transformation? No one in Ovid's text asks this question. Her
reflection gives Perseus the power to kill her, but it is power gained by
not gazing directly. So indirection, reflection, becomes the new means of
empowerment. Medusa is raped by Neptune because he looks at her;
Medusa is transformed by Minerva because the goddess will not look at
her; Medusa is beheaded by Perseus because he knows not to look at
her. As much as it is possible for anything to be so, the transformed
Medusa exists only as a reflection in a mirror. Because of the curse, she
cannot be seen except at the moment of death, and, although artists

from the Hebrews[10] to Roman stone carvers at Bath to Caravaggio have tried to represent her face, writers have left her curiously unfashioned.

Tobin Siebers argues that "the seemingly antithetical figures of Medusa and Athena are only two different expressions made by the same face. Medusa and Athena seem to occupy two poles, but double one another in crossing. . . . Once we detach our view from the mythological perspective of the community, the difference between the divinity and the monster vanishes."[11] To the extent that Minerva's anger at Neptune becomes objectified in Medusa, Siebers is quite right. But what interests me is the problematic of this "crossing." What response to female power prompts the construction of this paradigm? Freud's attribution of power is to one male-referential aspect of the head, and his concern is with male power, which leads him to dismiss Minerva as a castrated male and to discuss Medusa simply as a representation of the male fear of castration.[12] Must even a goddess be contained as one of two poles, as a marker for masculine power and experience?[13]

The problem of polarity raises the question of reflection as a means of representation, the distinction between the mirror and the painting or text. Any sort of representation is a doubling. The artist—writer or painter—creates the initial image in her eye or imagination and projects that image onto a canvas or a page. The writer or painter who works with a mirrored image first sees, then projects, then reverses the figure. Is this triple representation a means of further distancing, of further objectifying a figure, or is it somehow meant to work as does a double negative? Siebers suggests that we move "toward a comprehensive theory of the sacred" by "conceiving of representations as an agent meant to contain violence."[14] But, if this is true, do we not also move toward a comprehensive theory of the political by conceiving of representations as an agent meant to contain power? By investing the political with the ability to contain power, we provide at least the fiction that as a text is generated in relation to the aesthetic rules of a society, so is power controlled in relation to social order. Texts that represent power are all attempts to define and contain power, but "to contain" does not necessarily mean "to diminish." Machiavelli used his text to quantify, to present, a neatly contained reflection of the power of a prince, but the image in the mirror of the text was also meant to empower the author. Writers can use their texts to reflect powerful figures at "twice their natural size," to borrow Woolf's phrase, but the glorified reflection is also meant to benefit the writer, the maker of the mirror. This sort of reflection is a commonplace, for its goal is the socially acceptable one of praise and reward. But what if, as in the Medusa story, "contain" *does* mean "to diminish"? Whether or not maker of such a mirror would articulate his agenda must surely depend upon the cultural climate and upon the relation of the writer to his patron or ruler.[15] Virgil, as Ariosto's Saint John suggests, creates a powerful Dido only to diminish her, but he does so in an effort to glorify Augustus Caesar through his fictive ancestor, Aeneas. The human woman Medusa is not merely diminished by Ovid's narrative, she is annihilated. Her metamorphosis is not that of Daphne or even of Acteon, for she is denied not only speech, but also thought and emotion. Of all of Ovid's transformations, Medusa becomes most completely a thing, an object with no human faculties, an identity whose self is entirely external and defined by other characters.

In the Galleria degli Uffizi hangs Caravaggio's painting of the Medusa. The image is painted as a reflection on a shield. The face, though horrified, is not horrific; it can be called beautiful.[16] But it is not the face of the Gorgon; rather it is the reflection that allowed Perseus to kill her.

TAIN: THE SHIELD OF PERSEUS

The surface off of which the image is turned, the *tain*, is the crossing point of the chiasmus of the mirror gaze. The term probably derives from the tin or other alloy painted on glass to produce a reflecting surface,[17] but has become the term for the surface itself. Surely the point of the Medusa story is that reflection is not the thing itself, that the mirror-image gaze is significantly different from the direct gaze. The differentiation must lie, therefore, on the tain of the mirror. Here the image is reversed by reflection. Thus is the tain of a mirror radically different from the canvas of a painting. Is it also different from a textual blazon?

The tain is that which sends back the reversed image to the eye of the gazer. It can be the tin alloy behind a glass or it can be the polished metal of a shield, the water of a pool, or even the surface of the human eye.

It can be the words on a page. As the violence of Medusa's story escapes the bounds of representation on shield or in a text, so the power of Elizabeth, the power of Cleopatra, the power of Eve escapes from the texts contrived by Spenser, Shakespeare, and Milton, texts contrived to contain that power. The woman imaged on the tain of the text strikes the reader with a different force than the power of the original figure— a diminished force, I will argue, a mediated force, as Medusa's image was mediated for Perseus by Minerva's gift and Ovid's ordering of his narrative. The *Faerie Queene, Antony and Cleopatra, Paradise Lost* are texts in which the various powers of female figures are reflected by textual mirrors, reflected, contained, and ultimately diminished. Although I do emphasize the metaphor of the text as mirror when I make that statement, I also mean that each author uses literal references to mirrors and extensive mirror imagery within each text.

Do these Renaissance texts become the shield of Perseus? Mediating the iconic, historic, sexual power of these three female figures by rendering them as reflected images? If so, then the element of recognition is further problematized. Unable to recognize an interior female self, the male Renaissance poet sets up a paradigm in which the female character can study her external image and ponder her interior self. Of course, any element of recognition must be a metafiction, as the poet cannot endow his own creation with the ability to recognize that which he has failed to imagine. That these episodes so often result in the women failing to recognize themselves is hardly surprising when viewed in this light, and yet as an imaginative solution to a problem of gender identity, the mirror scene would be very clever if it could shed the intellectual baggage of its canonical history. I find it extremely revealing that in their attempts to represent the female self, the two epic poets construct mirror scenes as a means of constructing interior female selves, and that their plots depend upon female failure to recognize the self, while the playwright gives us a female self that is ultimately disempowered by the mirror of history, the Jacobean shield of Perseus facilitating the double death of Elizabeth I. In all three works, the female characters succeed to the extent that they are allowed to come to terms with their reflected images. The images, of course, being the products of the male poetic imagination, tell us about the poet's idea of the female self and little or nothing about the selfhood of Renaissance women. Like so many descendants of Perseus, Spenser and Shakespeare and Milton gaze at the reflections they have constructed and claim victory.

At one angle, presumably, Perseus' shield would return to him his own reflection. Instead he angles it toward the Gorgon, his gaze meeting her reflected image, and this process of reflection becomes the source of his own power. Perseus does not re-present himself through the reflection on his shield, but he does realize himself, does become a hero through his use of that reflection. The finite point of realization of his power is located neither in Perseus himself nor in the face of the Medusa, but on the tain of the mirror, the tain of the mirror that reverses the image of the Gorgon and that allows the would-be hero to kill her and to use her. Then he can re-present her through his own narrative; she has become part of his story. Although he has felt fear, has been vulnerable to the fate of those who gaze, since becoming empowered by the mirror of mediation, he has gained control of that power, gained control of the image. Ovid's strategy of narration, at which we gaze on the tain of the text, reinforces this shift in power.

How does the tain work? What action in the Medusa narrative is presented, re-presented here? Is it an unmaking of Minerva's transformation or a re-placement? Is it the gaze that is displaced or the object of that gaze? I would suggest that the gaze is controlled and the power of the object is mediated. This makes the tain of the mirror at once more powerful than either the gaze or the object it reflects—it is, after all, the gift of a goddess. This is a good analogy for the texts I wish to discuss. The extent to which students and sometimes scholars discuss Britomart, Cleopatra, and Eve as though they were real women owes less to the power of their historical sources than to the power of the poetic representation of Spenser, Shakespeare, and Milton. Their textual representations of female selves have become more powerful and remained more immediate than the original objects—real or imaginary—of their poetic gazes. For of course there are two sets of mirrors at the heart of this study: the mirror within the text and the mirror of the text.

Minerva's act of transformation, which renders Medusa unseeable except on the tain of Perseus' shield, can be seen as more than a metaphor for the author's act of writing Eve or Cleopatra or Elizabeth onto the tain of the text. In each case, the representation of the woman on the tain disempowers her and empowers the one who gazes. This places the reader in the position of Perseus, but does not quite allow the author to be Minerva. In one sense, yes, the author gives the tain of the text to the reader and allows the reader to look at the reflection of the woman. But, again, what is missing is the face of that woman. Although Minerva averts her eyes from the rape scene, these three writers give evidence of trying to see their female characters. Is Minerva able to look upon Medusa? We will remember that she hides her gaze behind her own shield, but a shield that deflects rather than reflects. If there is a relationship between Minerva and the author in this analogy, I would suggest that the author's gender parallels Minerva's shield. It stands between the real woman and the person with the power to reconstruct her. Minerva does not recognize herself in the ravished maiden any more than those three male poets can recognize themselves in their female creations. Both Minerva and the writers use a mediating surface to deal with the identity of the mortal woman. The tain of the mirror and the tain of the text thus assume a more important place in this paradigm of reflected knowledge. Perhaps Minerva never saw Medusa as a real woman; even if she did look, it would be without recognition. We can assume from other stories of gods' powers that she would not have been the victim of her own curse, so presumably she can look at Medusa the monster after her transformation, but still without recognition. If we carry this analysis into the realm of poetry, would the same not be true for the poet? He can look at his own creation, but he will not or cannot recognize a real woman. He can construct a woman who can seek to recognize herself in a mirror, but he cannot control the quality of reversal inherent in this mode of representation.

MIRROR: THE TWO VISIONS OF NARCISSUS

From classical Latin "to wonder, to admire," mirror (which has the same root as miracle) is thus a noun formed from a verb. "Mirror" as noun and as verb are two words less separable by grammatical distinctions than most homonyms. Not only does *mirror* signify both an act of gazing and the phenomenon generating the reflected gaze, but the term is also applied nonliterally to texts. This tradition, growing in metaphoric strength from Plato to Paul to Augustine, is most emphatically illustrated by the popularity of speculum or "mirror" as a title for medieval texts. "The aptness of the name lay partially in the inclusiveness which it implied. . . . So widespread was its use, especially from the twelfth through the sixteenth century, that historians of literature usually dismiss this question of its origin and multiple meanings with a casual reference to the uncounted examples of printed books and manuscripts to which the title was applied."[18]

Why do we look into mirrors? To see ourselves, of course, to know how we look, what we are. But not, precisely, to see or to know how we look to others. For the reflection in the mirror is not what others see; it is reversed. The reflection in the mirror is the gazer as seen by the gazer, an image represented by the chiasmus of reflection. The image of the mirror as an icon of vanity grows from this technical truth, as the story of Narcissus does not.[19]

Ovid gives us the story of Narcissus in lines 340–510, Book 3, of the *Metamorphoses* and the name Narcissus has become a commonplace for vanity, for self-love in narrative and poetry, existing somewhat discordantly alongside the iconographic tradition of vanity as a woman, usually a woman with a mirror. Not only does Ovid's story have implications beyond the commonplace for an historicized study of mirrors, but the figure of Narcissus raises subtle questions of gender and identity more often found in psychoanalytic discussions. Ovid tells us that Narcissus possessed a beauty so great that he was loved by both women and men. Narcissus himself serves as a sort of mirror, inclusively reflecting and reversing the emotions projected upon him: love and adoration become sorrow and resentment. As with the shield of Perseus and the pool in Narcissus's own story, the mirror surface itself is unchanged as it turns back images. In this story, only beauty—beauty beheld through the gaze—arouses love. Narcissus is indifferent to the love he arouses in the others who love his beauty unrequited; he evidently sees in these people who offer love no beauty sufficient to spark his own emotions. He is loved by and rejects both women and men, and it is a man who curses him: "'sic amet ipse licet, sic non potiatur amato!'" ["'So may he himself love, and not gain the thing he loves!'"] (1.405). The rejected lover's curse does not itself have the power to harm; once again we see the intervention of a female god. Indeed, if Nemesis had not heard the scorned young man's "righteous prayer," the implication is that Narcissus never would have found the pool "to which no shepherds ever came, or she-goats feeding on the mountainside, or any other cattle" (2.407–9). Not until he sees the image in the pool does he feel love. Ovid delays this moment through nearly half of the story—76 lines into a tale of only 170 lines. The narrator tells us: "se cupit imprudens et" ["Unwittingly he desires himself"] (1.425). Forty-six more lines go by before Narcissus discovers that the image is his own. Narcissus sees the object of his love as an unknown other, and cries "quisquis es, huc exi!" ["Whoever you are, come forth hither!"] (1.454). Not until lines 463–64 does he realize that "iste ego sum: sensi, nec me mea fallit imago; / uror amore mei" ["Oh, I am he! I have felt it, I know now my own image. / I burn with love of my own self"]. In Ovid's narrative, the youth seems unaware of his own beauty up to that moment of self-recognition in the mirror of the pool. Even then, it is not his own beauty but his own unattainability of which he speaks. This is not a story of vanity, but a story of the dangers of imperfect self-knowledge.

Narcissus' lack of vanity is an important element of Ovid's narrative, especially since Greek versions stress his self-pride.[20] Likewise, Ovid's version of the Narcissus story is significantly different from the medieval version of Ovid's Narcissus story, in which Christian moralists turned Narcissus into an icon of vanity and the mirror of the pool into the antithesis of the mirror of scripture. In the *The Romance of the Rose*, for example, the young man is said to be indifferent to others because he sees no beauty that surpasses his own: "But he, because of his great beauty, was so full of pride and disdain that he did not wish to grant

[Echo] his love, for all her tears and prayers."[21] And even in the less misogynist books by Guillaume de Loris's early pen, we find the element of blame not only central to the narrative, but partly elided onto women. After the death of Narcissus is duly recounted—"Thus did [Narcissus] receive his deserved retribution from the girl whom he had scorned"— the narrator directly addresses the women in the reading audience, concluding the narrative with the following moral injunction:

> You ladies who neglect your duties toward your sweethearts, be instructed by this exemplum, for if you let them die, God will know how to repay you well for your fault. (51)

Not only is Echo cited as the agent of Narcissus's death—called "just retribution"—but all women are warned in a dire sentence that seems completely unrelated to any elements of the narrative that precedes it. In Ovid, it is a man who asks the god of love to make Narcissus feel the pain of unrequited passion, but specifically a passion for himself that cannot be returned; in the *Romance of the Rose*, Echo's dying prayer is much more general—that Narcissus "might one day be tormented and burned by a love from which he could expect no joy"; furthermore, we are told, since "the prayer was reasonable, God confirmed it" (50). This may explain the line about "just retribution," but it leaves the warning to women as nonreferential as ever. There is, however, a context for that admonishment—the medieval tradition of allegorizing Ovid's verses as Christian tales of morality. As William D. Reynolds reminds us, the influence of that most famous of medieval revisions of Ovid, the fourteenth-century *Ovide moralisé* is only the locus classicus of a mind-set that rendered "the *Metamorphoses* as other commentators did the Old Testament, using the familiar Pauline explanation that everything is written for our instruction as justification for . . . supplying every episode . . . with a Christian allegory"—including identifying Perseus as Christ and Andromeda as the human soul.[22] The impulse to condemn women in what had been classically a tale of male identity cannot, however, be laid entirely at the door of the *Ovide moralisé*. As early as the twelfth century, we find in the French tale of "Narcisus and Dané" a version that not only expands the active role of the love-maddened, rejected woman, but—more significantly—a version in which Narcissus first identifies his image in the pool as feminine:

> "Being," he says, "that I see in there, how should I name you? Shall I call you a nymph, a goddess, or a fairy? Whoever you are, come out here and show

me your whole frame! . . . Alas! Does she understand me? Not at all! Perhaps [the water] is too deep? My God! She speaks and answers at once! I can see her lips move but cannot hear her. The water keeps her voice from coming, and I hear nothing. . . . Why does she not show herself? It must be either due to great pride or else she is not desirous of what I want."[23]

Here we see the gender identity of Narcissus problematized, as well as the vice of "great pride" attributed to a woman. Furthermore, the identification of the image in the mirror of the pool as feminine is consistent with another medieval interpretation and revision of this mirror story.

While discussing the *Erec et Enide* of Chrétien de Troyes, Jeanne A. Nightingale provides a discussion of the multivalent role of the mirror in medieval narratives.[24] Generalizing from the portion of the tale in which women are seen as mirrors of the knights' virtue, Nightingale argues for a generic paradigm in which the courtly lady becomes an "idealizing mirror" for the knight who must gaze at her constantly "to verify his progress and to ratify his very existence."[25] Linking this to the neo-Platonic discussion of the mirror, Nightingale suggests that

> In both traditions—the courtly and the cosmic—the mirror figure is used to represent the division between two worlds or two states of being, but since these two worlds appear identical, the mirror represents the locus of deception as often as it serves as a bridge to a higher level of reality. . . . Courtly love may be born in the eyes of the Lady, but if the lover becomes seduced by the image of the perfection he finds there and fails to perceive it as a dim reflection of that ideal toward which he must aspire, he will only alienate himself from the true object of his longing and share Narcissus' fate.[26]

Again we see the increasing intersection of the power of the woman and the power of the mirror in a version of the Narcissus story. While Nightingale's reading of the tale makes this largely Erec's fault, she leaves the more sinister implications of Enide's construction as a mirror unchallenged.

> Like Narcissus, or like Plato's deluded lover, Erec has become captivated by his own image, one that he himself has created in the person of Enide. For as he gazes into the mirror of her beauty, he perceives the image of himself as the perfected model—or "mirror"—of Arthurian knighthood, rather than the vision of the paragon he could yet become. he has made Enide reflect what he wants to see, to mirror his own sense of self-importance. He has chosen her as custodian of his public image, he has outfitted her from the queen's wardrobe so that she will appear a more fitting match for him, he has

even given her her name, "Enide," a feminine echo of his own. And now that he has made his "bele ymage" the single "source" of his gratification, it is Enid, in her role as image, who is blamed for deceiving him and luring him to his downfall.[27]

Obviously, I have cited this discussion of medieval texts at such length because so many of the elements of the narrative could apply to a discussion of Milton's Eve or Shakespeare's Cleopatra. Philippa Berry also makes this connection in the introduction to her book *Of Chastity and Power: Elizabethan Literature and the Unmarried Queen:* "The female beloved . . . was usually little more than an instrument in an elaborate game of masculine 'speculation' and self determination, for the philosophical enterprise common to both Petrarchism and Renaissance Neoplatonism used woman as a 'speculum' or mirror of masculine narcissism."[28] Not discounting the strength of either Nightingale's or Berry's arguments, we must not underestimate the distinction between the medieval mythographer's use of Ovidian paradigms and the images of poets and readers who could read the entire and uneditorialized version of Narcissus' failure to know himself. On the other hand, I would certainly not undervalue the influence of the medieval habits of thought and reading on an audience suddenly confronted with the "real" text. Ironically, Ovid's text would seem to be the revision to a reader in the 1580s or 1590s. That Ovid's Narcissus was not an icon of self-love would be the innovative idea with which the story might be reworked by Renaissance writers.

That this aspect of Ovid's story is largely forgotten by the modern reader (as it was denied to the medieval reader who focuses on the last fifty-six lines of destructive self-obsession) also argues for the power of Christian moral revisionism, even in an age that does not first and foremost define itself as Christian. Arguably, it would be the Renaissance reader, coming to the story in situ in Golding's 1565 translation of books 1–4 (which would also have included the Medusa story) or in one of the many post-1567 complete editions, who would have been more likely than the modern reader to consider the tale as a whole. But while the Renaissance reader or poet might have this advantage, he would at the same time be more heavily influenced by the conflation of the literal mirror with women. The lady with the mirror was a commonplace of decorative art as well as of literary iconography by the end of the Middle Ages. So the advantage of having a non-moralized (so to speak) Ovid to read could well have been mitigated by the cultural norm in which a woman's face appears in any key mirror.

Along with the distinction between recognition and reflection, this psychological re-gendering of the Narcissus story is the reason why I devote so much time to its implications. While the Medusa story depends upon the paradigm of the mirror, this is hardly its most famous feature; traditionally it is the Narcissus story that rises from the collective imagination when Ovid and mirrors are mentioned in the same breath. We find that elements of the two stories become intertwined in Renaissance texts. *Paradise Lost* may be the best example of this, but we find it in the other texts as well.

In the Narcissus story, Ovid does not explicitly distinguish between reflected and unreflected image. Indeed, the narrator tells us: "cunctaque miratur, quibus est mirabilis ipse" (1.424) ["all things, in short, he admires for which he is himself admired"]. But there is a difference, although we may not fully realize it until we have read the Medusa story. Those who gaze directly on Narcissus love him; they suffer because he does not love them; but they do not die.[29] Narcissus gazes upon his own image reflected in the pool and the ultimate result is death, a death, moreover, which is made all the more problematic in this context because it fulfills the first prophecy of Tiresias: "de quo consultus, an esset / tempora maturae visurus longa senectae, / fatidicus vates 'si se non noverit' inquit" ("When asked whether this child would live to reach well-ripened age, the seer replied: 'If he ne'er know himself'" (346–49). Is he then, himself, truly his reflected image?

Is there not a subtle difference even here? Not only is the image without substance, thus without dimension, but it is reversed by the mirror of the pool.

Here also the tain of the mirror has worked a change of life-and-death significance in an image, but a change that is a reversal, a mirror image of the change in the Medusa story. To gaze directly at the beautiful man is to become overpowered by love, but not ultimately disempowered by death; one still remains alive, able, for example, to plead or to curse. To gaze at the reflected image of the beautiful man is to meet death. Death awaits also for those who gaze directly at the horrific woman, while to behold her reflection is to overpower, to kill, both the female monster and, subsequently, one's foes. But this gender split may be too simple. We don't know what would happen to anyone else who gazed at either Narcissus's or Medusa's reflection. Perseus is acting on the instructions of Minerva and is otherwise hedged about with magic. What we can say is that both of these stories link power and identity with metamorphosis through mirror reflections. It is this paradigm—

and any gendered elements that it may include—which needs further explication.

The surfaces of the pool of Narcissus and the shield of Perseus act as literal mirrors; metaphoric and magical mirrors also figure prominently in literary history, although these categories obviously can intersect. For example, a literal mirror, such as the one Richard II calls for in Shakespeare's historical tragedy can become, in the context of that work, a metaphor for the difference between appearance and reality. The metaphoric mirror of Scripture[30] can employ a reference to a literal mirror, as Paul does in I Cor. 13. Or a literal mirror can be employed in a supernatural narrative without itself becoming a magic mirror, as when Perseus views the Medusa reflected in the mirror of his shield.

Suggesting that literary analysis is "concerned primarily with the relationship of a character to the magic mirror,"[31] Theodore Ziolkowski goes on to define the three major categories of magical mirrors to be found in literature: "the catoptromantic mirror that the viewer consults for information; the doubling mirror from which the reflected figure emerges to confront the viewer as his own 'double'; and the penetrable mirror that the viewer can enter in order to experience at first hand its reflected world"—finally calling the catoptromantic mirror "the oldest and most familiar of these categories."[32] That last statement seems to me to be questionable, as we should keep in mind that such quests for knowledge surely grew out of the properties of reflection. The magic may have been a first explanation without being a first experience. And it is only in this way that the catoptromantic mirror impinges on this study. When Britomart looks for herself, sees nothing, then sees Artegall, she has first gazed into what she thinks (through temporary lapse of memory) is a literal, simple mirror, thinking to see herself. The image of Artegall becomes more important and more problematic because it was not sought out in a catoptromantic mirror (well, it *is* catoptromantic, but Britomart has forgotten that), but instead found by seeming chance to return by eyes expecting a simple reflection.

THE PARADIGM OF THE MIRROR
IN THE PARADIGM OF THE TEXT

The mirror paradigm is related to the writing and reading of literary texts in a significant way. I began my work on this chapter by questioning the connection between classical and medieval mirror images and the use of the mirror image by Renaissance writers: the mirror of truth, carried over into the Renaissance in such texts as *A Mirror for Magistrates* and *The Steel Glass;* the mirror of vanity found in the *Romance of the Rose* and relocated into Eve's narrative in book 4 of *Paradise Lost;* the mirror of contemplation into which Rachel gazes in *Purgatorio* 27 and that Richard II breaks in act 4 of Shakespeare's play; magical mirrors from Arthurian romance, such as the one into which Britomart gazes in book III, canto ii of Spenser's *Faerie Queene.* If the multivalent image of the mirror, so important in medieval writings, has undergone some fundamental change in the Renaissance imagination, this change could be read as symptomatic of the ideological and artistic differences between the two periods. To say a change is symptomatic is not to proclaim it as definitive, for the real change at issue lies not in which of the multivalent mirror topoi Spenser or Milton might be using, but in the perception of reflection itself as a mode of representation. More importantly, all three writers in this study use the paradigm of reflection as a mode of representation for powerful female figures' sense of self. Removed from the Age of Elizabeth by both chronology and politics, Milton's use of this paradigm is the strongest argument for the inescapablilty of its cultural implications.

Reflection is a reversal, a crossing, a chiasmus of representation between the figure, the tain of the mirror, and the eye that sees the reflection. Because of this element of reversal, the paradigm of reflection in a mirror can be used as a subtle force for subversion by the imagination of a male writer representing a powerful woman. In Renaissance writing this heightened awareness of the element of the chiasmus includes not only the reversal of the specific image being mirrored, but reimagings of the influential classical and medieval sources and their contexts. Here I do not use "influence" as in simple source study, that which Rosemond Tuve once called the next-to-last infirmity of noble minds; I refer to the power that traditional paradigms of perception could have exerted on the the poetic imaginations of these three writers and their readers, power that could be re-imaged, privileged, or subverted, not merely reproduced. Nowhere is the complexity of Renaissance mirror imagery more available for study than in texts where the reflected image is that of a powerful woman. In this study I am arguing for both the recognition and the revision of a nexus ("Gordian knot" would be as accurate, if less trendy) of mirror traditions in three texts imaging powerful women: Spenser's *Faerie Queene,* Shakespeare's *Antony and Cleopatra,* and Milton's *Paradise Lost.* Ovid's Medusa narrative provides a most revealing subtext for discussions of these issues in the three texts I examine, for the story is both a paradigm of, and a metaphor for, the representations of gender and power. The three Renaissance texts show us just how variously the image of the mirror could be employed: the mirror as a literal glass surface or as an allusion to other mirror narratives, the mirror as the text itself or as the text holding "a mirror up to nature." If I seem to be using the term *mirror* inexactly, I am but mirroring the multiple uses of the term and of the concept in the texts I am studying.

In the last three years a number of studies have challenged our view of the construction of women in male-authored texts of the Renaissance. Most of these studies—which I will gratefully cite in later chapters— have ended quite naturally with the death of Elizabeth I. By pushing on to include Milton, I hope both to demonstrate the pervasive power of the Medusa paradigm and to dislocate this mode of representation from the specific historical presence of Elizabeth. Fatefully, a chronological discussion of the three texts allows me to discuss the powerful women— Britomart/Elizabeth, Cleopatra, and Eve—in reverse order of their historical chronology: a neat chiasmus.

So, again: Is the thing in the mirror, the other, the reversed image, stronger or weaker than the figure that generates it? Between Ovid's two mirror stories lies an answer: both. The image of Narcissus is stronger than the voice of the narrator, than the natural world around the pool, than the love of Echo, stronger than the identity of the real Narcissus. And it is the image itself that exerts power, for the moment when the young man realizes "*iste ego sum*" comes two-thirds of the way through the tale. It is the *image* of Narcissus that has outlasted most elements of the classical tale; it is the significance of the image that has to be made and remade by successive cultures, and that is most often used to discredit or disempower women. Medusa's reflected image, on the other hand, acts less powerfully on the gazer, but its effect is to make the gazer himself more powerful; so Perseus may gaze upon it and live to kill her and to use her monstrously real female face to kill others. The tain, the surface of the mirror—whether a pool or a shield or a text—has the power to displace by reversal, to displace perception, knowledge, power. Ovid gives us Medusa's story in reverse order: Perseus exercising his power with the Gorgon's head, Perseus rescuing Andromeda, Perseus telling an admiring crowd how he "won the Gorgon's snakey head." Then, at the very end of Book 4, almost as an afterthought and in response to a random question, Perseus tells the story of Medusa herself. We never see her face. Perseus tells the story of her rape second-hand, mentioning only that her hair was said to be beautiful; we never know what those who look on her metamorphosed visage see, for they die instantly; Perseus never describes what he sees mirrored on his shield, for his focus is on the power of the thing being reflected, not the thing itself. These two stories generate complex paradigms of perception and identity and power, paradigms made even more problematic by the medieval traditions that link the mirror of Narcissus to Vanity—a female figure—and that suggest that the power of the Gorgon was the power of sexual attraction.[33] The popularity of Golding's English translation gave Renaissance writers the freedom of an audience who could read Ovidian references through both the original stories and the traditional variations on those stories.

Shakespeare and Spenser make use of these narratives and other mirror imagery to describe, explain, justify, and displace the power of Elizabeth I. Spenser, writing for a living and aging queen, offers the monarch "mirrours more then one her selfe to see" (book III, proem), naming two mirrors—Gloriana and Belphoebe—but leaving unnamed the real mirror who is identified by the title of the book in which these lines appear: Britomart. In books III, IV, and V of his epic, Spenser fashions a narrative of reflection in which Britomart has her own mirror vision and begins a quest for identity that ends in book V when she is faced with a problem mirroring Elizabeth's own political reality. Britomart must privilege her own position without changing the position of all women (so she kills Radigund, the Amazon queen); and she must privilege the male-dominated social order without losing the means of her own empowerment (so she outlaws women's rule and *then* orders all the knights to obey Artegall); she must—as Spenser openly admits of Elizabeth—be both Gloriana and Belphoebe, public queen and private virgin. Spenser's fiction of dynastic epic ends with Britomart's words "farewell fleshly force." Like the canvas of the Siena/Sieve portrait of Elizabeth, the text of the *Faerie Queene* allows for this double vision. Within Spenser's text, Elizabeth, the Virgin Queen, can regenerate *herself*, as she generates and is reflected in the image of Britomart on the tain of this textual mirror.

Shakespeare uses the verb "to mirror" in a multiplicity of ways. A queen herself, Cleopatra seems at first blush as far from one whose epithet was "Virgin" as the imagination can reach, and I am not arguing—as I will with Britomart—that the Egyptian monarch is meant to be read directly and primarily as an Elizabeth figure. Still, she is an unsurpassed figure of female power in Shakespeare's works, but power that shares many properties with the tain of a mirror. In the major portion of the Cleopatra chapter, I will examine the ways in which other characters and Cleopatra herself generate images of themselves and of

her, images reflected back at the gazer from the mirror of this figure of
female power. The play itself possesses mirrorlike qualities as we see
a chiasmus—a crossing and reversal—of the identities of the two title
characters. Finally, in the last lines of the play, holding his text up to
reflect the nature of his own political world, Shakespeare mirrors a new
male ruler replacing a powerful older woman. James I identified himself
on his coronation medals as the Augustus Caesar of Britain. In the
closing lines of Shakespeare's play, Octavius (soon to be Augustus) orders
Cleopatra carried from her own monument and buried with Antony,
buried not as a queen but as a lover. (In Plutarch, Antony is buried in
Cleopatra's tomb and she is later placed beside him.) The play was written in 1606, the same year in which the tomb James ordered for Elizabeth was completed. With this tomb he marginalizes her as one of two
childless sisters, less importantly placed than she was originally beside
the first Tudor (with whom James later had himself buried) and less
importantly placed than James's mother, Mary Stuart. In death, therefore, Shakespeare's displaced queen gives us a political reflection of the
fate of the historical female monarch.

We see Milton exploiting both medieval and Renaissance readings of
the stories when he has Eve look without recognition at her own image
in a lake, when he has the voice of God speak, almost verbatim, the
warning of Ovid's narrator to Narcissus, and when he puns on the word
"vain." Milton forces the subtext of Ovid into his own lines so completely
that now, when Milton scholars discuss this scene in book 4, we call it
"the pool scene," even though the word "pool" appears nowhere in Milton's text. The pool is Ovid's, and Milton is having his intertextuality
both ways: strictly speaking Eve never looks with love on that image
while knowing it is herself, and the "vain desire" of which she speaks
can mean "fruitless desire"; but the more available meaning of "vain"
tips the balance toward the medieval tradition of vanity and our image
of Eve is shaped accordingly. And yet, as recent critics have observed, if
anyone in Eden is narcissistic in the pejorative sense it is Adam in book
8 when he falls in love with what he calls "my Self / Before me." The
sight of Eve and "the charm of Beauty's power glance" (8.533) turns
Adam, not literally to stone, but away from his knowledge of God, of
whose image he loses sight at the moment Eve returns to him.

All of these mirrors, mirrors that so variously reflect powerful female
images, are mirrors constructed by men. These authors may, like Perseus, gaze into their mirrors and see constructions of the feminine; they
may offer those mirrors to their readers, but (also like the Ovid story)
these constructions are more the reflections of the power of the male

[author] than of the female figure. In the pseudo-Platonic dialogue *Alcibiades,* Socrates asks: "if some one were to say to the eye, 'See thyself', as you might say to a man 'Know thyself', what should we suppose to be the nature and meaning of this precept?"[34] He then goes on to set up an analogy between the eye seeing itself reflected in another eye and the soul seeing its reflection in God, concluding that "as mirrors are truer and clearer and brighter than the mirror within the eye, so also God is by his nature a clearer and brighter mirror than the most excellent part" of a man's soul.[35] As these authors offer us mirror images of the Other, we see also reflected in their mirrors the image of the eye seeing its reflection in another eye, another I—the image thus becoming both a reflection of self and a representation of a reflected woman, or even a reflection of other such dual reflections.

In a 1983 *Representations* article with three essays of commentary appended, Neil Hertz uses a 1792 British antirevolutionary editorial cartoon called "The Contrast," which makes reference to Burke's *Reflections on the Revolution in France,* published in 1790. Half of the cartoon depicts Britain calmly representing peace and justice under an oak tree, while the other half of the cartoon personifies revolution as a Medusa figure holding both a sword and a staff with a man's head on it.[36] As part of a larger argument, Hertz uses the cartoon to ask: "The question is, why should revolutionary violence be emblematized in this way, as a hideous and fierce but not exactly sexless woman?"[37] He continues, speaking of the writings of Tocqueville and Hugo and Maxime du Camp: "All three writers have produced intensely charged passages that are about a confrontation with a woman, a confrontation in which each finds an emblem of what revolutionary violence is all about." He calls these representations of female revolutionary figures "Medusa-fantasies" and says that these figures have in common the unnatural, the ideal of things reversed: "They are threatening to the extent that they raise doubts about one's own more natural ways of looking at things; and it is that threat that prompts these powerfully rendered Medusa-fantasies when they are offered as substitutes for a more patient, inclusive account of political conflict."[38] I bring these observations into my essay not only to prepare the way for some of the political insights I find that the story of Medusa and the mirror of mediation gives us into issues of gender and power in Renaissance texts, but so that I may also invoke the commentary of Joel Fineman in his essay responding to Hertz's argument:

> Hertz associates this point of view with the political left, or, rather, more precisely, with the political left as seen by the political right. That is to say, this

is the point of view that the counterrevolution fearfully attributes to that which it opposes: this is how the right imagines revolutionary imagination. In the same way, with regard to erotics, this is the point of view not exactly of Woman but of that which natural Man looks at with erotic dread and fascination. Again, this is a point of view that is more seen than it is seeing, natural Man's salacious, voyeuristic image of the gaze of his unnatural other, the Other to which, as Lacan says, there is no other.[39]

In Ovid's narrative, in Shakespeare's play, in the epics of Spenser and Milton, the representations of women and power—and in the Renaissance texts the thoughts, words, and actions of powerful women—are literally the imaginings of male writers. In a society where the forty years of female (although not feminist) power of Elizabeth had raised profound questions of natural order or relationship between gender and power, I suggest that it is possible to describe the male mind as possessing "the point of view that the counterrevolution fearfully attributes to that which it opposes: this is how the right imagines revolutionary imagination." For all that we may now judge Elizabeth no feminist, however theologically and nationalistically we explain the objections raised to the influence of Henrietta Maria upon Charles I, and no matter how consistently Milton scholars ignore the possible influence of writers such as Rachel Speight, we must not discount the extent to which these seemingly uncontrolled women could disturb the cultural imaginations of male writers.

As I do not wish to present a traditional source study of the use of Medusa imagery in three Renaissance texts, neither do I wish to imply that this will be primarily an historical (although I would argue that it could be called historicist) study of the cultural discontents caused specifically by the rule of Elizabeth or the influence of Henrietta Maria or the writings of seventeenth-century women or the debatable power of women in Puritan politics—although Elizabeth certainly is a direct point of reference for two of the texts. Rather, I wish to examine these texts as products of a cultural climate where female power had become more public and therefore more frightening, evoking a variety of responses, some more conscious than others. I present the Medusa paradigm not as a formula for reading, but as a metaphor for the issues I wish to discuss within these three texts. To adapt the words of Madelon Gohlke to my own topic:

Much of what I am going to say about [the Medusa story and the representations of the powerful female self in these three Renaissance texts] depends on a reading of metaphor. It is metaphor that allows us to subread, to read on the margins of discourse, to analyze what is latent or implicit in the structures of consciousness or of a text. A serious feminist critic, moreover, cannot proceed very far without becoming paranoid unless she abandons a strictly intentionalist position. To argue sexism as a conspiracy becomes both foolish and absurd.[40]

So as I "subread"—read on the margins of these three texts—I will heed Gohlke's warning about a "strictly intentionalist position" even as I argue for some examples of deliberate disempowerment of the feminine. For it is possible to see both: that which is thoughtfully represented by a culture in response to historically composed expectations, and that which is revealed about a culture through those assumptions that are made without definitive articulation.

We can see the first and last faces of Medusa only in our imaginations. With Spenser's allegorical representation of a living English monarch, Shakespeare's Egyptian queen centered in an historical canvas placed in a contemporary frame, and Milton's representation of the first woman we see how the selfhood and the power of women—from the politically immediate to the historic to the mythical—can be mediated, re-imaged, celebrated, and diminished by the tain of a text. Unlike Ovid's Medusa, we have in Eve, in Cleopatra, in Elizabeth, an untransformed figure extrinsic to the text, but we also have the intrinsic representation that the author reflects on the tain of his text. This study is about turning, about the chiasmus of perception that exists both between the real and the image and between the image and the eye. In each of these three Renaissance texts, that chiasmus, turned on the tain of the textual mirror, always serves to alter relationships between and among the woman's gender and her power and her sense of self.

3

Elizabeth is Britomart is Elizabeth: this sex which is not won

I see and sigh (because it makes me sad)
That peevish pride doth all the world possess;
And every wight will have a looking-glass
To see himself, yet so he seeth him not.
Yea, shall I say, a glass of common glass,
Which glist'reth bright and shews a seemly shew,
Is not enough: the days are past and gone
That beryl glass, with foils of lovely brown,
Might serve to show a seemly favored face.
That age is dead, and vanished long ago,
Which thought that steel both trusty was and true,
And needed not a foil of contraries,
But showed all things even as they were indeed.
Instead whereof, our curious years can find
The crystal glass, which glimpseth brave and bright,
And shows the thing much better than it is,
Beguil'd with foils of sundry subtile sights,
So that they seem, and covet not to be.
　　　　　　　　　—George Gascoigne, *The Steel Glass*

In his 1576 satire Gascoigne makes distinctions between types of mirrors: the common glass or beryl glass, an earlier form of mirror that by its "foils of lovely brown" flatters a favored face in "seemly shew," has been replaced by the modern crystal glass that "shows the thing much better than it is." This crystal glass, with its reflection "beguil'd with foils of sundry subtile sight" is constructed so that the thing or person can be seen as "brave and bright"—or at least seeming to be so. Seeming, Gascoigne implies, will be enough for those who gaze into the crystal glass that overgoes the "seemly" reflection of common glass; if they seem brave and bright and better than they are, that is enough and they are beguiled with the ultraflattering image and thus covet no more. By con-

69

trast, the steel glass, whose age is called "dead, and vanished long ago," offers a reflection that is "trusty" and "true" and sufficient to itself, not needing to be contrasted with real sight; reality is not a "foil of contraries" for this mirror. Instead the steel glass represents reality. Gascoigne's narrator declares: "Since I desire to see myself indeed— / Not what I would, but what I am, or should— / Therefore I like this trusty glass of steel."[1]

Applying Gascoigne's distinctions to Spenser's poetic constructions of the mirrored Britomart/Elizabeth, I would suggest that in the proem to book III he offers Elizabeth what he claims to be a set of common glasses, in which she can see the "seemly shew" of the images of Belphoebe and Gloriana. As Britomart looks into her own literal mirror within the narrative, however, we find references to all three of Gascoigne's mirrors. The mirror made by Merlin is represented as a "mirrhour plaine," implying either the common glass or the steel glass; but it is also called a "mirrhour fayre" and "right wondrously aguiz'd," suggesting the properties of the crystal glass. The longest passage about the mirror itself—which I will discuss in more detail within this chapter— claims that it

> vertue had, to shew in perfect sight,
> What ever thing was in the world contaynd,
> Betwixt the lowest earth and heauens hight

a description that sounds much more like Gascoigne's valued steel glass.

Reading Gascoigne's Renaissance satire of self-knowledge with Spenser's mirror-filled allegory lends us some contemporary insight into Spenser's complex paradigm of variously represented mirrors. The poet of *The Steel Glass* warns "such as be historiographers / Trust not too much in every tattling tongue, / Nor blinded be by partiality," but only twelve lines later urges poetry to abandon preaching and flattery and to "dote not upon Erato," but to "invoke the good Calliope."[2] As he constructs *The Faerie Queene* with elements of historiography, partiality, preaching, and flattery, Spenser nevertheless gives us an epic that is closer to a steel than a crystal glass. Like the shield of Perseus, however, the text itself is a mediating mirror. As we look into the mirror of the text, we may see a reflection of the queen as she looks; but what we see is not the image that meets Elizabeth's eyes, nor can we meet the direct force of her glance even as we look into the same mirrors. Did Spenser hold a common or a crystal or a steel glass up before the eyes of his monarch? Is the glass he offers to the queen the same sort of glass he offers to the common reader? To begin to answer these questions, we must turn to the poem.

PAINTING ON MORE THAN MIRRORS: THE NARRATIVE OF REFLECTION

Although he names Elizabeth in both the 1590 and 1596 dedications of his epic, Edmund Spenser inscribes the name of his queen in no line of his poem. Even in the proem to book III, partly phrased in direct address to the monarch, he never writes the name Elizabeth, using instead pronouns, titles, and the representations of other writers. In these five stanzas Spenser conflates the trope of poetry as a speaking picture with the trope of the mirror of truth found in a text. In books III, IV, and V of his poem, Spenser simultaneously employs these two metaphors of representation to construct a triple vision of Elizabeth: the queen as she is popularly represented by sixteenth-century artists and writers; the queen as she wishes to be seen in relation to her own self-constructed image; the queen as a woman who is also a ruler in a society that genders political power exclusively male, a society that provides no models for the selfhood of powerful women. In dedicating the poem to her he subscribes to the fiction of a monarch of the arts, a ruler who nurtures creative endeavor as assiduously as she supervises her nation's defenses. In the letter to Raleigh and the proem of book III, he achieves the second representation: the queen is both the invisible Gloriana and the virgin Belphoebe in her public and private selves. And yet, even as Spenser offers the word "selfe" to Elizabeth, he suggests only the distinction between a public surface and a private surface—between Gloriana or Belphoebe; there is no reference to interiority. Only in the third vision, with its implicit promise of Elizabeth and the more complexly constructed Britomart, do we find any artistic or imaginative space for the representation of an interior self. The third, and most realistic of the representations, is the most politically significant. This third vision has little to do with the first two, is indeed in conflict with the first two visions, and therefore constitutes a radical poetic act that must be so carefully represented that it is done—literally and metaphorically—with mirrors.[3]

Saying that the royal houses of Europe were "consciously—intensifying the mystique of monarchy" as rulers felt the need to assume "more and more of a messianic role in an age that had witnessed the breakdown of the universal church and the shattering of the old cosmology," Sir

Roy Strong argues for the consequent importance of images of the monarch.[4] Recent work on the "Siena/Sieve" portrait and on the "Rainbow" portrait[5] has established in impressive detail just how true this statement had become for court artists in the last years of Elizabeth's reign. Strong's assertion, I will argue, also holds true for the work of Edmund Spenser as he produced what may be considered the greatest portrait of Elizabeth's reign: Britomart. Spenser's Elizabeth portrait surpasses all the painted panels, however richly encoded with meaning, because, through the force of epic narrative, it can figure forth a changing image, an image confronted by physical and political realities, an image thus altered by those confrontations. Because this changing portrait of ink on paper is linear, it presents the identity of its central figure to the eye only gradually, as the media of the poet's allegory and the poem's narrative ultimately construct the mirror image of a virgin whose motherhood is fictive merely.

Spenser introduces the analogy between a poetic representation and a painting in the proem to book III by speaking of Elizabeth's virtue of chastity as interior, "the pourtraict of her hart, / If pourtrayd it might be by any liuing art" (III Proem. 1.8–9).[6] In the next three stanzas he develops the conceit of the poem as painting, making it the controlling principle of representation for the legend of Britomart.

> But liuing art may not least part express,
> Nor life-resembling pencill it can paint,
> All were it *Zeuxis* or *Praxiteles*:
> His daedale hand would faile, and greatly faint,
> And her perfections with his error taint:
> Ne Poets wit, that passeth Painter farre
> In picturing the parts of beautie daint,
> So hard a workmanship aduenture darre,
> For feare through want of words her excellence to marre.
>
> How then shall I, Apprentice of the skill,
> That whylome in diuinest wits did raine,
> Presume so hight to stretch mine humble quill?
> Yet not my lucklesse lot doth me constraine
> Hereto perforce. But O dred Soueraine
> Thus farre forth pardon, sith that choicest wit
> Cannot your glorious pourtraict figure plaine
> That I in coloured showes may shadow it,
> And antique praises unto present person fit.

(III Proem. 2–3)

Having suggested the impossibility of a single painting being able to "figure plaine" all aspects of Elizabeth, Spenser goes on to suggest the medium of poetry as the only means of representing so "glorious" a figure. As David Lee Miller observes: "Thus *poetry* can cap the sequence of forms that are inadequate to their original while still leaving open a space for the emergence of *allegory* as an alternative to the poetics of sensuous realism."[7] Spenser offers first not his own but the poetry of Raleigh as a true picture of the monarch:

> But if in liuing colours, and right hew,
> Your selfe you couet to see pictured,
> Who can it do more liuely, or more trew,
> Then that sweet verse, with *Nectar* sprinckeled,
> In which a gracious seruant pictured
> His *Cynthia*, his heauens fairest light?
>
> (4.1–6)

Spenser goes on, however, in the last stanza of the proem, to displace the artistic achievement of Raleigh, overgoing it with his own as he offers not a single classical figure, but a mirror; not a single mirror, but "mirrours more then one" (4.6) will Elizabeth find in the single text that is Spenser's poem. This, then, is Spenser's version of Sir Christopher Hatton and another knight challenging each other as to who could present "the truest picture of hir Majestie to the Queene"; one presented a flattering picture, the other a mirror.[8] On this point I agree with Louis Adrian Montrose: "What the poet conventionally deprecates as his inability to produce an adequate reflection of the glorious royal image is [in the proem of book III] the methodical process of fragmentation and refraction by which the text appropriates that image, imposing upon it its own specificity."[9] Put more simply, I would suggest, the text appropriates the image of Elizabeth as she wishes to be seen in the 1580s—a real woman who is at once a monarch, a public virgin, and yet the mystical and metaphoric mother of her people—and replaces that image with a representation that is unequivocally iconic. In the complex representation of Britomart as an Elizabeth figure, we are first shown a remarkably detailed exploration of the interior female self, only to see that interiority displaced as Britomart defines her public identity and acknowledges that the manifestation of her female power is undercut by her attention to her interior identity. Realistically, in political terms, Elizabeth's multivalent public image is impossible.[10] While seeming to validate this multivalency, Spenser argues (beneath the veil of allegory that is Britomart) for the historical, social, and personal choices that have trans-

formed Elizabeth from a woman into an icon. He presents his argument
in the story of Britomart, whose gender identity is represented not on
the surface of a canvas, but on the tain of a mirror.

The poetic story—the [hi]story of Elizabeth's "ancestor" Britomart—is
foregrounded by the proem of book III and by the generic expectations
generated by Spenser's invocation of Ariosto's multiplot dynastic epic,
only to be gradually erased by the narrative of books III, IV, and V. If
the story and the narrative[11] were consistent, we would find a wedding
in book V; instead we find Mercilla and lose sight of Britomart as she
bids "farewell to fleshly force" (V. vii. 40.9) and the fiction of dynastic
motherhood. Using as pigment the fiction of a dynastic epic and framing
his portrait with allusions to two epic couples—thus overgoing the
painter of the "Sieve" portrait—Spenser offers to the queen a text
framed by her own multivalent image but mirroring her in the single
figure of Britomart.[12] The multiple nature of Elizabeth's public image—
monarch, virgin, mother, warrior, lover, goddess—is daunting enough
to make any artist "fear through want of words her excellence to marre"
by highlighting one aspect of this image at the expense or to the exclusion of another. I agree in part with Elizabeth J. Bellamy that one quest
(I would not say the "ultimate quest") of the poem is "the poet's unsuccessful effort to nominate Elizabeth"[13]; I would argue, however, that
intrinsic to the failure to name Elizabeth is Spenser's success at representing her. The paradigm of dynasty becomes a fiction, a prop, an
element of representation, which enables both the historical and the
psychological reality of the portrait. Monarchy and dynasty are complexly and inextricably linked, but to avoid any suggestion of failure
on Elizabeth's part, Spenser must find a way to transcend the dynastic
paradigm. To represent her even in relation to (to say "as" may be over-
stating the case) a woman with a sense of self, he must problematize the
proem's mirror topos by including Britomart as the principle Elizabeth
figure. By setting up the complex metaphor of portraiture and mirroring, Spenser begins this delicate task. In the proem of book I, Spenser
calls Elizabeth herself the "Mirrour of grace and Maiestie diuine"; in
the proem of book 3 he offers his own text as "mirrours more then one"
in which Elizabeth can see herself. Naming Gloriana and Belphoebe as
two of those mirrors, Spenser leaves unnamed his major representation
of Elizabeth—unnamed in the proem, but named in the name of the
book: Britomart.[14]

When we look at the images in the text, we realize that—whatever
Spenser may have said in the letter to Raleigh or in the proem to book
III—Britomart is the figure who mirrors the queen. Setting aside the

invisible and perpetually deferred Gloriana, let us examine Elizabeth, Belphoebe, and Britomart. Britomart and Elizabeth both have or have had fathers who were kings and from whom they learn, however indirectly, about the business of life; Belphoebe has no father, only sunbeams. Neither Britomart nor Elizabeth has a mother; Belphoebe has two: Chrysogone and Diana. Britomart has no sister, being her father's "onely daughter and his hayre," and Elizabeth has only the Catholic Mary—a half-sister who the Protestant Spenser would happily have equated with "none" and who was literally dead anyway. Belphoebe has not only a sister in Amoret, but a twin. Both Britomart and Elizabeth spent their childhoods as heirs of powerful men, as women in training for masculine roles (although not in the martial mode falsely described by Britomart) with no apparent attempts made to resolve the resulting confused gender-identity. Both were well-educated: Elizabeth's learning being legendary and Britomart having an extensive knowledge of at least Ovid and English history, as we learn from her exchanges with Glauce in III. ii and iii. Britomart, we observe in stanza 23 of canto ii, realizes in a general way that most women married and that "her life at last must lincke in the same knot"; but she had no object of desire, and the vision of Artegall takes her so much by surprise that she does not recognize (or refuses to recognize) its existence.

Elizabeth, being her father's daughter, would have been more than aware of the institution of marriage, but that awareness must have brought with it a lesson about the hazards of matrimony from the viewpoint of a woman who would inherit a throne. And her half-sister Mary's marriage to Philip of Spain would have taught her a lesson on marriage's dangers to both foreign and domestic empowerment—one reason, no doubt, that she became a professional virgin. Much like Britomart, Elizabeth looked for images of self and saw visions of male power; she had to fashion her female power for herself. Britomart is referred to by many of the same epithets as Elizabeth: "royall Maid" and "most noble Virgin." Although Britomart is told by Merlin that she will be a mother (a role that doesn't find a very realistic analogy in the fifty-three-year-old Elizabeth), the crowning achievement of Britomart's dynasty will be another "royall virgin" (III. iii. 49.6) who will reign with a "white rod" that must have some generative power, for Merlin concludes: "But yet the end is not." If this imaging is really there—and the similarities up to the dynastic prophecy are hard to ignore—then Britomart's struggle with her sexuality and with her union with Artegall become a minefield for Spenser. If we make the inescapable association between Britomart and Elizabeth while reading Britomart as a dynastic mother, then we

may conclude that Spenser is here trying, albeit delicately and by inference, to figure forth the sort of marriage and succession counsel to
which Elizabeth's subjects had long subjected her. But not only does
Elizabeth's age argue against such a reading: Britomart's behavior after
her mirror vision of Artegall is a tissue of ambiguous responses, contradictory actions, and ultimate denial that cannot simply and dismissively
be placed within the paradigm of the dynastic epic.

The seemingly simple metaphor of the mirroring text that Spenser
employs in the Proem is dislocated by the unarticulated representation
of Britomart as the major Elizabeth figure. The text is still Elizabeth's
figurative mirror, but Britomart's literal mirror also becomes a looking
glass for the monarch's eyes, as Britomart, the queen's mirror image,
looks into a mirror while the queen looks at her. This is very close to
the paradigm of the Medusa story. In the last chapter, I raised the question of the position of the reader in this paradigm. As Elizabeth looks
at her reflection turned on the tain of the Britomart text, we might find
a neat answer to this question. But Britomart herself finds a mirror
vision that gives her an image that is not her own. As Spenser doubles
the equation of the Medusa reflections, we may confidently seek a
greater degree of complexity in the representation of female identity
and power than resides even in Ovid's powerful narrative.

Dido/Britomart/Aeneas: gender in the "world of glas"

Beginning very much "in the middle of things," book III opens the
epic-within-an-epic that continues through books IV and V. As in the
Aeneid, we are presented with one canto of present-tense action and two
cantos of history.[15] The mirror scene and the rest of canto ii and all of
iii are supposedly told as Britomart's way of explaining to Red Cross
how she came to be as she is; but it is significant that these two cantos
are narrated not in the first person, as Aeneas tells us his story to Dido—
and, indeed, as Odysseus tells his to the Phaeacians—but in the third
person. Spenser thus objectifies Britomart as a speaking picture, which
is why we speak of her as a figure not a "character," and depersonalizes
her experience for the reader from enactment to representation. This
shift violates the story (Red Cross does, after all, ask Britomart directly,
not a third party) thereby heightening the tension between story and
narrative already present in book III. This tension is generated by
Spenser's secret depiction of Elizabeth through the presentation of Britomart. That Spenser gives us Britomart's earliest history through the

narrator rather than in first-person would seem to contradict my argument that here we see the representation of an interior female self. On the contrary, I would suggest that this strategy allows us to see how difficult it is for Britomart to recognize the elements of her selfhood, problematized as that female selfhood is by her inherited position of male power and her mirror vision. Spenser simultaneously gives us the evolution of an individual woman's self-awareness and the evolution of a strategy for the poetic representation of that selfhood. That Britomart's self-awareness is imperfect and ultimately ephemeral may leave the twentieth-century reader unsatisfied; on the other hand, that Spenser—a sixteenth-century male working within the formalized genre of allegorical epic—gives us an interior female self with any degree of development is remarkable.

The word "secret," as an adjective (often linked to "fear") and as a noun, is associated with Britomart from her first appearance in the poem, III. i, and reiterated through all her key episodes—the mirror vision, Merlin's cave, the House of Busirane, her first sight of Artegall, Isis Church—right up to her rescue of Artegall from Radigund and her disempowering of herself and all women rulers. "Secret" at first seems a dissonant note to sound in the presentation of so public a figure, but the work is a significant signal to the reader, suggesting both the secrets of Britomart's interior self and the open secret of Britomart's poetic identity as a figure of the even more public Elizabeth.[16] The reader knows the secret of Britomart's identity, but not her story; the reader knows Elizabeth's story, but is not yet fully aware of the complexity of her representation in Britomart. Because we know Britomart's identity as the Knight of Chastity, her problems in Malacasta's Castle do not initially seem as strange as they should. The trouble Britomart encounters in III. i springs from her failure to recognize the elements of sexual secrecy in Malacasta's castle and the expectations placed on her by those paradigms of sexual identity. The tapestries Britomart sees on Malacasta's walls are described in detail for us by the poet/narrator, who gives pride of place to the story of Venus leading Adonis to some "secret shade" (35.6) where she "secretly" (36.6) courts him and attempts to enjoy his love "in secret" (37.2). The repetition of *secret* as a descriptive term in three consecutive stanzas is hard for the reader to ignore, but, despite the fact that she is herself a walking icon of sexual secrecy, Britomart fails to read properly, fails to see the significance of the Ovidian narrative. Initially, the reader is not greatly surprised by Britomart's failure to read the tapestries, for it might be argued that a secret knight of chastity has yet to confront openly the forces of antichastity.[17] At any rate, after recognizing no threat, secret or otherwise, in the Castle's decor, Britomart fails either to see the danger of the "secret darts" (51.8) Malacasta throws at her or to anticipate the danger of Malacasta coming with "secret purpose" (60.3) toward her bed. Thus she receives her first wound, and with it realistic proof that keeping gendered sexuality private is not a successful strategy for avoiding sexual problems in either the public or the private sphere. The first bloody wound Britomart sustains is not the first blood she spills, as we discover in III. ii; on the importance of Britomart's bleeding I would agree with Bellamy's analysis:

> Spenser's very act of writing the imperial history of Tudor empire, then, becomes dependent on a symbolic breaking of the hymen, the spilling of virginal blood (Elizabeth's, Britomart's) that can color the blank page of history—virginal blood that identifies painful wounding with male (and imperial) authority, female blood that must be shed within an overdetermined interplay of menstruation, defloration, and birth in the name of dynastic continuity.[18]

That this dynastic continuity will prove to be fictive makes the "secret" meaning of the blood all the more central to Spenser's allegory.

That Britomart fails to see secrets that are plain to the reader is not surprising. I think the point here is that the reader, not Britomart, should become sensitized to the word "secret" and come to associate it with Britomart's encounters with sexuality, for sexual identity and its inextricable relation to selfhood is a secret Britomart tries to keep from herself—and I am deliberately blurring the boundaries between "sexuality" and "gender identity," because they are thus conflated in the text. Therefore, when we are finally given the details of Britomart's first encounter with gender identity in relation to sexuality in III. ii, we may be expected to remember and reflect upon the knight's failure to read properly the story of Venus and Adonis and to act properly in Malacasta's castle. This forces us to question Britomart's success at recognizing the basic elements of female selfhood with which she is confronted in III. ii.

Britomart's rejection of sexual identity is more graphic than any version of Adonis' withdrawal, and yet she seems to recognize neither the figure nor the revision of his story. To be fair, Britomart's situation as she perceives it in III. ii is closer to those of Daphne, Syrinx, and even Philomela; that Spenser offers her the Venus and Adonis narrative rather than one of these female-victim narratives is our first hint that the poet will not be presenting an early-modern female Bildungsroman. The naive reader of III. i may not expect the Knight of Chastity to

know the story of Venus's sex-denying lover. But when we realize that
Britomart is familiar with such Ovidian oddities as Myrrhe, Biblis, and
Pasiphaë (ii. 41), we must recognize Britomart's reading of the tapestry
for what it is: a failure of awareness that amounts to suppression of
knowledge. Britomart's secret fears, generated by the mirror vision in
III. ii, have been neither assuaged nor displaced by her transmogrifica-
tion from a weak, sick girl into a successful knight; they have merely
been placed below the level of what Spenser constructs as her immediate
consciousness. Spenser figures this forth by playing on the immediate
ignorance of the canto 1 reader. When we are later given Britomart's
history of secret fears about the secrets of sexuality, we remember the
Malacasta episode and are forced to reread it.[19] Britomart misreads and
is wounded because of her failure to recognize the sexual lessons she
has already been shown. Her failure of recognition is also a failure of
interior self-awareness.

This failure, which equates with denial, goes far to explain the lies
Britomart tells to Red Cross at the beginning of canto ii. Denying the
reality of her own girlhood, she gives Red Cross a tale that elides the
childhoods of Virgil's Camilla and Tasso's Clorinda—significantly, two
women who live and die not only as warriors but as virgins. And once
again Spenser forces the naive reader into an inescapable misreading,
offering no reason to disbelieve or even to question Britomart's tale of
a martial childhood. Not until we reach the end of canto ii do we learn
that Britomart's hands were "weake" and knew not the use of "dreadfull
speare and shield" (ii. 53.3–4). As there seems to be no necessity for
Britomart to tell this lie, we can read it as a revising and re-presenting
of history and of her identity before she looked into Merlin's mirror. As
psychologically significant as this appears, taken with her next lie—her
reason for seeking Artegall—the significance of Britomart's remaking
of her own self-representation becomes frighteningly clear.

After providing herself with a masculine childhood—coming as close
as she can to self-denial and self-revision by seeing herself as the knight
in the mirror—Britomart tells Red Cross that she seeks Artegall because
he "hath vnto me donne / Late foule dishonor and reprochfull spight"
(ii. 8.7–8). Red Cross expresses surprise at hearing this and speaks well
of Artegall. Upon hearing Artegall praised, Britomart "woxe inly wondrous glad," her joy compared by the narrator to that of a loving mother
who sees a baby she as carried for nine months "in the deare closet of
her painefull side" (11.1, 7). This is an amazing simile. Britomart's reaction to news of Artegall is linked not only to gender and to sex, but
to motherhood. Furthermore, her gladness is specifically described as

interior, both physically ("in the deare closet of her painefull side") and in her pleasurable acknowledgment of it ("woxe inly wondrous glad"). We must find, therefore, all the more amazing her outward, verbal response: she accuses Artegall of rape. The interiorized emotion is thus eclipsed by the invocation of an act that violates physical interiority. Both rape and pregnancy are functions of sexual identity, but to follow the image of a happy pregnancy with the charge of of rape suggests serious problems of consistency within one woman's sexual awareness. Shifting the focus of her accusation from what has supposedly been "vnto me donne," she speaks of "A simple mayd" upon whom Artegall did "worke so haynous tort, / In shame of knighthood, as I largely can report" (12. 8–9). Doctor, I have this friend. . . . Britomart is able to present externally the identity of Artegall only in terms of physical violation, even as she denies the internal pleasure she feels at the thought of him.

While the naive reader of these lines may (must) be puzzled by the seeming contradiction presented by Britomart's accusations in stanzas 8 and 12 and her joy in stanza 11 and "secret ease" (8) and her pleasure in stanza 15—this is nothing to the effect her lies have on the reader who knows the whole truth—a truth that is unfolded a mere two stanzas later as the narrator begins the flashback to Britomart's first sight in the mirror. As informed readers, forced by Spenser to reread Britomart's lies with the reflected knowledge of the truth, we must ask two questions: why this particular sort of lie and why does she need to lie at all? Red Cross already knows that she is a woman, so the necessity of finding some knightly reason to be seeking Artegall no longer exists. That she charges him first with dishonoring herself and then with dishonoring some nameless maid shows that she still associates Artegall with sexuality that is somehow harmful to her and from which she needs to distance herself, even as she seeks him. Her reaction to the masculine is now more mixed than it was following the mirror vision, but it is still overwhelmingly negative. Her sense of selfhood is certainly more problematic. We also realize that, since her Amazon childhood is a fiction, Britomart's desire for a male-defined identity has grown out of, rather than being manifested within, the mirror vision. Spenser, as he does with the Malacasta episode, once more uses narrative placement to privilege the topos of reflected knowledge associated with mirrors in general and Britomart's mirror vision in particular. Britomart has still failed either to externalize or to internalize her own vision of sexuality beyond the parameters of the mirror vision. Like Milton's Eve, she never sees herself, but is shown—by a supernatural male agency generated by the male narrator—a masculine image that will give her an identity that is only a name: Mother. She rejects her place in this paradigm as she replaces the gladness of childbirth with the charge of rape in her speech to Red Cross. On the other hand, she makes that speech while presenting a male exterior identity and fictionalizing the internal identity of an Amazon who from childhood has felt contempt for female-identified actions. As with the representation of Elizabeth, this complex representation of Britomart's identity begins on the tain of a mirror.

The exact nature of the mirror in which Britomart sees Artegall is not easy to ascertain.[20] When we first hear of it in III. i. 8.9 the narrator calls it "*Venus* looking glas." The next mention, as "a mirrhour plaine" (ii. 17.4), is quickly superseded by its description as the work of Merlin's "deepe science, and hell-dreaded might, / A looking glass, right wondrously aguiz'd, / Whose vertues through the wyde world soone were solemniz'd" (18.7–10). This famous "world of glas" (19.9), given by Merlin to King Ryence so that the latter might never be surprised by foes' attack, is now presented as an instrument of public policy, neither "plaine" nor having to do with Venus. Its location in her father's private space—which Bellamy calls "one of Book 3's many hidden, womb-like enclosures where thresholds are approached but never quite transgressed"[21]—further problematizes her experience with it. That the mirror is so variously represented serves to foreground the ambiguity of the mirror tradition—more correctly, traditions—available to the late sixteenth-century writer or reader.[22] As Gascoigne suggests, there is a temporal element linked to the popularity of various sorts of mirrors, so in an allegory that uses the history of ancient times to shadow contempory events, the valence of a crucial mirror would be constructed with deliberate and necessary ambiguity. The reader is not sure exactly what sort of mirror this is, and neither, apparently, is Britomart. Again, as with the narrative of Britomart's quest, we are given information that must be revised and reread in light of subsequent contradictory facts— a narrative strategy that enacts the process of reflection.

As the mirror of Britomart's father had been "a famous Present for a Prince" (21.6) and of strategic importance to the prince's kingdom, we must find it all the more strange that Britomart, Ryence "onely daughter and his hayre" (22.4) seems to know nothing of its properties, although she has access to it. If she had known its purpose, she would not have expected to view herself in "that mirrhour fayre" (22.6). That she does seek for herself "in vaine" comes as no surprise to the reader (although it does raise questions about Artegall's status as one of Ryence's foes) as the narrator's description of its power precedes Britomart's viewing by only three stanzas:

It vertue had, to shew in perfect sight,
What ever thing was in the world contaynd,
Betwixt the lowest earth and heauens hight,
So that it to the looker appertaynd;
What euer foe had wrought, or frend had faynd,
Therein discouered was.

(19.1–6)

If Britomart knew what the reader now knows about this mirror, fear would not be an inappropriate response.

But does she know? After first seeking in vain—that telling pun—for her own face, Britomart, "auizing [generally glossed as 'remembering'] of the vertues rare, / Which thereof spoken were" (22.6–7), thinks again and looks once more to see that which might "to her selfe pertaine" (22.9). According to the narrative of stanza 23, the particular "that" for which Britomart looks is a husband: "So thought this Mayd (as maydens use to done) / Whom fortune for her husband would allot" (5–6).

What we must question now is exactly how much about the mirror Britomart does remember. She recalls enough, albeit belatedly, to look not for herself but for someone "that mote to her selfe pertaine," but does she also remember that the mirror was devised to present the foe or the feigning friend? This question makes a reading of stanza 23 all the more vexed. Spenser's language in stanza 23 figures forth quite vividly the psychological construct we now call the subconscious;[23] Britomart is not actively seeking or thinking about a husband, but the idea is in her mind. We see the interior self in action, as it were, even though Britomart's thoughts do not articulate a conscious process of self-examination. Nevertheless, these thoughts are at least as self-referential as they are focused on the idea of a future mate, and (as in Milton's remake of this scene) the shadow of narcissism flits across the glass evoked both by this self-interest and by the pun on "vaine." Furthermore, her tacit acknowledgment that a woman's identity is, in the usual course of human events, eventually linked to a man's identity places her thoughts of a future husband well within the parameters of self-examination. If Britomart recognizes anything about the mirror's purpose, does she therefore subconsciously see her inevitable husband as a foe? Is Spenser trying to show the workings of Britomart's mind or to plant ideas in the minds of his readers? Or to figure forth a political situation in which any alliance was somehow disempowering? Stanza 26 would seem to answer "both" (or "all"): for Britomart—while seemingly unaffected [she viewed well, liked well "ne further fastned not, / But went her way" (2–3)]—is actually the unknowing victim of Cupid's secret

arrows, her private self wounded in the arena of public policy that is
the mirror. That she looks twice, first unthinkingly and privately, then
with knowledge of the political function of the glass, and sees herself in
neither context is at least as significant as the fact that she sees a male
figure. In both attempts she is seeking knowledge of or pertaining to her
"selfe"; in neither does she gain such knowledge. Similarly, the reader is
told that she is unaware "that her vnlucky lot / Lay hidden in the bottome
of the pot" (4–5). "Unlucky lot"? This phrase and the description of
"the false Archer, which that arrow shot / So slyly" is the language with
which Virgil speaks of Dido, language that evokes a male/female paradigm that includes not Achilles, but Aeneas.[24] Dido became "unlucky"
when she was placed by the gods in a position where her private emotions became a threat to the public good. By using the mirror, an instrument of public policy, for private (however heedless) pleasure, Britomart
may have placed herself in a similar position. The sort of self-
examination that the mirror allows Britomart is possible only because
she is the daughter of a public figure; by offering her a mirror vision
in which the elements of the public balance, if not outweigh, the private,
Spenser may be questioning the extent to which a princess can possess
a private self.

After her mirror-vision, Britomart falls ill and speaks "fearefully,"
arguing with her nurse that it is not love from which she suffers—"But
mine is not (quoth she) like other wound" (36.1)—"For no no vsuall fire,
no vsuall rage / It is, O Nurse, which on my life doth feed, / And suckes
the blood, which from my heart doth bleed" (37.3–7). She describes
what she has seen in the mirror by negatives: "Nor Prince, nor pere it
is" (37.8), "Nor man it is, nor other liuing wight," but "th'only shade and
semblant of a knight, / Whose shape or person yet I never saw" (38.1,
3–4). Citing as the source of her misfortune "my *fathers* wondrous mirrhour" [emphasis mine], Britomart goes on to detail her ills:

> Within my bleeding bowels, and so sore
> Now ranckleth in this same fraile fleshly mould
> That all mine entrailes flow with poysnous gore.
> (III. ii. 39.2–4)

Granted that *ranckleth* is a key term for love wounds in *The Faerie Queene*
(Arthur's in I. ix and Marinell's in IV. xii), nevertheless, Britomart's
symptoms described in these lines sound much closer to discomforts of
the menstrual cycle than to the "ulcer" she diagnoses in herself. This
literally internal marker of the feminine coincides with Britomart's attempt to know herself psychologically, as allegorized by the mirror scene.

ıysical and the psychological are closely linked in the representa-
' female identity, and Spenser's Elizabeth figure is horror-struck
by both. The vision of Artegall, which replaces the nonimage of herself,
generates in Britomart both physiological and psychological reactions,
each unpleasant, the first, however, necessarily and naturally linked to
female sexuality, the second a sign of conflict over that sexuality. This
denial of or lack of recognition of her private female self causes Britomart's public activities to suffer from this vision-generated weakness;
her "princely" identity has been diminished—or reversed—by the vision
of a male:

> Thenceforth the feather in her loftie crest,
> Ruffed of loue, gan lowly to availe,
> And her proud portance, and her princely gest,
> With which she earst tryumphed, now did quaile.
>
> (27.1–4)

and Glauce observes that she no longer "tastest Princes pleasures" (31.6).
In addition to her physical diminishment and pain, Britomart also becomes "Sad soleme, sowre, and full of fancies fraile" (27.5) and experiences both bad dreams and a loss of sleep.

Glauce, although she initially feels "feare, least loue it bee" (31.1),
ultimately tries to comfort Britomart with the argument that it *is* love
from which she suffers; moreover, she argues, it is a good and natural
love, if Britomart will only accept it as such.

> "Daughter," (said she)[25] "what need ye be dismayd?[26]
> Or why make ye such Monster of your mind?
> Of much more uncouth thing I was affrayd,
> Of filthy lust, contrary unto kinde;
> But this affection nothing straunge I finde;
> For who with reason can you aye reprove
> To love the semblaunt pleasing most your mind,
> And yield your heart wheche ye cannot remove? . . ."
>
> (40.1–8)

Glauce refers to Britomart's mind twice in these eight lines and argues
that it is in Britomart's power simply to decide, mentally to "yield" and
to acknowledge this vision as pleasing to her—to accept this vision as
having a natural place in the development of her identity as a woman.
But just as Milton's Eve sees Adam as "less fair," Britomart has made "a
Monster of" (interestingly, not "in") her mind, and both women are told
that they are wrong and must revise their reactions to these mirror

images. And what, may we not ask, must Elizabeth be making of all this if she is, as invited, gazing into the mirror of the text? She is given an allegorical representation of a young woman's curiosity about both herself and the sexual identity of self that is linked to marriage. But rather than seeing the young woman flourish and develop in this quest for self-knowledge, Elizabeth is confronted with a female prince made physically ill by the conflict between elements of her public and private selves. Spenser pushes the analysis beyond the flat representations of Gloriana and Belphoebe when he sets out to allegorize Britomart's mental struggle with her body's physical manifestations of womanhood. To stress the conflict between the interior and the exterior, Spenser provides Glauce's arguments as an explication of the sort of interior selfhood Britomart fears to acknowledge.

Glauce goes on to make a secondary argument, however, through an interesting list of negative examples. Rather than reassuring Britomart with stories of happy wedded normalcy, Glauce catalogs three unnatural love stories (41), telling Britomart that her love, "Though strange beginning had" (42.2), is by contrast good.

> "Not so th' Arabian Myrrhe did set her mynd,
> Nor so did Biblis spend her pining hart;
> But lov'd their native flesh against al kynd,
> And to their purpose used wicked art:
> Yet playd Pasiphaë a more monstrous part,
> That lov'd a Bul, and learnd a beast to bee.
> Such shamefull lustes who loaths not, which depart
> From course of nature and of modestee?
> Sweete love such lewdnes bands from his faire companee."
>
> (41)

The implications of the examples are not lost on Britomart. Although she declares herself to be a little eased (43.1) that her "loue be not so lewdly bent, / As those" (2–3), she remarks bitterly that at least those lovers found "Short end of sorrowes" (8) while her own fortune is to suffer endlessly, to "feed on shadoes, whiles I die for food" (44.3). Making the obvious comparison between herself and Narcissus, she similarly concludes that she is worse off "then Cephisus foolish child" (6) whose mirror vision had a substantive correlative. And yet the prophecy of Tiresias was that Narcissus would only come to grief if he came to know himself. To this Glauce once more offers comfort stained with the sinister, suggesting that the body of Britomart's vision might "learned be by

cyphers, or by Magicke might" (45.9) and vowing "by wrong or right /
To compasse thy desire, and find that loued knight" (45.8–9).

After what the narrator calls Glauce's "chearefull words" (47.1) raise
the spirits of the "sick virgin" (2), Britomart is able to sleep. The next
day the two repair "Vnto the Church" for a religious exercise as odd
and contradictory as the stanzas of comfort preceding it.:

> They both vprose and tooke their readie way
> Vunto the Church, their prayers to appeale,
> With great deuotion, and with litle zeale:
> For the faire Damzell from this holy herse
> Her loue-sicke hart to other thoughts did steale;
> And that old Dame said many an idle verse,
> Out of her daughters hart fond fancies to reuerse.
>
> (48.3–9)

Not surprisingly, considering the quality of their devotions, Britomart
returns home only to relapse into "her former fit." We should not be
surprised that a visit to a (presumably) Protestant church has failed to
simplify the identity of a powerful female virgin. Now, however, we are
told straight out by the narrator that Britomart's problems are psychological and stem from a lack of self-knowledge: "the royall Infant fell /
Into her former fit; for why, no powre / Nor guidance of her self in her
did dwell" (49.1–3). Abandoning both reason and religion, Glauce now
tries a series of folk remedies that also prove unable to "slake the furie
of her cruell flame" (52.2). At the end of the canto, Britomart is left to
waste away, suffering from a "hart-burning brame" (4) and "like a pyned
ghost became, / Which long hath waited by the Stygian strond" (5–6).

Why is this so difficult? Britomart's agony of denial and Glauce's wildly
overdramatic responses are not necessary to the story itself unless that
story is not a narrative of dynasty, but a representation of a unique
woman who can find no self-image in any mirror. Such figures are not
thick upon the ground in literature, and Spenser has carefully prepared
us to see Britomart as the image of one of the few powerful women
whose sexual identity had been displaced by her political power.[27]

The word-picture of Britomart being consumed by the cruel flame
of a love that is somehow wrong again brings to mind Virgil's Dido.[28]
Britomart, shot by Cupid's arrow, feels the physical response to her
vision of Artegall, suffers from bad dreams, tells her female confidante
of her pain, is told by Glauce that what she feels is only natural—"No
guilt in you, but in the tyranny of loue" (40.9)—is not entirely comforted

by this, seeks comfort in the Church, and remains the victim of burning love. Dido, in book 4 of the *Aeneid,* turns for comfort to her sister, Anna:

cum sic unanimam adloquitur male sana sororem:
"Anna soror, quae me suspensam insomnia terrent!"

(8–9)[29]

Anna's response argues that love should not be viewed as unnatural:

Anna refert: "O luce magis dilecta sorori, solane perpetua maerens carpere iuventa, nec dulcis natos, Veneris nec praemia noris?"

(31–33)

Dido, heartened by Anna's opinion,[30] goes to the temple to seek confirmation: "Principio delubra adeunt, pacemque per aras / exquirunt" (56–57). But, as the narrator explains, her state of mind is such that she cannot benefit from whatever the exercise of religion might offer:

Heu vatum ignarae mentes! quid vota furentem quid delubra iuvant? Est mollis flamma medullas interea, et tacitum vivit sub pectore volnus.

(65–67)

Unhappy Dido still burns with ill-fated love: "Uritur infelix Dido"(68).

If Spenser is using the story of Dido to tell Britomart's history, this solves what otherwise seems to be a problem with conflicting discourses. The problems raised by such a reading, however, seem—initially at least—even more troubling than the problem it lays to rest. But Spenser, in canto iii, does not leave Britomart within the paradigm of Dido; he allows her to follow in the footsteps of Aeneas.[31] While this will allow him to continue his dynastic fiction, the strategy raises some obvious problems of gender identity for Britomart. In the resolution of those problems—deferred until book V—lies the answer to the riddle of "mirrors more then one."

In book III, canto iii, which opens with four stanzas of references to classical "Antiquitie" (2.1), Britomart follows not only the footsteps of Aeneas, but also those of Odysseus, Dante the Pilgrim, and Bradamante. Before she can go out and up toward a desired goal, Britomart must first go down and inward to learn the nature of that goal.[32] Guided by Glauce, Britomart finds Merlin "low vnderneath the ground, / In a deep delue, farre from the vew of day" (7.7–8). Critics often link this scene to Bradamante's encounter with Merlin's ghost in Ariosto's *Orlando Furioso.* Except for the persona of Merlin, however, the paradigm is much closer to book VI of the *Aeneid* than it is to Ariosto's poem. Bradamante does not seek Merlin; she arrives in his tomb as the immediate result of a lie and trick by another figure in the poem. Furthermore, she has no prior knowledge of her dynastic role or of the knight with whom she will fulfill that role. Like Aeneas, Britomart is led underground by a female guide, and while she is not as aware of her fate as is Aeneas, Britomart deliberately seeks underworld counsel about a problem of which she is acutely aware. Spenser's Merlin, like Anchises, provides the entire dynastic story himself, not relegating the specifics to another as Ariosto's Merlin does to Melissa. After hearing the dynastic history, Britomart—like Aeneas—is changed and pursues her public destiny with vigor. Bradamante is directed, not revitalized.

Britomart arrives in Merlin's cave in the shadow of Dido, inflamed by an imperfectly understood passion and weakened by a lack of self-knowledge. She leaves somewhat comforted and with a specific goal of public identity, reshaped into the model of Aeneas. Her gender, however, does not conform to the pattern she must follow. After giving the reader a glimpse into the troubled interior self of Britomart in canto ii, Spenser offers Merlin's advice in canto iii as a solution to her public identity; her sick psyche, however, has been left unaddressed by dynastic prophecy. Like the artist of the "Sieve" portrait of Elizabeth, Spenser presents the allusion to a male Aeneas in a female figure, although the tradition of epic romance provides for the poet a solution not available to the painter. At Glauce's "foolhardy" (52.1) suggestion, Britomart dons her father's armor and identifies herself with the figure presented to her by her father's magic mirror—the least problematic representation of herself available to her. That Glauce introduces her suggestion with a catalog of women-warriors is, I believe, less significant than her remarks about Britomart's person:

> Ne certes daughter that same warlike wize
> I ween, should you misseeme; for ye bene tall,
> And large of limbe, t'atchieve an hard emprize,
> Ne ought ye want, but skill, which practize small
> Will bring.
>
> (53.5–9)

Britomart can become "a mayd Martiall" (9) because she can be made to look and act like a man. But, in secret, she remains a woman. This secret, however, is one of which only the reader has full knowledge, for Britomart herself seems (still) as confused about her sexuality, as anyone might be who sees her in armor. Furthermore, as Glauce here mentions four women-warriors by name, it is interesting to note the presence or absence of women in other chronicles within the epic. Britomart and Elizabeth, the alpha and omega, are the only women either named or referred to by Merlin in his dynastic prophecy. In the section on the History of Britain in book II canto x there are at least twenty (it is sometimes difficult to be certain of gender) women mentioned. In the final historical narrative, III. ix, however, Venus provides the only female presence. This representation of the importance of women in history is significantly inconsistent. As Glauce dresses Britomart to represent a man, she is also inconsistent. Mentioning four women-warriors by name, her most detailed story is of one whom she refers to as "a *Saxon* Virgin" (55.5). Britomart is forced to ask for the Virgin's name, which is Angela—from which name, says Glauce, her people began to name themselves "Angles." By her nonchronological grouping of the five women, Glauce gives the places of priority (Bunduca first, Angela last) to virgin warriors, grouping the warriors who were also wives and mothers in a position of lesser rhetorical significance. As Cavanagh points out, this construction of Britomart in relation to the other women-warriors leaves her, oddly, standing alone. "The new warrior also betrays no explicit debt to the female warrior tradition which the narrator claims [in the opening lines of canto iv] to miss. . . . Her place within the lost tradition of warrior women remains obscure."[33]

After the narrator concludes the flashback of both the mirror vision and prophecy, he returns the now-knowledgeable reader to the narrative present, the encounter with Red Cross, and presents what seems at first to be an externalization of that vision and prophetic gloss: Britomart's apostrophe to the sea in III. iv. 7–10. Hamilton calls this speech an allegorical projection of "her inner emotional disorder into nature's disorder" (337 n), and so it appears as Britomart begins:

> Huge sea of sorrow, and tempestuous griefe,
> Wherein my feeble barke is tossed long,
> Far from the hoped hauven of relief,
> Why do thy cruell billowes beat so strong,
> And thy moyst mountaines each on others throng
> Threatning to swallow up my feareful life?
>
> (iii. 8.1–6)

As we read to the end of the stanza, however, we find that Britomart is not projecting her own emotions on the disorder of nature, but rather internalizing—unsuccessfully—the disorder of nature into her own body:

O do thy cruell wrath and spightfull wrong
At length allay, and stint thy stormy strife,
Which in these troubled bowels raignes, and rageth rife.

(8.7–9)

If Britomart were able to locate the storm of which she "thus com-
playnd" (7.9) as within her own "troubled bowels," then she could allegorize and thus objectify her own troubles; the physical, sexual sea of
troubles upon which she sees the "feeble vessell" (9.1) of her own identity
being controlled by the "bold and blind" (9.9) figures of "Love my lewd
Pilot" (9.6) and the "Botesawine" Fortune (9.7), the former having "a
restlesse mind" (9.6) and the latter knowing "no assuraunce" (9.7). So
that her "ship" may survive the irrational guidance of these two, Love
and Fortune, Britomart calls upon "Thou God of winds" (10.1), Aeolus,
who—according to Comes via Hamilton—represents reason (Hamilton,
338 n). If reason rules Love and Fortune, she argues, the storm will
become "some gentle gale of ease, / The which may bring my ship, ere
it be rent, / Vnto the gladsome port of her intent" (10.3–5) where "I
shall my selfe in safety see" (9.6).

But Britomart is not a text thus to be allegorized; as the representation
of woman, a complexly public and private woman, she cannot be so
neatly dis-membered, not even by her "self." We see here the problem
of Britomart's *ek-sistence,* to borrow a term from Luce Irigaray. "Ek-
sistance" is "existence as conscious separation or differentiation from
nature: the state of being opposite to that generally ascribed to the
feminine."[34] Britomart's attempt to explore her interior self by allegorizing her emotional state foregrounds the impossibility of this mode of
representation: a woman is not a sea, a ship, or a storm. In feigning
poetry men have long described women as such, but when a woman
tries to use these metaphors to analyze her own interior self, they prove
inadequate and the fiction of representation is unmasked, revealing a
male-generated fantasy. Because she is no poet, Britomart uses the language of male-dominated lyric, and it fails her. As she described the
mirror vision by negatives, Britomart can only describe herself in terms
of what she is not.

As Britomart ends her attempt to allegorize her sexual fears, Glauce
once again intervenes to remind her that good is supposed to come of
her sexuality, raising here the public, dynastic good of those who will
"fetch their being from the sacred mould / Of her immortall wombe, to
be in heauen enrold" (11.8–9) in an effort to soothe Britomart's internal,
secret, private fears. And once again we are presented by a conflict of

narrative discourse and poetic action: after the narrator tells us that Glauce's elevated, dynastic interpretation of sexuality has "recomforted" (12.1) Britomart, Spenser brings onto the shore Marinell, a pure young man whom Britomart promptly prepares to attack (13–14), hears "with deep disdaine" (15.1), and smites with "so fierce furie and great puissaunce" (16.2) that she leaves him "tomblen on an heape, and wallowd in his gore" (16.9). "The martiall Mayd stayd not . . . to lament" the hurt of the man who tried to set boundaries for her, but rides ahead over beaches strewn with gold, pearls, and other jewels, and "despised all; for all was in her powre" (18.9).

We have here no Camilla who will pause, even in battle, to seek for glittering treasure—"femineo amore praedae et spoliorum." Camilla along with *"Penthesilee"* and *"Debora"* are mentioned by the narrator in the first two stanzas of this canto as examples of "Antique glory," which cannot compare with Britomart "As well for glory of great valiaunce, / As for pure chastitie and vertue rare" (3.3–4). Britomart is more brave, more pure, more chaste, and more virtuous than these women warrior/ virgins, and—as we must read from the implicit comparison with Camilla's specifically sterotypical female love of plunder—less feminine.[35] Benson's reading of this passage foregrounds this issue:

> The superior of the ancient heroines in their field of endeavor, [Britomart] is not an Amazon, and in her balance of accomplishments and virtue she provides a transition between "antique glory" and Elizabeth. She is the ideal immediately in view when the poet praises nonmilitary Elizabeth. By means of her, the Queen, none of whose "goodly deeds" is cited, holds a position superior to the greatest women of history without being the brutal kind of woman demanded by the questions raised in the first stanza.[36]

If the picture of Britomart that we see in III. iv were the final vision, the completed portrait as it were, I would be in complete agreement with Benson. But not only is Britomart in search of a more complex sense of identity than we find in the Italian texts against which Benson builds her reading, but that complex sense of identity—that sense of selfhood—is represented as an identity in transition, neither psychologically nor historically static. We see elements of this transition in the microcosm of her apostrophe to the sea and the events that follow it. Nor is the final shape of her metamorphosis by any means clear. Benson says that Britomart "never is torn between love and duty; her love is her duty."[37] If this were true, Britomart would be a much more simple figure to read.

In her "feigning fancie" Britomart "did portray" Artegall as "Wise, warlike, personable curteous, and kind" (5.7, 9), these "selfe-pleasing thoughts" feeding "her wound" not with healing, but rather making it worse: "her smart was much more grieuous bred, / And the deepe wound more deepe engord her hart" (6.1–4). Fulfilling what appears to be her function in the poem, to act as a "gloss" on Britomart's problems with sexuality, Glauce offers comfort, not by bringing Britomart to terms with the immediate reality of sexual difference, but by displacing that immediate reality with a lofty, future-tense vision of dynasty. The immediate result is that Britomart rises to attack yet another man, yet another version of that internalized mirror vision. Not until the House of Busirane does Britomart, who never sees the Garden of Adonis, see and begin to recognize external projections of her internal sexual fears.

Glauce's role in the Britomart story is as much psychological as iconographic. Certainly it is a rich composite of other supporting personae of literary adventures. While knights in Arthurian romances often have squires whose presences and absences are not always logically accounted for, Glauce's presence and absence in the poem is clearly linked to Britomart's psychological struggles with sexuality. In addition to the paradigm of Dido and Anna, her role as a mother figure in Britomart's III. ii illness is an obvious one, even if she did not keep referring to Britomart as "daughter." She tries and fails to explain Britomart's sexuality as normal and something that should be gladly accepted, and this failure leads to the visit to Merlin—a journey also initiated by Glauce, just as the Sybil instructs and accompanies Aeneas. After leaving Merlin's cave it is once again the nurse who suggests the ploy of dressing as men; this gender confusion is certainly traditional and, in the generic context, probably unavoidable, but it does not make Glauce's task of reconciling Britomart with her sexuality any easier.

Glauce is with Britomart at the beginning of III. i as "an aged Squire" (4.3), and she is not individually mentioned among the "all" who spur after Florimel, and yet Britomart is alone when she comes upon the Red Cross Knight in combat with Malacasta's champions. What happens to Glauce? If we think about her at the time, it is only to include her in the "all" who pursue Florimel. But at the beginning of canto iv, after Britomart has parted from Red Cross at the end of canto iii, we find Glauce present and serving the martial maid, mentioned as casually as though she had been there all along. Her absence during the Malacasta episode and the retelling of the mirror and Merlin stories is unaccounted for. Her presence in canto iv, however, is required for the same sort of dialogue we find in III. ii. Britomart complains of the problems generated by sexuality (iv. 6–10) and must be "recomforted" by Glauce.

And again in IV. vi she serves as sexual mediator, this time between Britomart and Artegall himself, as well as between Britomart and her fears about sexual reality.

The problematic pronunciation of Glauce's name makes the level of the pun on "gloss" unclear. We know it must be a dissyllable, but cannot ascertain whether the *c* should be hard or soft. If it is soft, however, the resonance of the pun becomes inescapable. Edmund Spenser uses gloss as we would, meaning "an accompanying explication," in *The Shepheardes Calendar* epistle: "Here-unto hue I added a certain Glosse or scholion for the exposition of old wordes and harder phrases."[38] In the "old wordes" of Chaucer, who is praised at length for his language, "glosse" and "Glauce" could be very close. And as Glauce first emerges as a figure of importance when she tries to gloss the mirror vision for Britomart, the triple pun of a reflective surface is also tantalizingly available.

Whether we are to read her as a "gloss" on Britomart's sexuality or as a projection of that within Britomart that is striving to understand and accept sexuality or as an external force provided by the poet to remedy some flaw or lack in his female hero is—as Scudamore says of the purpose of Venus's veil—"hard to know" (IV. x. 41.2). What we *can* know, however, is that whenever Britomart must confront directly some iconographic presentation of sexual conflict, she does so without Glauce's presence. When she first looks into the mirror, then in Malacasta's Castle and Busirane's House, as she hears of the Venus statue, during her dream in Isis Church, Britomart is alone, without the mediation of Glauce's sexual knowledge. Nor is it possible to argue that Glauce disappears after having accomplished her purpose. Britomart's actions in V. vii show that her ambiguity about her sexuality is still unresolved. What Glauce's final disappearance may support, however, is the argument that Spenser is presenting Britomart as having moved beyond the boundaries of traditional sexual advice and counsel.

In III. xi Britomart, without Glauce, is "Greatly—dismayd" (22.1) by the wall of flame at Busirane's door, although one might argue that this is simply common sense recognizing "The cruell element, which all things feare" (22.4). But as she enters Busirane's house, we see that she is remembering the lesson of canto i. Not again guilty of failure to recognize sexuality when she sees it, after walking through Busirane's first illustrated room, Britomart "backward cast her busie eye / To search each secret of that goodly sted" (xi. 50.2). Although, even after much reading, she cannot "find what sence it figured," ix. 50.5) or "wist not what it might intend," 954.9), Britomart learns enough from the injunc-

tions "*Be bold*" (50.4) and "*Be not too bold*" (54.8) and from what she sees
on the walls to refrain from taking off her armor or sleeping "Fore
feare / Of secret daunger" (xi. 55.6), thus watching the Masque of Cupid
"In secret shade" (xii. 27.5) while keeping a "secret stand" (28.9). Here
she is paying attention to the dangers of sexuality (as she was not in
Malacasta's castle), using a "busy" eye to examine the Ovidian manifestations of Busirane's power. She confronts Busirane and almost completely
overcomes—she does sustain another wound—the fear he represents,
although she overcomes it without understanding it. Even Amoret
understands more than Britomart, as she pleads for the "knight" to
spare the life of the magus who has cast her in a spell and who alone
can release her. Revealing her own uncertainty, Britomart keeps her own
sexual identity a secret until she is well away from Busirane, even though
this causes Amoret some distress. Susan Frye has recently raised the
fascinating suggestion that the cantos of the Busirane episode "feature
a figure of Elizabeth that is simultaneously imprisoned, entertained with
spectacle and poetry, and raped."[39] Frye sets up her argument by the
suggested parallel between the structure of Busirane's House and the
floorplan of the privy chamber at Hampton Court:

> In effect, the text's first assault on female self-possession resides in the topog-
> raphy of tyranny and pain that Britomart must traverse to reach Amoret.
> Busirane's three rooms open sequentially, like Elizabeth's presence chambers
> at Hampton Court, described in 1598 as "adorned with tapestry of gold, silver,
> and velvet, in some of which were woven history pieces."[40]

This is an electrifying observation, but Frye refrains from enlarging
upon that one sentence of comparison, although she does provide a
floor plan of Hampton Court as it appeared in 1547. As I have already
suggested, I believe that the "text's first assault on female self-possession"
occurs in the mirror scene in Britomart's father's closet, early in book
II; but do I think the links between magic, male-dominated spaces, and
sexual fears generate same sort of mirroring we find between the House
of Pride and the House of Holiness in book I. Here, of course, the
structures are primarily psychological rather than simply architectural.

Without getting totally sidetracked into BUSIRAMA (or the Busirane
Tournament of Interpretation),[41] I would point out that once again the
reader is given information of deferred significance, a reflective narrative. As we read about the Masque of Cupid we can read it in terms of
Britomart's fears, even though she herself does not seem to do so. Not
until IV. i, however, do we learn that this is the masque that generated

in Amoret the sexual fears that manifest themselves as the figure of Busirane. So in a sense, Britomart succeeds because she is unaware of the implications of what she sees[42] (the same reason she failed at Malacasta's castle) while the reader is simultaneously unaware of the significance of her ultimate success with Busirane. This lack of awareness on both parts makes Britomart less a complex figure and more a masquelike representation of that which will free Amoret. At this point in the poem, Britomart has more in common with most icons than she does with most women and so, again within Spenser's poem, does Elizabeth. Indeed, in the 1590 ending of book III we have an example of poetic *pentimento*, as Spenser gives us the image of Britomart "halfe enuying" "that faire Hermaphrodite" (III. xii cancelled stanza 4), an image he replaces with books IV and V. Lauren Silberman points out that at "the conclusion of the 1590 *Faerie Queene*, both Britomart and Spenser's reader are onlookers";[43] so, I would stress, is Elizabeth. Frye writes:

> On her quest to discover the meanings she embodies as Chastity, Britomart once again witnesses Chastity constructed through the association of love, forced courtship, and rape . . . the language of Busirane the magician is also the language of Spenser, and both rely on the figurative relations between eros and magic to bind their female audience.[44]

Although we are on dangerous ground when we begin to think and speak of Elizabeth in the same way we think and speak of Britomart and other female figures in the epic, we are tempted onto this ground by the poet himself.

As Leigh DeNeef has suggested, central to the allegory of *The Faerie Queene* may be the fiction of the reader watching Elizabeth reading the poem.[45] But even if this *is* a fiction, it is the operative fiction of the poem, and we are still confronted by the problem of Britomart's relation to Elizabeth's mirrors more than one. Britomart's private, female self is kept secret, deferred by circumstances, by other figures in the poem, and most of all by herself, just as Elizabeth's public image as nonvirginal female was deferred by herself by lines such as those she wrote to Parliament in 1563: "though I can think [that marriage is] best for a private woman, yet I do strive with myself to think it not meet for a prince."[46] In Britomart, the public and private are less clearly demarcated. Every time Britomart comes close to gaining a realization of her female self—as in her first encounter with Artegall—she is described in terms of diminishment. And yet, the poem and the tradition argues, she must accept—nay, achieve—the realization of that female identity, for it is here that her true female power resides in motherhood. Maureen Quilligan argues that "Spenser may counsel his female readers to follow Belphoebe's example of virginity, but the chastity he truly extols is Amoret's; it is the chastity not of a virgin queen, but of a wedded wife."[47] If Quilligan is right and Spenser is really celebrating Amoret over Belphoebe, perhaps Britomart's presentation as a conflation of the figures of Dido and Aeneas constitutes the middle ground that will keep Elizabeth—married to no man but to a nation—from taking dangerous offense at the "hail wedded love" theme.[48] This would explain why Britomart does not recognize Amoret's sexual fears as her own. It does not explain, however, how we are to read either Britomart's sexuality or her sense of self.[49]

As long as Britomart's sexuality is located within the paradigm of dynastic epic, we must read it realistically. If, however, we see the dynastic construct as a fiction, as the poetic equivalent of an iconic symbol in a painting—such as the miniatures on the pillar in the "Sieve" portrait—we can look beyond this foregrounded image to the main figure. The image adds richness to the central figure, as the globe in the "Sieve" portrait adds a cosmic dimension to Elizabeth's monarchy; but the globe in the portrait does not suggest that Elizabeth literally rules the world. Neither does the fiction of dynasty mean that Britomart is going to marry and have children. As the eye moves beyond the globe in the portrait, so does the reader move beyond the suggestion of dynasty within the poem. Throughout book III and also in books IV and V, Britomart's sexual image is reflected, deflected, refracted, and finally deferred. By choosing to begin Britomart's odyssey of self-knowledge with a literally untrue but metaphysically and psychologically significant mirror image, after calling attention to Elizabeth's mirror images in the proem, Spenser is foregrounding the traditional topos of the mirror only to subvert it. By displacing Britomart's vision of herself, by forcing her to at least gesture toward an acknowledgment of an interior self, and by forcing her to attempt to reinscribe her identity again and again in Elizabeth's textual mirror, Spenser offers us a mirror image that displaces truth. It is a vision that by its inherent trope of reversal, the chiasmus, defers truth beyond the bounds of the text into the the world of pragmatic and psychosexual politics—or perhaps dislocates truth from that world *into* the text. The image of the mirror becomes the portrait of an image: Elizabeth.

How, then, can we read Elizabeth looking into the textual mirror/portrait of Britomart's quest and what does this double reading tell us about the function of Britomart's interior self? By watching Elizabeth watch Britomart turn herself from a woman looking for a husband to beget a dynasty into an icon figuring forth the elements of just rule to achieve immortality, a process she completes only in book V. The casualty here, of course, is any construction of an interior self. Icons intrinsically lack interiority. In representing Britomart as a multivalent portrait of Elizabeth, by constructing a sense of interior selfhood for Britomart, by having her fail to reconcile that interiority with the external realities of her political power, Spenser acknowledges the power of the interior female self only insofar as he represents it as something to be rejected in favor of the public good of a public figure.

For the moment, let us suspend our acceptance of Spenser's heavy-handed references to the dynastic epics of Virgil, Tasso, and Ariosto, just as I have suggested that we set aside the limitingly literal references to Gloriana and Belphoebe in book III's proem. If we don't think of Britomart primarily as a future wife and mother, what does she then become? One answer is: an icon of female power internally beset by secret sexual fear. True, Britomart endears herself to us as we follow the development of her private fears, because she seems more like a flesh and blood girl/woman than any other figure in the epic. But as the cantos roll by, she becomes more and more objectified and public as we are privy to fewer and finally none of her personal thoughts and reactions. In canto ii of book III Britomart starts out with all of the psychological and physiological baggage of a flesh-and-blood woman. How, then, does she turn herself into an icon? By going through the looking glass of public policy on the tain of the text, though the chiasmus of perception that turns her from an icon of the female into a female icon, from a reflection of psychosexual dynastic potential with some sense of an interior self into a portrait of public female power.

A LOOKING GLASSE FOR MARIED FOLKES?

[a woman should strive to please her husband] whose face must be hir daylie looking glasse, wherin she ought to be alwaies prying, to see when he is merie, when sad, when content, and when discontent, where to she must alwayes frame hir own countenance.

A brief and pleasaunt discourse of duties in Mariage (1568)[50]

for even as a looking glass if it be a good one, doth shew the countenance of him that glasses himselfe in it: So it beseems an honest wife to frame her selfe to her husbands affection and not to be merry, when he is melancholy, or jocund, when he is sad, much lesse fire when hee is angry.

A Looking Glasse for Maried Folkes (1610)[51]

If Britomart is one of Elizabeth's mirrors, what happens when Britomart comes face-to-face with her own mirror vision? In IV. vi Britomart sees not a mirror vision, but a flesh-and blood-Artegall. Significantly, much of this canto's vocabulary reflects for us the mirror scene in book III. By reading IV. vi in the context of these mirror tricks of identity, we may uncover a more complex and possibly disturbing correspondence between Britomart and Artegall than is suggested by the conventions of dynastic marriage, and may also find between the dynastic pair and Elizabeth a more direct correspondence than usually suggested by critics; we will certainly discover a most complex presentation of the correspondence between sex and temporal power. Here again Spenser foregrounds the traditional topos of the mirror only to subvert it. From her departure from Merlin's cave in book III, Britomart has possessed the power of a successful knight. While other areas of power and knowledge have been presented as unavailable to her, her prowess as the Knight of Chastity has remained undamaged. But it is not as a male knight that she can claim the promised power of dynastic motherhood, and it is not as a mother that her power can be seen as an image of Elizabeth's—Elizabeth who was neither a man nor a mother. If Britomart wishes to recognize and claim the power of dynastic motherhood, she must abandon both those elements of her internal self that are disturbed by this paradigm of female identity and the public power she now possesses as an outwardly male knight. If Britomart is to keep her immediate public power, to make it her own, she must do what Elizabeth did; she must somehow move from the level of dynastic reality to the iconographic reality of allegory.

In book IV, canto vi, Britomart recognizes Artegall in a face-to-face confrontation—as opposed to their anonymous meeting in IV. iv. Although she clearly defeated him in canto iv and has just acquitted herself honorably in anonymous battle in stanzas 10–13 of canto vi, when Britomart "Beheld the louely face of Artegall" (26.2) and begins "it to her mind to call, / To be the same which in her fathers hadd / Long since in that enchaunted glasse she saw" (26.4–6), she immediately begins to manifest symptoms of physiological feminine weakness as significant as those in canto ii of book III. At seeing the fleshly manifestation of her mirror vision "her wrathfull courage gan appall, / And haughtie spirits meekely to adaw" (26.78), and when she hears "the name of *Artegall*, /

Her hart did leape, and all her hart-strings tremble, / For sudden joy, and secret feare withall" (29.1–3). This "secret feare," when discussed at all, is generally read as fear of sex, an interpretation that I do not wish to discount, but rather to amplify by suggesting that it may also be fear of losing her male empowerment. Britomart's initial illness in book III seems at first to be generated by the vision of the male Other that she wished to become but was not.[52] We subsequently understand, when given the information of III. ii. 27–52 to reflect back on our reading of III. i–ii. 26, that she fears what she sees in the mirror because of what that Other may force her to become: a publicly sexual figure whose name, Mother, is derived from her relationship to male husband and male child. Between her meeting with Merlin and this sight of Artegall, Britomart has been granted a gender reprieve, a space and time in which she can function as a man while seeking out her putative female destiny. Since her initial anxiety was not assuaged, and only partially displaced, by the quest for Artegall, we should not be surprised that it resurfaces here as "secret feare."

Britomart's recognition of Artegall causes her to reflect the womanly weakness and secret fears she manifests in III. ii. What is perhaps more telling, however, is that—between seeing Artegall's face in stanza 26 and hearing his name in stanza 29—she is more immediately reflecting the actions and feelings initially manifested by Artegall, who has himself just mirrored her reactions in III. ii. When Artegall beholds the "celestiall vision" of Britomart's face, he becomes weakened and humbled, just as Britomart did before the mirror; his "benumbd" arm becomes "powrelesse" (21.3), and he too feels "secret feare" (21.3). The Medusa paradigm would be unambiguously obvious were it not for the reaction Spenser fashions for Artegall.

> And he himselfe long gazing thereupon
> At last fell humbly downe upon his knee
> And of his wonder made religion,
> Weening some heauenly goddesse he did see
> Or else vnweeting, what it else might bee;
> And pardon her besought his errour frayle,
> That had done outrage in so high degree:
> Whilest trembling horrour did his sense assayle
> And made each member quake, and manly hart to quayle.
>
> (vi. 22)

Like Britomart after her mirror vision, Artegall does not admit that what he sees is simply another human being.[53] In lines 4 and 5 of stanza

22 his thinking echoes that of Britomart in III. ii. 37–38, and his sex-linked physical reactions—trembling and quaking—mirror Britomart's own physical diminishment. Unlike Britomart, however, he finds a culturally acceptable context for his reactions, as he "of his wonder made religion" (22.3) and "turning his feare to faint deuotion, / Did worship her as some celestiall vision" (24.8–9). This does not grant Britomart even the power of the beautiful Medusa of the *Romance of the Rose* or Petrarch, for the power to act, to worship, is all Artegall's. Artegall, whose sexual identity is not in question, quickly externalizes his "secret fear" into the acceptable and objectifying framework of religious awe, much as Petrarch displaces his feelings for Laura onto the Virgin Mary in the closing lyrics of the *Rime Sparse*.

Britomart, on the other hand, internalizes her "secret feare" as quickly as possible, just as she did in III. ii. When Britomart hears the name of Artegall, her reactions mirror Artegall's—her arm, too, becomes weak, her sword drops, and she feels "secret feare" (29.3). But she seeks to hide her reaction from Artegall, from the others, and from herself:

> And all her vitall powres with motion nimble,
> To succour it [secret feare], themselues gan there assemble,
> That by the swift recourse of flushing blood
> Right plaine appeard, though she it would dissemble,
> And fayned still her former angry mood,
> Thinking to hide the depth by troubling of the flood.
>
> (29.3–9)

Here, in a reversal of her postmirror vision actions, she seeks to keep her reaction a secret from all observers.

Once again it is Glauce who steps in, here to help facilitate Britomart's confrontation with the physical correlative of her mirror vision. In the space between Artegall's reaction to Britomart (stanzas 19–24) and Britomart's mirroring reaction to Artegall (stanzas 26, 27, 29) we find one stanza about Glauce:

> But *Glauce*, seeing all that chaunced there,
> Well weeting how their errour to assoyle,
> Full glad of so good end, to them drew nere,
> And her salewd with seemely belaccoyle,
> Ioyous to se her safe after long toyle.
> Then her besought, as she to her was deare,
> To graunt vnto those warriours truce a whyle;

Which yeelded, they their beuers up did reare,
And shew'd themselues to her, such as indeed they were.

(25)

After Britomart acts out her part of the recognition scene, Glauce speaks three stanzas: the first (30) directed to both knights, telling them of their "secret fate" (4); the second (31) to Artegall, pointing out that he "may not disdaine, that womans hand / Hath conquered you anew in second fight" (2–3); and the third to Britomart, instructing her to "relent the rigour of your wrathfull will, / Whose fire were better turn'd to other flame" (2–3) and ordering her to "Grant him your grace" (5). At Glauce's words, both knights react: "Thereat full inly blushed *Britomart;* / But *Artegall* close smyling ioy'd in secret hart" (32.8–9). Both the inwardness of Britomart's blush and the word "But" suggest that Glauce may be less than successful in her attempt, begun in and continued from III. ii, to reconcile happily Britomart with her own sexuality. Once again Britomart's reaction to Artegall is linked to blood—here a blush—and once more it is figured as internal; unlike the menstrual blood of III. ii or the bloody wounds of III. i and III. xii, however, this blood remains internal, as does her emotional and psychological reaction to Artegall. Compared to the relatively detailed representation of interior selfhood we see in book III, Britomart's presence in book IV is presented primarily on the surface. Rather than learning more about her interior female self, we must read her exterior responses as they mirror those of the dominant male in the scene.

Glauce's speech to Artegall presents one of the strongest statements of female power in the entire poem: "For whylome they [women] haue conquered sea and land, / And heauen it selfe, that nought may them withstand" (31.4–5). Once again we see the narrative of the poem in conflict with the story, as this line is spoken to the male knight to whom Britomart is supposedly about to subordinate herself. Furthermore, Glauce's reference to Artegall's double defeat at the hands of a woman (line 2) not only strengthens the sense of paradox, but foreshadows his defeat and humiliation at the hands of Radigund. The lines of gender identity are very lightly drawn in Glauce's intervention, lightly drawn and easily transgressed.

In Artegall's wooing of Britomart we find a continuing conflict between the story and the narrative of the poem, a conflict that becomes a crucial element of Spenser's representation of Britomart in the remainder of book IV and in book V. In the confrontation scene, Glauce appeals to Britomart for a "truce," thus implying Britomart's control of the situation. In her three-stanza explication, however, it is to Artegall whom she first individually speaks, thus granting the male knight the place of privilege. Artegall, who was winning the battle when overcome by Britomart's beauty, is seen as at once gaining and relinquishing control. Britomart's initial martial control of the conflict is restored by her all-conquering beauty and affirmed by Glauce's appeal for truce. Having presented such a complex nexus of control, Spenser is able to begin the actual courtship story with the balance of power in question—a question that he manages to sustain rather than resolve, doing so by continuing the conflict between story and narrative.

At this point in the poem, and for a brief space only, the story of Artegall and Britomart as lovers follows very traditional lines. Artegall "with meeke seruice and much suit did lay / Continuall siege vnto her gentle hart" (40.3–4) while Britomart tries "with womanish art / To hide" (7–8) her wound of love. The language is that of courtly love, even unto the metaphor of the woman as a hunted thing brought "at the length vnto a bay" (41.3), right up to the inevitable point at which the woman capitulates. Here, however, is where the narrative begins to undermine the story. Britomart's response to Artegall shifts from the passive to the active as she "was content" (4) "to relent" (5) and finally "yeelded her consent" (7) to "take him for her Lord" (8), the active verb structures conflicting with Britomart's seeming surrender.

At this point Spenser switches the emphasis, with the story beginning to undermine the narrative. As the narrative discourse of stanzas 40 and 41 suggests that Britomart is more in control than does the story of those stanzas, so the story of stanzas 42–46 conflicts with the traditional narrative of a lady loath to be parted from her lover. That language of romance is subverted by the story that presents Britomart as a knight involved in her own quest, not as a locus that the male must abandon. "That all so sonne as he by wit or art / Could that atchieve, where to he did aspire, / He vnto her would speedily reuert" (43.5–7). The fact is, as the story speedily reminds us, Britomart will not be there to be reverted to; she will be off on her own adventure, which has not concluded with finding Artegall. As Britomart gazed into the mirror in III. ii, she began the chiasmic crossing of her quest for identity, initially locating that identity in the figure of Artegall. If Spenser were following the paradigm of gender identity suggested by the two quotes with which I opened this section, then all of Britomart's problems would resolve themselves as she gazed into the mirror of the man himself. Obviously, Spenser, while playing with these social expectations, makes a far different use of the topos of the mirror. Here, in IV. vi,[54] Britomart makes contact with the tain of the mirror, the man himself, and is reflected back on another journey of reimaging. Her process of self-knowing, begun by the earlier vision, is neither neatly concluded nor cleanly diverted by this scene; rather, she must seek further constructs of interiority to reach any sort of resolution about her identity. Only when her dream in Isis Church mirrors all that she has learned on her quest does she lose all elements of an interior self and become a public icon. This time the reflection will emerge from the chiasmus as the face of Mercilla, the face of Elizabeth.

It is very important, I believe, that between Artegall and Britomart's dawning physical passion in the recognition scene and its extension in the conflicted wooing of stanzas 40 ff., comes Scudamour's plaintive inquiry about Amoret. Rather than reading this as a comic incursion in a long-delayed love scene, I suggest that this serves as a reminder to the reader of a larger pattern being worked out; for Scudamour's quest will lead us to the Temple of Venus and to the vision of the hermaphrodite relocated from the 1590 ending of book III. That the Garden of Adonis is followed, not preceded, by the Temple of Venus makes some slight sense in the Scudamour/Amoret plot—not that this plot ever depends very heavily upon any form of logic—but is of the greatest importance in the larger pattern of Britomart's quest. If she were really going to fulfill on the literal-dynastic level the prophecy of Merlin by finding the man in the mirror and having children by him, would it not make much more sense to follow their meeting with a set piece of generative love rather than with one of sexual ambiguity? This is what Lauren Silberman calls Monday morning quarterbacking of the allegory. We want Britomart to "win" the Super Bowl of dynastic epics, thus elements of hindsight enter into our reading, replacing what is with what we think should have been. In fact, the standard assumptions about reading Britomart as dynastic mother are made fourfold difficult by the Temple of Venus, Isis Church, by her own actions at the end of V. vii, and by the appearance of Mercilla as the key figure of female power at the end of book V. Might we not better question those assumptions than perform complex agonies of overreading on the poem?

I here raise more strongly my suggestion that we suspend our belief in Spenser's dynastic intentions, what I call his dynastic fiction. If we look at the poem in the way Spenser has taught us from book I on—as a fusion of form and meaning—we see two patterns for the Britomart story, neither of which leads to the nursery.

ODYSSEUS/BRITOMART/PENELOPE:
THE FICTIVE GLASS OF DYNASTIC MARRIAGE

For the meaning of Britomart's chiasmic journey within her own quest and within Spenser's dark conceit, we must look to Isis Church and to her dream where, as Kenneth Gross observes, "diverse levels of discourse . . . intersect within an almost obsessive construction of ambivalence."[55] Britomart's dream is the crucible in which the major elements of her gender-displacing mirror vision, her victory in the House of Busirane, and the hermaphroditic Venus of book IV come together; heating this crucible is the tension between two types of allegorical reality (or nonreality)—the dynastic "reality" of English history and the icono-graphic "reality" of Elizabeth's reign. Luce Irigaray's remarks on dreams are useful in the context: "Dreams are also riddles in that . . . they recast the roles that history has laid down for 'subject' and 'object.' Mutism that says without speech, inertia that moves without motion, or else only with the motions of another language, another script."[56] Dreams are also ways of figuring the sub- or unconscious, that most interior of selves. Through her dream, Britomart fuses the two allegorical fictions of female selfhood into one; she becomes mother not of a dynasty of Englishmen, but the generative source of a dynasty of virtues.[57] Gross argues that it is the dream in Isis Church, "as opposed to her early mirror-vision" that allows Britomart to find her "place within a mythic and political story";[58] I agree, but would argue that it is the dream that allows the quest for self-identity generated by mirror vision to end.

That Isis Church is intricately related to Britomart's other significant adventures is made immediately clear. Britomart arrives and enters "with great humility" (V. vii. 3.7), in contrast with her entry to Busirane's House where "resolu'd to proue her vtmost might" she "Assayld the flame" (III. xi. 25.1,4); Talus, like Sucdamore, is not allowed to enter. One way to read Talus's exclusion from Isis Church is to suggest that, as Scudamore is too much a physical manifestation of the sexuality being iconographically psychoanalyzed in Busirane's House, the iron man is too literal a manifestation of Justice to be allowed into the delicate balance of Justice and Equity. More to the point for this reading of Britomart, however, I would suggest that Talus is too closely associated with Artegall to be allowed to intrude on the scene where Britomart will finally gain knowledge of, and a means of, controlling her sexual identity. Furthermore, Talus belongs to Artegall's story, and—even though book V is named for him—the story and the narrative of Isis Church are a key frame in the almost-evolved representation of Britomart, a representation that ultimately has nothing to do with Artegall.

Upon entering the temple, Britomart stops to gaze at the wonders confronting her. This gaze, as Hamilton rightly suggests (410 n), is meant to recall for the reader her gazing into the mirror of Venus and at the statue of Cupid in Busirane's House; but while she gazes into the mirror first in vain and then in bewilderment and at Cupid's statue unable "her wonder [to] satisfie" (III. xi. 49.8), these are not her reactions in Isis Church.

> She wondred at the workemans passing skill,
> Whose like before she neuer saw nor red;
> And there uppon long while stood gazing still,
> But thought,that she there on could neuer gaze her fill.
>
> (vii. 5.6–9)

This is fascination, not incomprehension; to "wonder at" a skill is to understand, or at least appreciate, something about the accomplishment. After being shown the statue of Isis, Britomart reacts:

> her selfe vppon the land
> She did prostrate, and with right humble hart,
> Vnto her selfe her silent prayers did impart.
>
> (7.7–9)

Britomart has herself seen the statue of Cupid, and she has heard Scudamore's description of the statue of Venus. When Britomart prays "Vnto her self," she prays not just silently, as this phrase is usually glossed, but literally *to* herself. What she sees in the Isis statue forms a palimpsest of iconography with elements of those other statues; the text is the nature of her own sexual identity and must be read within herself and thus must be read psychologically, in a dream.

To say that Britomart, in her dream, identifies with or becomes the Isis statue is too easy. As her dream begins, Britomart is clearly separate from the Isis figure: "Her seem'd, as she was doing sacrifize / To Isis" (13.1–2). "All sodainely" (4) she sees herself "transfigured" (4), her "linnen stole to robe of scarlet red" and her "Moone-like Mitre to a Crowne of gold" (5–6). But while the Isis statue, as described in stanzas 5 and 7, does wear a golden crown, the only colors mentioned with her linen garments are silver and gold. The red of Britomart's robe is the blood red of the psychosexual physical wounds she receives in III. i and xii, as well as the red of the flames that soon (stanza 14) threaten her self-generated "felicity"; this blood, however, is now fully externalized. Britomart and the Isis statue do not become one. In stanza 15 we are told that the crocodile awakes from under "the Idols feete" (2). Most critics concur with Hamilton that the female pronouns of these stanzas refer to both Britomart and the Idol/Goddess she is becoming. This presents no serious problem until we come to the point where the crocodile is beaten back by "the Goddesse with her rod" (15.9). Britomart, whose dream appearance is so carefully described in stanza 13, has no rod. Britomart and the Idol are two separate figures.

The crocodile is Artegall, seen first as a "she" just as Britomart first wished to see him when looking for her own image in the magic mirror. Iconographically linked to the twisted, fatally wounded dragon at Cupid's feet (III xi 48) and the snake "whose head and tail were fast combyned" (IV x 40.9), which constitutes Venus' legs and feet, the dream crocodile represents to Britomart a threat that she perceives as male, the treat of sexual difference, of female sexuality trapped within the dynastic paradigm. What we see in stanzas 15 and 16 is indeed prophecy, but not the dynastic prophecy of the priest's interpretation. It is a prophecy of what might be if Britomart continues to follow the path the poem has set for her; it is a warning. If we read all the female pronouns as referring to Britomart (except for the clearly linked "Goddesse with her rod"), and read "Goddesse" and "Idole" as Isis, we see the following pattern of action.[59]

Britomart is happy, though puzzled, by her transformation into the red garments of sexuality, just as she has outwardly accepted, but not without doubts and fears, her role as dynastic mate for Artegall as foretold by Merlin (an acceptance that also involved a change of clothing). When she is threatened with the reality of sexual desire, the flames, she sees Artegall—the reality of her mirror vision—as a possible source of rescue. Although the crocodile does devour the flames that threaten Britomart and the world of her dream, he then becomes himself a threat as he turns "her likewise to eat" (15.8). Britomart is saved from being internalized by the crocodile, and she is saved by the goddess who beats back the beast and humbles it—as Radigund has done to Artegall, as Britomart herself did in IV. iv. In its humble state, the crocodile makes himself low before Britomart's feet and seeks her love—just as Artegall did in IV. vi. Britomart accepts his suit and becomes pregnant by him, bringing forth "a Lion of great might" (16.6)—just as Merlin tells Britomart she will do in III. iii. 29–30.

The dream, although an interior construct, here actually figures interiority of self less directly than does the narrative of Britomart's illness in book III. Here Britomart is at once spectator and participant in the allegorical representation of her potential sexual identity; in book III she lacked that objective distance. In a sense, Britomart's dream tells her nothing that she did not already know. But it presents to her unavoidable connections between events that she has perceived separately and over a long time. Her reaction, therefore, becomes the most significant part of the entire episode. She awakes "full of fearefull fright, / And doubtfull dismayd through that so vncouth sight" (16.8–9). These puns on "maid" (in its various spellings) and "dismaied" are another way in which Spenser employs the devices of narrative to subvert the dynastic argument of his story. Red Cross puts the two meanings together for us when he asks "this Briton Mayd . . . what . . . Made her dissemble her disguised kind" (III. ii. 4.5–7). In stanzas 30 and 40 of the same canto we find the pun in Glauce's words directed to Britomart: "What vncouth fit . . . Hath . . . Chaunged thy liuely cheare, and liuing made thee dead?" (30.7–9); "Daughter (said she) what ned ye be dismayd / Or make ye such Monster of your mind?" (40.1–2). She has in some sense been "dis-maid" since her encounter with the mirror, where the word is stressed: "So thought this Mayd (as maydens use to done)" (23.5) of a husband; as she droops in stanza 27, the narrator comments "She wist not, silly Mayd, what she did aile" (7). In the Busirane cantos, Britomart is "Greatly . . . dismayd" (ix.22.1) by the flames, yet not at all "dismaied" (xii.37.3) by the quaking of the house as she holds the sword over Busirane's head, and yet is again "much dismayd" (vii. 42.3) by the sight of the "goodly roomes" vanishing utterly as she and Amoret depart. In IV. vi the punning includes Artegall as "he her made / To giue him ground" (12.7–8). By his attack, however, Britomart is "no whit dismayd" (14.6) even as his sword strikes her "horses hinder parts" (13.6) and she is forced to dismount and lay aside her enchanted lance. When Artegall sees Britomart's face, the pun on maiden seems to be located within his identity: "At last fell humbly downe vpon his knee, / And of his wonder made religion" (22.2–3) and asks her pardon for his "errour frayle" (6) "Whilest trembling horrour did his sense assayle / And made ech member quake, and manly hart to quayle" (8–9).

In the Isis Church scene, Britomart is ultimately and permanently "dismaid." After looking at the statue, beneath it "did the warlike Maide her self repose" (V. vi. 12.1); she awakes from her dream "doubtfully dismayed through that so vncouth sight" (16.9). Never again is Britomart called "Maid." After she defeats Radigund and rescues Artegall, the uses of "made" figure forth Britomart's empowerment: she asks Artegall "What May-game hath misfortune made of you?" (40.2), then proceeds to free the other captive knights. "And magistrates of all that city made" (43) and "Made them swear fealty to Artegall (43.6). Britomart begins her journey as a "Maid," struggles with being "made" and "dismaied," and is finally "dismayd" by the Isis dream, then becomes a maker. Radigund is never referred to as a "Maid," while Mercilla, icon of justice, is called "a mayden Queene of high renowne" (V.viii.17.2). Britomart, as the shadowed reflection of Elizabeth, represents all forms of female identity without now literally experiencing any of them.

After awaking thus "dismayd" in Isis Church, Britomart lies awake the rest of the night and thinks about what she has seen, but the result of those thoughts is to add "melancholy" to her doubt and fear. True, when the priest gives his dynastic reading of the dream, Britomart is "much iased in her troublous thought" (24.2), but the dream that the priest is reading is not the dream Britomart has.[60] Britomart is not Isis in her dream; Isis is a force able to subdue the crocodile to which Britomart submits. This "misreading" is not the priest's fault, for he can only read what he was told, told by Britomart "As well as to her minde it had recourse" (20.3). What the narrator is telling us with this line is that Britomart does not or cannot tell the whole truth of the dream. As Irigaray observes, "But [the dreamer when awakened] restricts himself to reframing, remarking, or 'analyzing' [the dream's] contours, restratifying its stages, so that order, good 'conscious' order, may prevail. Elsewhere."[61] Britomart denies the reality of what she has dreamed just as she denied the reality of what the mirror vision offered her. In a discussion of interiority, the denial of a dream is more significant than is the denial of an external vision, and Spenser uses this distinction to represent Britomart's loss of interior selfhood. We see her re-casting of her dream with the priest as a construct of the subconscious still at work, but that unmade subconscious is leading her toward an external, iconic identity that denies any sense of female interiority. While it is possible to see mirror visions, magic prophecies, and dreams as modes of representation that need not be privileged as "reality" within the world of the poem, actions and scenes presented in the narrative of present-tense action when Britomart goes forth "To seeke her loue" (24.7) cannot be similarly disprivileged. When Britomart fights with and kills Radigund, she subdues the part of female power and identity that can, by its very existence, be read as a threat to male empowerment. She is not, however, able to place herself within the male-dominated paradigm of the dynasty, because of the circumstances in which she finds Artegall. Artegall, like the crocodile of her dream, has been humbled by a woman. Indeed, Benson argues for the direct influence of the Medusa narrative on the encounter between Artegall and Radigund.[62] Britomart awoke from her dream "dismayd" by her "vncouth" union with just such a figure as she now finds Artegall to be. Britomart must find a place for herself within the poem, but that place cannot be with Radigund whose female power threatens the natural order and continuity of life; nor can it be with Artegall whose male power has been compromised by defeat at the hands of one woman and rescue at the hands of another, a spectacle that dismays Britomart as much as does her dream. That she could revise these patriarchal values seems not to occur to Britomart—or Spenser—as the martial maid stands before Artegall:

> abasht with secrete shame,
> She turned her head aside, as nothing glad,
> To have beheld a spectacle so bad.
>
> (38. 3–5)

Like Elizabeth, Britomart, in the closing stanzas of canto vii, feels responsibility for the larger social order without being able to find any place for herself within that order. Spenser foregrounds this disordered order with a reference to Homer.

> Not so great wonder and astonishment,
> Did the most chast *Penelope* possesse,
> To see her Lord, that was reported drent,
> And dead long since in dolorous distresse,
> Come home to her in piteous wretchednesse,
> After long trauell of full twenty yeares,
> That she knew not his fauours likelynesse,
> For many scarres and many hoary heares,
> But stood long staring on him, mongst vncertaine feares.
>
> (39)

Britomart's wonder, astonishment, and uncertain fears are indeed greater than Penelope's, for—as Spenser here cleverly reminds us—it is Britomart who has been out having the adventures *and* remaining chaste while Artegall has donned woman's clothes and done the very woman's work of Penelope and her ladies, with none of the Greek queen's strength or cleverness, but through his own failure. Britomart is presented as at once greater than the best of both Penelope and Odysseus— an androgynous image not unlike the Dido/Aeneas allusions of book III—while Artegall is both less powerful than Penelope and more wretched than the king disguised as a beggar. Britomart's new identity, while more powerful than in the Dido/Aeneas paradigm, owes nothing to an interior sense of self. After her dream, after killing Radigund, after seeing Artegall disgraced, Britomart is represented entirely through her actions; her thoughts and feelings are dismissed from the text with a single line: "farewell fleshly force."

In a reversal of the book III mirror scene, Artegall is now the gowned figure performing domestic tasks and Britomart is the victorious knight. What can Britomart do when she is confronted with such a vision? She can renounce her part in it. All of her five questions in stanza 40 also question the justice of a society that can both define roles of sex and power and then make those roles inaccessible to one who is placed by circumstances in an ambiguous role. As closely as he dares, Spenser is depicting the predicament facing Elizabeth when she ascended the throne. In stanzas 41–43 Britomart deals with her situation in much the same way Elizabeth came to terms with hers; in stanzas 44–45 the poet provides, as did Elizabeth, a rhetorical smoke screen that will prevent the radical action from threatening the sensibilities of the established order.

"FAREWELL FLESHLY FORCE": THE FIRST FACE OF MEDUSA

> Ah my deare Lord, what sight is this (quoth she)
> What May-game hath misfortune made of you?
> Where is that dreadfull manly looke? where be
> Those mighty palmes, the which ye wont t'embrew
> In bloud of Kings, and great hoastes to subdew?
> Could ought on earth so wondrous change haue wrought,
> As to haue robde you of that manly hew?
> Could so great courage stouped have to ought?
> Then farewell fleshly force; I see thy pride is nought.
>
> (40)

After asking her five questions in stanza 40, Britomart answers herself with the only solution available to her: "Then farewell fleshly force." That the power is Britomart's alone is represented by the narrative, which contains not one word about the feelings, speech, or reactions of Artegall. But a dynastic marriage requires two significant partners. By showing Artegall to be insignificant in relation to Britomart, Spenser explodes his fiction of dynasty. When Britomart rejects the physical representation of Artegall—so radically reversed from that armored mirror vision—the literal, fleshly dynastic level of empowerment is no longer a possibility; the interior female sexual identity is no longer necessary; there remains only the power of the icon. In stanzas 41–43 Spenser presents his most carefully crafted conflict between narrative and story.

Thenceforth she streight into a bowre him brought,
And causd him those vncomely weedes vndight;[63]
And in their settde for other rayment sought,
Whereof there was great store, and armors bright,
Which had bene reft from many a noble Knight;
Whom that proud Amazon subdewed had,
Whilest Fortune fauourd her successe in fight,
In which when as she him anew had clad,
She was reuiu'd, and ioyd much in his sembalance glad.

(41)

The story restores Artegall's male garments, outlaws female rule, and returns Artegall to the action of the poem, leaving Britomart "sad and sorrowful." The narrative, on the other hand, shows us a Britomart who never gives up, and indeed adds to, her control of the action. It is on the level of action that her powerful identity resides, however; her interiority is not represented, although her struggle to escape from or indeed to renounce such interiority is arguably present from the first canto of her story. In stanza 41, as Artegall is being doubly redressed, all of the active verbs are Britomart's actions; Artegall is presented only in the passive. The very difficult action of stanza 42 mirrors the policy of Elizabeth when she found herself on the throne, following the rule of a wrong-thinking woman.

So there a while they afterwards remained,
Him to refresh, and her late wounds to heale:
During which space she there as Princess rained,
And changing all that forme of common weale,
The liberty of women did repeale,
Which they had long vsurpt; and them restoring
To mens subiection, did true Iustice deale:
That all they as a Goddesse her adoring,
Her wisedome did admire, and hearkned to her loring.

(42)

She must privilege her own position without changing the position of all women; she must privilege the male-dominated social order without losing the means of her own empowerment. She must, as Spenser openly admits, be both Gloriana and Belphoebe, public queen and private virgin. She must, in fact, be both in one; she must be Britomart as she has been so complexly presented in books III, IV, and V. The female power that she "restores" to men's subjugation is the female power linked to physical force, to blood, and to the "secret feare" of sexuality, the female

power of dynastic reality. The male poet who has constructed an interior
sense of selfhood for Britomart, who has so constructed that self as to
leave it incompletely known and thus unrecoverably unrecognized by
the woman, now removes even the possibility of interiority to foreground
the public identity of his Elizabeth figure. The concept of female power
as interiority is completely restored to the commonwealth of men's subjectivity. Britomart, the narrative tells us, changes the "forme of common
weale" by "restoring" women to "mens subiection," even though it is the
men who need to be "restored." Stanza 42 constitutes a double negative
of story and narration that cancels itself out. In stanza 41 Britomart
restores Artegall's private person to his place in the social order. In
stanza 43 Britomart restores Artegall's public person to a position of
control by making all of the other captive knights swear allegiance to
Artegall.

> For all those Knights, which long in captiue shade
> Had shrowded bene, she did from thraldome free;
> And magistrates of all that city made,
> And gaue to them great liuing and large fee:
> And that they should for euer faithfull bee,
> Made them sweare fealty to *Artegall*.
>
> (43)

But, just as if stanza 42 did not exist, it is still Britomart who is giving
the orders. Her actions are still presented in the active voice, the mens'
in the passive. At the end of stanza 43, Artegall leaves—ultimately still
in the passive—"Vppon his first aduenture, which him forth did call" (9).

In stanza 44 we find the rhetoric of romance masking the actions of
political power. Through Britomart Spenser acknowledges that the social order depends upon establishing the honor of the Knight of Justice
and that "his honor, which she tendred chiefe, / Consisted much in that
aduentures priefe" (3–4). Having cleared the way for Artegall to succeed
when "he redeemed had that Lady thrall" (45.8)—that Lady who will
be Belge and/or Irena, not Britomart—Britomart departs from the
scene and from the poem. When she bids farewell to fleshly force she
finally accomplishes that for which she has been striving since her first
sight of Artegall in the mirror, a way "her anguish to appease" (45.5).
She renounces the physical world and her place in it as a woman; by
privileging iconographic lessons of Busirane's House, the Temple of
Venus, and Isis Church above the discourse of dynastic prophecy and
the elusive construct of selfhood, Britomart moves out of the poem as

a fleshly force so that she may appear, as does Elizabeth, as an icon of justice.

In the figure of Mercilla, we see Spenser's final mirror trick: Britomart's quest for a recognizable identity refracted by the mirror of the text into a culturally and historically safe image of female power. Mercilla is a textbook example of the allegorical representation of an abstract virtue; the question of her interior selfhood cannot conceivably arise. In stanzas 27–34 of V. ix, Spenser offers us Mercilla, described by what might be termed the greatest hits of Britomart's iconographic encounters: the statue of Cupid in Busirane's House, the figure of Venus as seen by Britomart and the reader through the words of Scudamore, the Isis Idol, and the Isis Church dream. Mercilla represents a state of permanence, of peace; she alone of all these iconic presentations is seated, and seated on a royal throne. She is clothed not with "a slender veile" (IV. x. 40.7) or "garments made of line" (V. vii. 6.4) and trimmed with silver fringe or—most specifically—"Nor of ought else, that may be richest red" (V. ix. 28.3), but with "a cloth of state" that is "like a cloud" and yet itself gives off light "with bright sunny beams, / Glistring like gold" and "shooting forth siluer streams" (28.1, 6–7, 8). These imperial coverings are made distinct from the earlier garments by their association with temporal power. Like Venus, Mercilla is surrounded by fluttering putti: "A flocke of litle loues. . . . With nimble wings of gold and purple hew. . . . Whose shapes seem'd . . . like to Angels" (IV. x. 41.2–5); "those litle Angels" on "their purpled wings" (V. ix. 29, 1–2). Like both Cupid and Venus, there are figures prostrate at Mercilla's feet; but rather than the lovers of the tapestries (III. xi. 49.3–5) or "great sorts of louers piteously complayning" (IV. x. 43.2), "kings and kesars at her feet did them prostrate" (V. ix. 29.9). Like the Isis statue, Mercilla holds a scepter, and, like the Idol and Britomart in her dream, wears a crown. But the sword at Mercilla's feet is "rusted" because of "long rest" (30.6), signifying the peaceful years of reign achieved by one who accepts herself as an icon. The animal at Mercilla's feet, in contrast to the wounded dragon, the self-consuming/generating snake, the twisted and the seductive crocodiles, is a "huge great Lyon" (33.4), the symbol of royal power. This is the lion of Britomart's dream, the lion Britomart herself becomes in her fight with Radigund, the lion of Merlin's prophecy, and hence even the ancestor of Una's lion. Mercilla's lion is the most physical, vital element of her iconographic presentation, and for that very reason it is kept chained and "coller bound," so that its strength and courage might not overpower with their physical force the abstract nature of Mercilla and the virtue that Mercilla represents. Rather than having her identity as a woman challenged, Mercilla possesses a power "that all the world dismayde" (30.9).

In the Isis Church dream Britomart begins to recognize her identity as a dynastic mother; but the vision of that identity, compounded of past and present knowledge and of dynastic prophecy, leaves her "doubtfully dismayd." The priest counsels her to tell him her troubles, using almost exactly the same words as Glauce in III. ii: "Say on," urges the priest, "the secret of your hart" (19.6). Britomart leaves the dreamworld just as she left the mirror. She has dreamed of bringing forth the lion of Merlin's prophecy, but has gone forth from that dream to fight Radigund and to be described herself as both a "Lionesse" and a "Lion" (30.1, 7). She becomes not the mother of a "fleshly force," but an icon that has neither sex and both sexes, both Dido and Aeneas, both Odysseus and Penelope, but no interior identity of her own. The offspring of an icon must be an abstraction: not of flesh and blood but of public policy, of justice that will overcome all secret fear—secret male fear of female power or secret female fear of loss of power. Representing male power is unproblematic; representing female power in a mode that is neither Madonna nor monster is tricky. It must be done, as it were, with mirrors. The mirror is Elizabeth's as she holds the text, and the metamorphosis of Britomart is thus confined to the limits of representation set by Elizabeth's own self-image. The real power, however, belongs to the maker of the textual mirror: the male poet. Spenser does not simply construct either Britomart or Elizabeth as a Medusa figure. If that image were in his mind, he could not make the casual reference to Medusa when Britomart removes her helmet and reveals her hair in III. ix., nor could he use the image of Artegall transfixed before Radigund in book V. The larger pattern of a woman disempowered by means of a male-controlled mirror, this paradigm of selfhood made unknowable by reflection speaks to the enormous imaginative hold that the Ovid's mirror narratives exerted upon the Renaissance mind. That Spenser uses the mirror vision at once as a means of constructing an interior female self, as a barrier to the realization of female power, and as the metaphor for the allegory of his text demonstrates both the multivalent power of the mirror and the significant inevitability of its link to the representation of woman.

As for the larger pattern of the poem, this explains why we look for an end-of-book set piece built for Britomart and find instead Mercilla's court. The book-V representation of Mercilla is a palimpsest of the iconography of Britomart's mirror vision and quest: the House of Busirane, the statue of Venus that so suggestively mirrors the "faire *Hermaphrodite*" of Britomart herself in the 1590 ending of book III, the statue of Isis, Britomart's dream, and Britomart's final battle with Radigund— an overgoing both of the Isis Church dream-palimpsest and of Britomart's final actions in the poem. The only sense of self we find in the icon of Mercilla is the choice between two public images: in stanza 37 of canto ix she converts herself as queen to herself as judge, as Hamilton's note suggests. It is this public construct of female power that enables Artegall to go forth actively in canto x. The flesh and blood Britomart of III. ii has become an icon of justice and has thus been reinscribed, metamorphosed as the perfectly allegorical Mercilla, Mercilla who can clearly—not secretly—be read as a representation of Elizabeth. The cumulative iconography of Britomart's dream reenters the narrative of the poem through and in the figure of Mercilla, an iconographic representation of Elizabeth. The dream, then, constitutes an interior space within the narrative of the poem, a interior space for reflecting the various images of the title and the proem of book III. Through this interior reflection, Britomart exits as a dynastic heroine so that she may reenter the poem as an icon of justice. As Spenser anoints the historical wounds left by Mary Stuart's execution with the balm of Duessa's trial he is also giving us the closing vision of his Elizabethan mirror trick begun in book III. We are faced with the reality of a poem that gives us not a dynasty of English women and men, but a dynasty of ideas, of virtues. Britomart and Artegall and their dynasty have become a fiction that is first deflected then transcended by the complex icon of political reality that is Spenser's portrait of Elizabeth in the last years of her reign. In this portrait, Elizabeth is not represented as the simplistic duality of Gloriana/Belphoebe. Spenser moves beyond this safe and conventional construct to the more complex (and potentially more dangerous) task of representing the queen as he sees her: a woman who must have had to recognize a previously unknowable interior self. That Britomart is ultimately represented as an icon of justice is as conventional as the Gloriana/Belphoebe paradigm, but the adventures and changes Britomart undergoes between her girlhood and her renunciation of "fleshly force" form too intimate a portrait of a woman who must find and keep a place of power in a male world for Spenser to present them openly as images of the queen. And yet, ultimately, Spenser does take the safer route. He never says that Britomart is Elizabeth and he never says that he is turning Britomart into Mercilla. From behind the veil of allegory, the poet accomplishes these manipulations of representation by employing the mirror-trick of reflection. That the mirror ultimately fails to reflect an interior female self foregrounds the question of whose eyes could possibly meet that reflection with recognition.

4

Cleopatra: the tain of the mirror

For a free woman, there can be no relationship with men other than war. Especially when it is a case of love: the closer one gets to the enemy, the more necessary it is to be violent because of the violence within him, and, paradoxically, the more necessary it is to distance oneself from him. . . . Because the Amazons don't make war for reasons that men understand. . . . They conduct their war not to kill but to take hold. . . . They have to seize male strength. But they must take it alive. . . . It is the invention of a union that is the opposite of rape and masculine abduction: but it takes place on enemy territory . . . they marry only the men they have conquered. To be an Amazon is to be faithful to the law of reversal: one must repeat the act that proves or symbolizes that she is not captive or submissive to a man. One has to have won; but this victory does not have the meaning of a masculine triumph. He dominates to destroy. She dominates to not be dominated; she dominates the dominator to destroy the space of domination. Because the one knocked down is helped to his feet. And she leads the one who is "conquered" into her world—a world he has never dared imagine. There waits a festival: a woman who is not a slave.
　　—Hélène Cixous, "Achilles is Penthesileia is Achilles"

I begin the Cleopatra chapter with this epigraph by a twentieth-century feminist because, as the Gascoigne quote set the contemporary stage for the problems of mirroring and identity in Spenser's epic, so does this passage from Cixous give us remarkable insight into the cultural constants and mutations in the dynamics among gender and power and identity in Shakespeare's play. In her essay, Cixous argues against the cultural construction of the Amazon as a monstrous creature. In some scenes within the drama, Cleopatra is represented as a monster—a monstrous construct that would be thus labeled not only in the seventeenth century, but in our time as well. Indeed, we have only to look at the press clippings of Hillary Rodham Clinton to see how our society reacts to a powerful, beautiful, aggressive woman who has influence, sexual and otherwise, over an even more powerful man. We should not be surprised to find the elements of the female monster in Shakespeare's Cleopatra; what is amazing is that we also find some of the wonder described in Cixous' analysis. Cleopatra does lead Antony, however briefly, into "a world he has never dared imagine." This world calls him back again and again from his Roman world, ultimately to his ruin. But again, we see this ruin figured more as the failure of Roman society to value human emotion than any sort of perversion in Cleopatra's world. It is, however, a fight to the death between the two value systems. Shakespeare could imagine and try to represent something of the war of which Cixous speaks, as he constructs a woman whose "victory does not have the meaning of a masculine triumph." That Shakespeare's representation relies so heavily upon the concept of reversal, however, does not signal the same sensibility that Cixous evinces when she says that to be a powerful woman, specifically an Amazon, "is to be faithful to the law of reversal: one must repeat the act that proves or symbolizes that she is not captive or submissive to a man." On the contrary, Shakespeare's use of reversal, much of it accomplished through the paradigm of the mirror, is a product of the very cultural assumptions which Cixous speaks against. Shakespeare's construct of the powerful Cleopatra contains many, if not all, of the elements of Cixous' Amazon. The playwright's ultimate disposition of these elements of gender, power, identity, and selfhood, however, is of course a product of his own culture, not of ours.

". . . NOT MORE MANLIKE . . . NOR . . . MORE WOMANLY"

Of all the women in all of Shakespeare's plays, Cleopatra is arguably the most powerful, as well as the best representation of an interior female self.[1] Not only is she a ruler in her own right, not only does she dominate those around her through force of personality (a force that is only partly due to her recognition and use of her sexual identity), but she—unlike any other major female character in the tragedies—keeps speaking after the scene in which the male protagonist dies. Indeed, Shakespeare alters the generic convention of title characters breathing and speaking their last in act 5 by having Antony expire in act 4, thus leaving all of the last act for the death of Cleopatra. True, she does not speak the play's closing lines—no women ever does that, with the semiexception of Rosalind in the persona of a male actor—but, of course, neither does any other tragic hero. And yet Shakespeare's Cleopatra is not an unproblematic representation of an interior female self, of female power, or of a female who has been completely successful by the standards of male power; but neither does she lack interiority, power, or some measure of political success. The elements of identity, gender, and power are so tightly wrapped around these two historical figures, the Egyptian woman and the Roman man, that reading them (the elements or the characters) separately becomes both frustrating and confusing. The playwright's emphasis upon Plutarch's *Lives* makes the distinction between history and drama equally murky. As if that were not enough, the parallels between the burial of the historical Cleopatra in Plutarch, the fictional Cleopatra in the play, and the historical allusions to the reburial of the contemporary figure of female power, Elizabeth I, are deliberately conflated in the play's final lines.[2] Shakespeare has given us a dramatic version of the perspective portrait Cleopatra mentions in act 2: from one perspective we see one set of images; from another we see something else entirely. Catherine Belsey acknowledges the multivalency of Cleopatra's final visual identity when she describes the queen's death:

> A woman, at once whore and mother . . . who simultaneously refuses the feminine, the figure of Cleopatra is thus plural, contradictory, an emblem which can be read as justifying either patriarchy on the one hand or an emergent feminism on the other. Or perhaps and icon of the contest between the two.[3]

How, in all of this, can we see only—or even primarily—Cleopatra the character? Not easily, if we cling to generic expectations generated by the title. In the most obvious sense, Shakespeare has blurred our vision by the contradiction of calling the play *Antony and Cleopatra,* while relegating the former to near-comic death in act 4 and giving the latter a splendid set piece in act 5, the dramatic space traditionally reserved for the death of the tragic hero. Up until this point in the play, Shakespeare violates our expectations about gender and power and representation; wile simultaneously reminding us that we "should" be seeing Antony as the hero, the playwright makes Cleopatra into the image that most constantly fills our eye. No sooner has she spoken her last, however, than is her status diminished both verbally—by Charmian who speaks of her as a "lass" and a "princess," not as a great queen—and physically, by Octavius who removes her from her royal monument. But these act-5, scene-2 revisions are only the last in a long series of metamorphoses of

Cleopatra, a series of changing images that begins with the first lines of the play.

Unlike the poets who give us Eve and Britomart, Shakespeare does not present a literal mirror among his many strategies for reflecting the political and sexual and personal powers of Cleopatra or for representing such elements of interiority as we find in the character. Considering that the Egyptian queen is much nearer the medieval and Renaissance commonplace of a beautiful, vain woman holding a looking glass than either the first woman working in her garden or the martial princess on her quest, this is very surprising. He does, however, profoundly employ the concept, the paradigm, of reflection as a means of representing the identity of Cleopatra—both her public identity and some elements of an interior self. Additionally, subtly, Shakespeare evokes aspects of the Medusa story through a variety of images, the most important employing the process of reflection itself, and the most obvious using snakes. If this were the source study I claim it not to be, Shakespeare's representation of Cleopatra would be the most central example in my argument, for the invocation of Ovid's mirror/monster narrative is so self-consciously employed in relation to female power. In a discussion of the paradigm of Medusa as a characteristic of male attempts to represent female interiority, however, the play constitutes perhaps the least concrete locus for my argument.

As Hamlet claims an inwardness which "passes show," Cleopatra seemingly attempts to externalize her every nuance of emotion. Her character exhibits some remarkable elements of self-knowledge, but the comments she makes to her women and to Enobarbus often take this self-knowledge and display it as merely uncontrolled speech. As I examine these evidences of self-knowledge turned into objects of public display, I will also argue for an attempt on the part of the playwright to construct some interiority for Cleopatra. The strongest evidence for this argument comes late in the play, as Cleopatra's grief gives her an interior identity which—although it generates one of the most spectacular death scenes in the Shakespeare canon—"passes show" as a direct representation, for it is largely constructed through the paradigm of reflection, the reflection of her identity, and the identity of Antony. The moon that is left behind after Antony's death is itself a body that reflects light. Cleopatra's suicide reflects and reverses the unsuccessful Roman death of her lover, even as it (quite unnecessarily in the context of the plot) includes the serpents that evoke the Medusa myth.

In *The Common Liar* Janet Adelman both discusses and contextualizes the association of Cleopatra with serpents:

we will remember that she herself is the serpent of old Nile when her baby the asp nurses her asleep. Despite our Freudian expectation, serpents are frequently associated with women: the female serpent is a dangerous enemy, whether she is Python's dragoness companion or the feminized Satan of medieval painting. The composite image of woman and serpent serves as an emblem for the attraction and repulsion felt toward women; in fact, it serves to express an enticement which is felt as dangerous precisely because it is so enticing. Lamia, Scylla, the mermaid-sirens, Medusa, and Spenser's Error all express the same fear: and they are Cleopatra's common ancestors.[4]

Nevertheless, the serpent imagery, as well as some direct and indirect references to the Gorgon that I will discuss later, constitute neither the most interesting nor the most significant of the Medusa paradigms in the play. The play itself functions as a reflection, as a series of multivalent reflections by which Cleopatra's image is radically metamorphosed: there is the formalistic reflection of Cleopatra's identity in relation to both her gender and her power, presented in the first scene and reversed in the final scene; there is the metaphoric reflection as the identity of Antony (and others) is reversed by reflecting on to and then off of the tain of Cleopatra herself; there is the historicist reflection of an older female ruler being replaced and revised by a younger male with imperial designs. Some of these reflections allow for the limited development of an interior female self, but ultimately the play demonstrates the inability—the refusal of—society to acknowledge a woman as anything other than an icon. And so this play, which at first glance might seem to be the most tangentially related of the three texts I discuss in this study, thus lies at the heart of the argument.

Antony and Cleopatra is held together by a tissue of images, words, and actions that are reversed as they are replicated by reflection. The play opens and closes with a Roman man, who has no cause to like her, speaking about the Egyptian monarch. Philo speaks of her as a slut (revising the implications of her name in the title), while five acts later Octavius Caesar uses language more politic and speaks of her as a royal enchantress (revising her robes of state into a becoming outfit, as it were); the first Roman speaker would separate the queen from his leader for the greater glory of Antony and the Roman Republic, but Octavius joins the pair in eternal sleep, both the general and the queen diminished and subordinated to the future glory of Augustus and the Roman Empire. In act 1 scene 1, Cleopatra speaks before Antony; in act 4, scene 15 she interrupts his death speech to keep speaking right on through act 5, that space traditionally reserved for the death and last words of tragic heros. Her first speech diminishes his reputation; her last speeches apotheosize him. In act 1, Octavius speaks of the reactions of the Romans to Antony's stay in Egypt, Romans who "do bear / So great weight in his lightness" (1.4.24–25); then in act 4, scene 15, Cleopatra says "How heavy weighs my lord! / Our strength is all gone into heaviness, / That makes the weight" (32–34) and "All" echo her: "A heavy sight!" (40); but in act 5, scene 2 Cleopatra's language transforms both Antony's supposedly irresponsible lightness and his self-inflicted heaviness, punning on "light"—"His face was as the heav'ns, and therein stuck / A sun and moon, which kept their course, and lighted / The little O, th' earth" (79–81)—and speaking of his actions as joyous: "His delights / Were dolphin-like, they show'd his back above / The element they liv'd in" (88–90). When Antony abandons Cleopatra in Egypt and betrays her love by remarrying in Rome, she does not diminish her queenship by more than a few seemingly customary fits of temper; when Cleopatra betrays Antony at the Battle of Actium, he most uncharacteristically turns and follows her to his humiliation and ultimate ruin. His action triggers for her a characteristic emotional scene; her action triggers in him an uncharacteristic betrayal of his own code of behavior. This trope of reversal is also found in the play's allusions, where—far from giving us Cleopatra as Dido—Shakespeare reverses the roles in this representation of an African queen, with Antony himself speaking of Dido and *her* Aeneas. Linda Woodbridge uses this dislocation of gender and power roles to protest the frequency with which critics refer to Cleopatra generically as "the archetypal woman: practicer of feminine wiles, mysterious, childlike, long on passion and short on intelligence."[5] Woodbridge's impatience with those critics is certainly justified, since we find throughout the play that the elements of gender identity and power are very unconventionally represented in both characters. Indeed, unconventionality lies at the heart of most of the play's actions and representations of identity.

Can one imagine a woman thrown by her ardor into the men's zone, and who says: "It's him. It's you. It's the unique one. And I can't make him mine"?

Certainly unimaginable in conventional society, where woman's desire cannot shoot straight like that but must take a thousand detours to express itself, and so often resign itself to the comedy of eloquent silence. Because in ordinary existence, woman does not announce, does not begin things. It is agreed that she will not go after the object of her desire. Courtly love is two-faced: adored, deified, assimilated to the idol that accepts homage, she has the rank and honors of the Virgin. Conversely, and the same position, in her powerlessness, she is at the disposition of the other's desire, the object, the prostitute.

Under these conditions, what is a woman's desire? What is left of it? What shows? What culpable impulse is cut off?[6]

Again, Hélène Cixous was not writing about Shakespeare's play in this passage, but her questions speak to the representation of Cleopatra we see in act 1, scene 1, the Cleopatra whose first words "shoot straight" and ask for the love she is sure is rightfully hers. Both the opening speech of Philo and the point in their conversation at which Shakespeare has Cleopatra and Antony enter prepare us to see a woman transgressing the boundaries of conventional behavior by both Roman and English standards. And yet if we look carefully at what she actually says and does, the image changes; from the conventional point of view it changes for the worse, as Cleopatra speaks freely of both love and politics. Antony's "goodly eyes" may "bend, now turn / The office and devotion of their view / Upon a tawny front" (1.1.2, 4–5),[7] but as we look and listen closely, we find that this "front" is only one aspect of her character. Yes, the first words we hear (hers, not Antony's, is the first speech of the pair) are of love, but, as Irene G. Dash points out:

the close interweaving of her roles as sexual being and political person becomes immediately apparent . . . [as] talk of love quickly gives way to discussions of political strategy when a messenger from Rome enters with news. Compared with Antony's wish for a brief summary of the message, Cleopatra repeatedly insists, "Nay, hear them, Antony" (19), "Call in the messengers" (29), and again later pleads with him to attend to them. Although she refers to those back in Rome with mockery . . . [throughout the scene] Cleopatra's advice that he listen to the messenger beats a refrain.[8]

Throughout the play Cleopatra will talk of both love and politics, because in her Egyptian, female worldview the two need not be separated. Unlike the Roman soldiers and their Roman leader, Cleopatra makes no separation between the public and the private. This is why we find her interiority figured so differently than that of Britomart. Not only do the conventions of genre demand externalization of selfhood, but Shakespeare constructs this particular dramatic character as one for whom the externalizing of any interior thought or emotion is not only possible but natural. We should not, however, make the mistake of assuming that this process of externalization is uncontrolled on Cleopatra's part; indeed, her statements in act 1 show us that she picks her moments of display with great care.

Whether or not Shakespeare presents this with blame or praise is a topic for intense debate, but Cleopatra's manipulation of Antony in act

1, scene 3 certainly runs contrary to the values espoused by conduct
books of the late-sixteenth and early-seventeenth centuries.

> See where he is, who's with him, what he does.
> I did not send you. If you find him sad,
> Say I am dancing; if in mirth, report that I am sudden sick.
>
> (3–6)

These famous instructions of Cleopatra to Charmian could indeed be
the mirror image of a passage in Edmund Tilney's 1568 *Brief and pleasaunt discourse of duties in Mariage,* in which, during an after-dinner debate Lady Julia argues that a woman should strive to please her husband
"whose face must be hir daylie looking glasse, wherein she ought to be
alwaies prying, to see when he is merie, when sad, when content, and
when discontent, where to she must always frame hir own countenance."[9] This image of the husband as the mirror in which the wife
should see herself was evidently a popular one, for it occurs in Robert
Snawsell's *Looking Glasse for Maried Folkes* that was originally printed in
1610 and reprinted in 1631. Here, in yet another debate, four women
are talking. Eulalie (called in the preface "wellspoken" as opposed to
other women variously described as "scold" and "proud malapert") says
that when her husband is sad she

> would not then laugh and dally with him, and play the tom-boy, as many
> women are wont to do in such a case, but I put upon me a sad countenance
> also, and lookt heavily; for even as a looking glasse if it be a good one, doth
> shew the countenance of him that glasses himselfe in it: So it beseems an
> honest wife to frame her selfe to her husbands affection and not to be merry,
> when he is melancholy, or jocund, when is is sad, much lesse fire when hee
> is angry.[10]

Of course, it is always difficult to know how to read such evidence. It's
very tempting to accept these paradigms as the norm. On the other
hand, we could conclude that the presence of these good, husband-
mirroring wives of the conduct books implies that many women of the
period behaved as Cleopatra advises, and that Tilney and Snawsell were
mounting a counterattack. This is a fascinating question quite beyond
the scope of my study, but because the issue of women's conduct is discussed using the paradigm of the mirror—metaphor is really too weak a
word—I include the quotes as evidence of a cultural association between
women and mirrors in relation to conventional behavior and gender
identity.

Arguing that the gender roles in Shakespeare's play are not reversed but polarized—"gender divisions remain constant"—Carol Thomas Neely reads the sad/dancing/mirth/sick lines as "merely a subtle, self-conscious, and inverted example of the responsiveness that is characteristic of Shakespeare's women."[11] What is inverted is the perspective. Here Cleopatra is not responding to Antony's moods—she will not herself actually become either mirthful or sudden sick; rather she is composing false representations of herself that will cause him to respond as she wishes. She loves him, but her love takes the initiative, the active role that seeks—or, more to the point, assumes—control; certainly, to borrow Cixous' phrase, this is a role reversal "unimaginable in conventional society," whether Roman or English, and, in fact, it seems to shock Charmian, who urges her queen to follow more conventional lines of behavior.

One of the most obvious reversals operating within the play is the representation of the story of Dido and Aeneas. Since the story of Antony and Cleopatra in the center of Aeneas' shield was used by Virgil to foreground the Roman values of his hero's descendant Octavius/Augustus Caesar and to declare those values superior to those of Mark Antony (so popular and so recently defeated) it is hardly surprising that we find Shakespeare picking up Virgil's "history" and using it for similar editorial ends. As Janet Adelman argues:

That Antony creates his own version of Aeneas does not imply that either he or Shakespeare was deficient in knowledge of the classics; nor is it merely symptomatic of Antony's tendency to see everything as a reflection of his own state. Antony is one in a long line of reinterpreters of Virgil. The story of Dido and Aeneas presents the archetypal conflict of public and private values: Aeneas's choice of empire over love is susceptible to reevaluation by those who are not certain that civilization is worth the enormous sacrifices that it asks in the *Aeneid*.[12]

In Shakespeare's play, the chief of those who reevaluate is Antony. In act 4, scene 14 he cries out for the lover whom he believes has abandoned him, calling for love itself, "Eros," to be the agent that sends him to join his queen.

> Eros! I come, my queen!—Eros!—Stay for me!
> Where souls do couch on flowers, we'll hand in hand,
> And with our sprightly port make the ghosts gaze.
> Dido and her Aeneas shall want troops,
> And all the haunt be ours. Come Eros, Eros!
>
> (50–54)

Even more interesting than the amazing name Shakespeare bestows upon Antony's servant is the language that the Roman leader brings forth in this speech. He calls Cleopatra "my queen," a phrase used more by a courtier than an equal, and certainly not the words of a superior. Antony both images a reversal of the book-6 encounter between Dido and Aeneas in the underworld—giving them a Hollywood-style happy ending—and he then usurps that re-presentation as a mirror for himself and Cleopatra. Like the phrase "my queen," his wording of "Dido and *her* Aeneas" (emphasis mine) signals the shift in power from the Roman leader who subordinates the private to the public in favor of the queen who has tried to value both. We see him both revise Dido's story (making it hers rather than Aeneas') and reenact Dido's last scene, a scene precipitated in both texts by the actions of Rumor, what Shakespeare calls "the common liar" (1.1.60). Like the Queen of Carthage, Antony cannot count on help from those around him to end his life. Both Antony and Dido are forced to wield the sword themselves and neither achieves the goal of instant death. Dido lingers wordless on her funeral pyre until she is released by the merciful gods; Antony lingers and is carried to Cleopatra's funeral monument where he is allowed to say little more than "I am dying, Egypt, dying" (4.15.18). After Antony's death, as Janet Adelman points out: "Instead of a Dido hard as flint (*Aeneid* 6.471) in her rejection of Aeneas in the afterlife, we have a Cleopatra 'marble constant' for death to meet with Antony."[13]

Cleopatra's response to Antony's claim that he is "a Roman by a Roman / Valiantly vanquish'd" (4.15.57–58) is reflected in Cleopatra's stated desire to take her life "after the high Roman fashion, / And make death proud to take us" (87–88), a desire that she fulfills even as she redefines its terms. Unlike Antony whose death is prompted by and performed as a series of mistakes, Cleopatra knows exactly why she is dying; she has an accurate assessment of both her political and personal situation and makes a decision based on both. If it were only Antony's death that inspired her—as he claims hers was for his self-slaughter—she could have died immediately while she still held undisputed power in her monument with knives and poisons at her disposal, an antique Juliet. But it is not until she assesses her political future as unacceptable in act 5 that she goes forward with her plan. Once she decides to act, she does so not only with the active help of all those who serve her, but also with decisive speed, enormous dignity, and beautifully articulated opinions that still mingle inextricably the public and the private: five lines after she expresses her hyperbolic fear that Iras will reach Antony's lips before she does, she tells the asp "O, couldst thou speak, / That I might hear thee call great Caesar ass / Unpolicied!" (5.2.306–8). Two lines later she speaks of her baby at her breast, then calls again for Antony, and dies. In his act-4 death, Antony begs for the last of many thousand kisses, for wine, for an opportunity to speak; Cleopatra creates her own opportunity and has "Immortal longings" (281). Antony's last words are "I can no more" (4.1.5.59), while Cleopatra's last line forms a rhetorical question to which she has already supplied the answer. The question, which requires less than a full clause—"What should I stay—" (5.2.313) is answered by the self-willed death that cuts it short.

With serpents and sexuality and stiffening bodies everywhere, we can certainly suggest that Shakespeare is using the Medusa story to some end. But even here we find a reversal. If there is a blood-freezing Medusa in this play it is Antony, not Cleopatra. While the sight of the dead Antony makes Cleopatra "marble constant," the effect she has on Antony is just the opposite: she softens him. In act 3, scene 11, after the Battle of Actium, when Cleopatra exclaims "I little thought / You would have followed" (55–56), Antony responds:

> You did know
> How much you were my conqueror, and that
> My sword, made weak by my affection, would
> Obey it on all cause.
>
> (65–68)

Throughout the play we hear others speak of Antony's transformation. In the opening speech of the play, Philo orders Demetrius: "Take but good note, and you shall see in him / The triple pillar of the world transform'd / Into a strumpet's fool" (11–13). These are but the last lines of Philo's speech which, as Barbara J. Bono points out, describes the physical degeneration of Antony:

Two strong spatial images inform his [Philo's] speech: Antony has declined or bent and in the process has lost shape or definition . . . an erect "triple pillar" has become an effeminate "strumpet's fool." He dotes, rather than loves; his dotage "o'erflows the measure"; his eyes "bend"; his heart, in a punning play on "temper," softens its martial ferocity to lover's submission. . . . The speech approves Antony's heroic energy, but would harness it to the service of Roman ideals of measure, public authority and conquest. Philo fears the "motion" Cleopatra induces in Antony as a dissolution of his nature. . . .[14]

But Philo's judgments do not constitute the only example of the hardened, phallic image of Antony the warrior being "transform'd" by his

association with Cleopatra. Scene 4 of act 1 brings us to the famous
insult uttered by Octavius, that Antony:

> is not more man like
> Than Cleopatra; nor the queen of Ptolomy
> more womanly than he.
>
> (5–7)

As Lepidus tries, mildly, to defend Antony ("His faults, in him, seem as
the spots of heaven, / More fiery by night's blackness" [12–14]), Octavius
argues that his behavior signals a profound change, as Antony is not
merely filling "vacancy with his voluptuousness" (26), but has regressed
into the irresponsible state of a child (28–33) and is no longer the model
of a soldier who could drink horse piss (61–62). The horse "stale," of
course is only one of a litany of examples of Antony's former toughness
as a soldier. To this Lepidus can only say "'Tis pity of him" (71).

Early in act 2, scene 5 Cleopatra supplies us the anecdote that could
have given rise to Caesar's criticism, and it is, she tells us, but one of
many:

> That time? Oh times!
> I laugh'd him out of patience; and that night
> I laugh'd him into patience; and next morn,
> Ere the ninth hour, I drunk him to his bed;
> Then put my tires and mantles on him, whilst
> I wore his sword Philippan.
>
> (18–23)

All of the verbs in this speech are active and it is Cleopatra who is the
force behind them. Antony is represented in the passive voice, even to his
being dressed. Neely calls this speech "Cleopatra's exuberant memory of
hers and Antony's unique drunken exchange of clothes" and argues
that it "is given its joyous point by the secure and satisfying gender roles
in which the two ordinarily exist," citing the lines that follow this speech
to support her reading.[15] But there is no reason to believe that this
behavior is unique, for Cleopatra speaks of "times"; and the next lines,
uttered upon the entrance of a messenger, "O, from Italy! / Ram thou
thy fruitful tidings in mine ears, That too long have been barren" (23–
25) suggest, by both Cleopatra's use of the imperative and her graphic
language, a relationship that is far from conventional, a relationship
with at least elements of reversal. The lines which Neely cites as indicative
of "secure and satisfying gender roles" sound more like a command to

perform aural rape by proxy than evidence of anything "ordinary."[16] But even if they constitute, as Neely suggests, a reference to the established sexual relationship of Antony and Cleopatra, we are shown a relationship in which Cleopatra issues the imperatives.

It is in this scene that we hear two direct references to Ovid's mirror stories, and both come from Cleopatra as she responds to the news of Antony's marriage. When the messenger asks (with some reason) if he should lie, Cleopatra replies:

> O, I would thou didst;
> So half my Egypt were submerg'd and made
> A cestern for scal'd snakes! Go get thee hence!
> Hadst thou Narcissus in thy face, to me
> Thou wouldst appear most ugly.
>
> (93–97)

The brief reference to Narcissus—raised in the subjunctive only to be dismissed—is both expected and a surprise. We expect it because of its link to vanity, which is in turn linked to female beauty; we are surprised because in all of the lines about Cleopatra's beauty, her indulgences, and her faults, this is one fault that no one attributes to her. When she lies on her couch in her palace, she holds not a mirror but a pen. Her catalog of her lovers is not offered in support of her own attraction, but as a tribute to her present lover. Cleopatra goes beyond the Narcissus image, dismissing it because it has no meaning for her, no power over her. She loves herself, of course, but not in vain. She associates neither herself nor Antony with the face mirrored in the pool. She does, however, invoke more centrally the other Ovidian mirror narrative as twenty lines later she says to Charmian, seemingly of Antony:

> Though he be painted one way like a Gorgon,
> The other way's a Mars.
>
> (116–17)

The idea of a perspective painting, one that figures different images when viewed from different angles, is at least as interesting in the context of this argument as is the reference to the Gorgon. In fact, the shield of Perseus could be considered a type of perspective painting: from one angle the eye sees the face of Medusa, from another the face of Perseus, and both are reversals. But why does Cleopatra pair Medusa—always "the" Gorgon, although there were three—with Mars? Mars is obvious as an Antony reference, and considerable ink has been spilled over the

Mars/Venus paradigm in this play, but it is Perseus whose face shares the tain of the mirror with Medusa. For obvious reasons Cleopatra would not want to see Antony as a Perseus figure, as this would cast her almost inevitably in the role of Andromeda or the only other female in the scene, Medusa herself. Perhaps she sees this halfway through her simile—one of her most characteristic qualities is that she revises herself even as she speaks—and simply substitutes the most logical figure from mythology for the name of Perseus. Perhaps we are being shown an active unconscious conflating two narratives. In either case, her simile becomes itself a perspective portrait for the reader, a surface that can be variously evaluated, depending upon the angle from which it is read. I find it most significant that Shakespeare has Cleopatra speak of perspective painting, of multiple images, of double identities, for in his play it is the Queen of Egypt who is primarily presented in this fashion, as the tain of a mirror that generates an image both mutable and multiple.

"AND DIE / WITH LOOKING ON HIS LIFE": THE MIRROR OF THE I/EYE

In her compendium of imagery, *Cleopatra: Histories, Dreams, and Distortions*, Lucy Hughes-Hallett writes of the Egyptian queen and her suicide as follows:

> Cleopatra died: her name did not. She aspired to immortality and she won at least the kind that lasting fame affords. But that fame was to have a curiously chameleon-like character. A mirror rather than a portrait, her image has passed through as many changes as it has had spectators, for those who have tried to see her, to reimagine and reproduce her image, have instead seen and displayed themselves in her.[17]

Although Shakespeare's Cleopatra is only one of the enormous number of representations Hughes-Hallett discusses, her choice of the image of the mirror that reflects not the queen but the representer is particularly apt for a discussion of the play. The image of reflection that provides the paradigm of representation for Shakespeare's Cleopatra appears fleetingly in act 1, scene 4, it is the image of Cleopatra's former lover Pompey reaching climax while gazing at his own reflection in Cleopatra's eyes:

> and great Pompey
> Would stand and make his eyes grow in my brow;

There would he anchor his aspect, and die
With looking on his life.

(1.4.31–34)

What Cleopatra says of Pompey could in some measure be said of every character—certainly every male character—who comes in contact with her. The images generated when Antony and Octavius gaze at her are, of course, the most important, but we find a most revealing example in the description, both visual and editorial, of her which Enobarbus provides back in Rome. The most famous portion of this verbal portrait, of course, is taken almost word-for-word from Plutarch. After he presents the set piece of Cleopatra on the barge, however, Enobarbus continues to describe Cleopatra's traits as reflections of what he sees as Antony's virtues. As Lepidus earlier suggests that Antony's faults seem almost beautiful, so Enobarbus speaks of Cleopatra, hopping through the public street, being blessed when she is riggish (2.2.239). As Bono points out, this portion of Enobarbus' speech has a different source and therefore a very different connotation: "Lucretius's invocation of Venus is the source for Shakespeare's additions to Plutarch's description of Cleopatra at Cydnus. The Venus genetrix not only of the Roman race but of all things under heaven, she conceives the good and dispels evil."[18] Because Antony "cannot" leave Cleopatra, her flaws become his virtues in the eyes of Enobarbus. When Menas speaks of Octavia as the ideal wife, having heard Enobarbus say she possesses the Roman virtues of "a holy, cold, and still conversation," he is rebuked by Enobarbus who claims than Antony cannot value those characteristics because they are not his own (2.7.122–26).

Pompey may have "died" while looking at his own reflection in Cleopatra's eyes and Enobarbus may look at Cleopatra and see a reflection of what he sees (or wishes to see) in his Antony, but the character whose reversed gaze is most central to the play is, of course, Antony himself. Antony gazes at Cleopatra almost unceasingly, as sight is the sense most often mentioned by him and others who describe him with Cleopatra. And yet, to an almost shocking extent, he never truly sees her. What he sees are his expectations of how a lover, a mistress, a wife, a queen will act; he projects those expectations onto the tain of the mirror that is Cleopatra and they are reversed, always surprising him. The question Cleopatra asks to stem Antony's tide of abuse in act 3, scene 13, "Not know me yet?" (157), does transform his invective to loving discourse, but the unspoken answer to that question is "No"; no, he never truly knows her because he never truly sees her.

In act 1, scene 2, Antony and Enobarbus anticipate a confrontation with Cleopatra in which she "dies instantly" (141) and exhibits "cunning past man's thought" (145); while, in some measure, both of these predictions come true in act 1, scene 3, Cleopatra does not react to Antony's departure with grief or to Fulvia's death with glee as the two men imply she will—quite the reverse. She astounds Antony by upbraiding him because he does not show enough grief for his late wife:

> O most false love!
> Where be the sacred vials thous shouldst fill
> With sorrowful water? Now I see, I see,
> In Fulvia's death, how mine receiv'd shall be.
>
> (62–65)

After this display, she is restored only by the knowledge that he will *leave* Egypt as her "soldier, servant, making peace or war / As [she] affects" (70–71). In this scene Cleopatra acts contrary to Antony's expectations, but by doing so she manipulates him into the attitudes she desires. Here we see her earlier speech to Charmian made flesh. In this process of reversal, Cleopatra alters not only Antony's expectations, but also his action and speech. Four times, in lines 24 through 39, she breaks into his attempts to speak; after he conveys the news of Fulvia's death and hears Cleopatra's condemnation of his behavior, his speech reverses his scene-2 intentions. No longer does he plan to break off from Cleopatra; instead he goes forth using language more suited to a knight sworn to her service than to a triple pillar of the Roman world. Antony's perceptions and Antony's words are reversed after contact with the tain of the mirror that is the character of Cleopatra.

In act 3, at the heart of the play, we find a series of complexly represented reversed images. Here again we see the common qualities of the mirror and the perspective portrait. As Enobarbus makes up his mind to desert Antony, he is influenced by his changing perceptions of the images of Cleopatra and Antony. In scene 7 he speaks to Cleopatra with disdain, arguing that she should stay home from the war for two reasons. The first is that his efforts to understand her—not, significantly, to *know* her in the intellectual or physical sense—will distract Antony from his fighting.

> Your presence needs must puzzle Antony,
> Take from his heart, take from his brain, from 's time,
> What should not then be spar'd.
>
> (10–12)

To this complaint, so much more complex than the "not before the big game" image of horses and mares he mutters in an aside (6–9), Enobarbus adds his concern for Antony's (and his own) reputation:

> He is already
> Traduc'd for levity, and 'tis said in Rome
> That Photinus an eunuch and your maids
> Manage this war.
>
> (12–15)

Here we see a reversal not only of gender, but of class, as Enobarbus articulates the gossip of Rome that puts Cleopatra's servants, not the queen herself, in a position of power.

The debate over whether to fight on land or on sea is seen by Enobarbus as proof that this Roman gossip is not entirely false. The decision is itself an elemental reversal, as Antony takes to the sea in the Egyptian fashion. When Antony speaks of fighting at sea, Cleopatra responds as if there were nothing to debate: "By sea, what else?" (28). Both Enobarbus and a soldier who personifies the history of Roman conquest by land—"Let th' Egyptians / And the Phoenicians go a-ducking; we / Have us'd to conquer standing on the earth, / And fighting foot to foot" (63–66)—are not so much refuted as ignored by an Antony who repeats simply "By sea, by sea" (40), "I'll fight at sea" (48). And in scene 10 it is to a duck, "a doting mallard" (19), that Scarus compares Antony when he tell Enobarbus that their leader has fled after his lover: "we have kiss'd away / Kingdoms and provinces" (7–8). Both Enobarbus and Scarus agree with Canidus that things might have gone differently "Had our general / Been what he knew himself" (24–25).

If Antony is not "himself," then what is he? The implication is that he is some new image generated by Cleopatra. We do not know if Enobarbus is present in scene 11; he does not speak individually, and Antony is said to enter simply "with Attendants." It is after this scene, however, this scene in Antony himself tries to blame Cleopatra—"O, whither hast thou led me, Egypt?" (51) he asks before speaking of his "sword, made weak by my affection" (67)—that Enobarbus reverses himself and absolves Cleopatra, placing the blame squarely on Antony.

> CLEO. Is Antony or we in fault for this?
> ENO.   Antony only, that would make his will
>   Lord of his reason. What though you fled
>   From that great face of war, whose several ranges
>   Frighted each other? Why should he follow?
>   The itch of his affection should not then

> Have nick'd his captainship. . . . to course your flying flags,
> And leave his navy gazing.
>
> (13.1–12)

If Enobarbus' reversal of blame is not the result of his seeing Antony
first blame and then be restored by Cleopatra in scene 11, then to what
can we attribute the change? To some extent, we must return to the
image of the perspective painting: in act 2 Enobarbus saw Antony's virtues reflected on Cleopatra; he now sees Cleopatra's identity reflected
upon his general. Certainly his final reversal in act 3, his decision to
leave Antony, comes after he witnesses a remake of Cleopatra and Antony playing these reversed roles. This makes Enobarbus' accusation that
Antony has left "his navy gazing" into yet another resonance of the
Medusa paradigm. Speaking of the point in the battle at which Enobarbus averted his own eyes, he now describes those who looked on Antony's
actions as trapped in a seemingly perpetual gaze, just as are those who
gaze on the face of the Gorgon. Even here, there is an element of reflected horror; for it is not the mere fact of Antony's retreat that generates this reaction, it is the fact that all the Romans see his retreat as a
function of his union with Cleopatra. Her identity is now mirrored in
his actions. Enobarbus blames Antony rather than the Egyptian queen
in his scene-13 speech, but the subtext of that condemnation is Antony's
inability to look away from Cleopatra.

Later in scene 13, after Cleopatra has received a messenger from
Caesar, Antony mirrors Cleopatra's most emotional and unreasonable
words and actions. Here he usurps her speech, reversing the pattern of
act 1, scene 3 (which will be reversed once again in Antony's death scene),
and reversing the imagery he used in act 3, scene 11 to describe the
same relationship he now damns. Rather than a sword made weak by
affection, or the leader who cries only twenty lines before "Authority
melts from me" (13.90), Antony now declares he has grown hard with
anger:

> You have been a boggler ever
> But when we in our viciousness grow hard
> (O misery on't!), the wise gods seel our eyes,
> In our own filth drop our clear judgments, make us
> Adore our errors, laugh at 'u while we strut
> To our confusion.
>
> (110–15)

Here Antony seems to equate "true" sight of Cleopatra and her faults
with growing hard, a process that is then thwarted by "the wise gods"

who "seel our eyes" and "make us / Adore our errors." Antony continues
to reimage Cleopatra as a slut, as a "morsel, cold upon / Dead Caesar's
trencher . . . a fragment / Of Cneius Pompey's" (116–18), as a traitor,
implying that she has always been thus, while at the same time acknowledging that he himself is greatly changed, saying that Caesar is "harping
on what I am, / Not what he knew I was" (142–43). Cleopatra deflects
this outpouring—which is a perspective portrait reversal of her own
act-1, scene-5 cataloging of old lovers as a tribute to Antony—with her
single question "Not know me yet?" Then it becomes clear that he as
been "harping" on what she once "was," not the identity to which she
would now say "I am." This reversal is so rapid and so complete that it
goes unacknowledged by either Antony or Cleopatra. He moves in one
line from condemning her to being comforted by her, vowing to get
drunk with her and all his followers. Even here, she reimages him. Knowing that the time is past for private love games such as she extolled in
acts 1 and 2, she now provides Antony a public excuse for celebration
with her lie "It is my birthday" (184), thus giving the facade of dignity
to his self-indulgent desire to get drunk. For Enobarbus, who witnesses
this amazing double transformation, the reversal is complete:

> Now he'll outstare the lightning: to be furious
> Is to be frighted out of fear, and in that mood
> The dove will peck the estridge; and I see still
> A diminution in our captain's brain
> Restores his heart. When valor preys on reason,
> It eats the sword it fights with. I will seek
> Some way to leave him.
>
> (194–200)

Antony is no longer "himself" unless he is made so by the manipulation
of Cleopatra. The leader that Enobarbus once thought could be reduced
in power by his union with Cleopatra is restored to (an appearance of)
the state from which he as fallen, restored by the Egyptian queen. The
image of his leader has now become only a reflection of the image of
Cleopatra, and Enobarbus, thinking he has seen everything of each of
them, decides to leave. In this complicated nexus of perceptions, misperceptions, and revised perceptions, there are three issues I would like to
examine more carefully: Shakespeare's strategy that gives us the character of Enobarbus, himself engaged in a reversal of perception and loyalty,
as an observer-figure, as a marker for the revisions of Cleopatra's and
Antony's characters; the complex nature of those revisions, each set of
which reflects an element of change in the other; and the question of

Antony's exterior identity as it is represented in relation to Cleopatra's interior identity.

"I CAN BEHOLD NO LONGER"

So speaks Enobarbus at the Battle of Actium—an ironic decision, as it is his role as observer that most fully defines Enobarbus in act 3. He watches the romance in Egypt; he watches Romans plot; he watches Antony choose to fight at sea; later he watches his defeated leader turn on Cleopatra; he watches—at least once, possibly twice—as Cleopatra restores Antony from hysterics to some appearance of Roman order. At the center of all this watching, he does not watch the battle. Why is the gaze of Enobarbus given such a position of privilege in act 3? The answer lies, I believe, in the role Enobarbus fulfills in the first two acts, where he is both the voice that urges (while playing devil's advocate) Antony toward Roman reason—certainly Cleopatra sees him in this light when she speaks of Antony being "dispos'd to mirth, but on the sudden / A Roman thought hath strook him. Enobarbus!" (1.2.82–83)—and yet the voice that explains and mediates Antony's behavior in Egypt to his fellow Romans (2.2 and 2.6). In these early acts of the play, Enobarbus speaks to and for Antony; after act 3, scene 7, when his advice about fighting on land is ignored, he speaks to Cleopatra and to the audience in asides, but his relation to Antony is that of an observer; in act 4 he leaves Antony only to find that he did not know his leader as well as he thought, and his death is his response to his acknowledged misperception. It will be Cleopatra's servants who "can endure / To follow with allegiance a fall'n lord," who "conquer him that did [their mistress] conquer," and who earn "a place i' th' story" (3.13.43–46). Enobarbus leaves Antony because he believes the Roman is destroying himself; because he has left Antony, Enobarbus himself is destroyed. Here too we find the sort of balance that could be called "measure for measure," but that contains the crucial element of reversed perception. The point at which this perception is reversed lies in the sight that he does not watch, the Battle of Actium—the Battle of Actium that Virgil puts at the center of Aeneas's shield. From Shakespeare's reflection of this act of history Enobarbus turns his gaze. Because he can gaze no more, he turns from Antony, and because he turns from Antony, he dies. The metamorphosis of Enobarbus is but one action in this dramatic whole, but it is an action that is set in the paradigm of reversed perception.

If Enobarbus does not literally see Antony as a reflection of himself—

or more hierarchically, himself as a reflection of Antony—we neverthe-less find in the representation of Enobarbus' sight of his leader key elements of both the Narcissus and the Medusa narratives. Enobarbus wants Antony to reflect all the Roman values he holds so dear; indeed, if Antony can be said to embody those values, then Enobarbus can con-struct himself as Antony's reflection. But for Enobarbus to gaze directly at Antony while he is acting in a non-Roman (or anti-Roman) fashion would be the death of Enobarbus. So, at the Battle of Actium, he averts his eyes. Ironically, in act 3, when he sees Antony as the reflection of a strength that is really Cleopatra's, he chooses an action that will lead to his death. If any character in Shakespeare can be said to have died from looking, that character is Enobarbus. He looks at Antony and believes he sees a false image; he looks at Cleopatra and thinks he sees a monster, but this image is transformed into the reflection of that which he loved: Antony. His final reversal of perception, when he knows without physical sight that he was wrong to leave Antony, brings on his death. He realizes that Antony does indeed both embody and reflect the values he honors. Like Narcissus, he is in love with an image he cannot possess because it is to some degree his own reflection; like those who look directly at Medusa, he is struck down by a power that is beyond the control of the object of his gaze.

"BUT SINCE MY LORD IS ANTONY AGAIN, I WILL BE CLEOPATRA"

From the first scene of act 1, when Cleopatra says "I'll seem the fool I am not. Antony / Will be himself" (1.1. 42–43), the issue of Antony's self arises again and again, to be left unresolved by Octavius' closing declaration that Cleopatra will be buried "by *her* Antony" (5.2.358, em-phasis mine). But that last line is deceptive, for the question is not simply to whom Antony belongs, but whether Antony's "self" resides in his glorious past or in his immediate actions. As Philo somewhat confusingly observes of his leader:

> Sir, sometimes when he is not Antony,
> He comes too short of that great property
> Which should go with Antony.
>
> (1.1.58–60)

What, then, is Antony? We see him leave Egypt answering Cleopatra's claim that "my oblivion is a very Antony, / And I am all forgotten"

(1.1.90–91) by declaring that "thou residing here, goes yet with me; /
And I hence fleeting, here remain with thee" (103–4). Such sentiments
work very well in John Donne's love poetry, but are too metaphysical to
have much meaning in a drama set over most of the Mediterranean.
Antony returns to Rome, but once there he tells Octavia "If I lose mine
honor, / I lose myself" (3.4. 22–23). Through all of Antony's transformations of "self," Cleopatra remains that which she has always been: a
constant in flux. Her image of self is ever-evolving, a fact she celebrates
by reveling in memories, even when those memories contradict the point
she is making about the present. Her famous act-1, scene-5 review of
her past lovers, up to and including Antony, is the perfect example of
this. When Charmian teases that she once spoke of Julius Caesar as she
now speaks of Antony, she brushes contradiction aside: "My salad days,
When I was green in judgment" (73–74). When, at the end of the play,
she decides to die in the "Roman fashion," she does not reject her Egyptian identity, she merely adds another dimension to her self.

Ultimately, Antony's "self" seems to be defined by the audience to
which he is presenting it; but since that audience is so often a mix of
Romans and Cleopatra and her court, he is really a "self" only insofar
as is the crocodile[19] he describes in act 2:

> It is shap'd sir, like itself, and it is as broad
> as it hath breadth. It is just so high as it is, and moves
> with its own organs. It lives by that which nourisheth
> it, and the elements once out of it, it transmigrates.
>
> (2.7. 42–45)

When Cleopatra says she will "be Cleopatra" now that Antony "is Antony
again," what has she been in the interval? Has she been the Antony
figure? Has he been Cleopatra?

Speaking of Antony and Cleopatra's deaths in the pattern of the play
as a whole, Barbara Bono also argues for the trope of reversal, from
"Philo's moralistic framing of the [first] scene" to the suicide of
Cleopatra:

> But Philo's interpretation of the lovers' action is a noteworthy one, grounded
> in centuries of orthodox interpretation of the *Aeneid* and the virtues of Roman
> culture. . . . This judgment is effectively reversed by Cleopatra's imaginative
> transformations as, through the divided catastrophe of the play, she turns
> Antony's suicide into her triumph. . . . In *Antony and Cleopatra* Cleopatra has
> to force reappraisal of the potent Roman historiographical tradition, the myth
> of the Roman mind. She does so not as transcendent *dea ex machina*, but as
> immanent enactor of fictions.[20]

For all her mutability, Cleopatra never suggests that she is not herself. That definition of "self" simply contains more elements than does Antony's. When Antony is himself, it is by Roman standards of public conduct. Ironically, in act 3, we see this Roman "self" being reconstructed and nurtured for Antony not by the agency of Enobarbus or by other Roman prompts, but by Cleopatra.

"NOT KNOW ME YET?"

If we look at the death of Antony in act 4 as he self-defines it, we must consider that his most constant identity has been one who knows neither others nor himself. Certainly he does not know Cleopatra, although she knows him almost completely. Before he dies in Cleopatra's monument to which he has been ignominiously lugged, Antony offers Cleopatra political advice on the situation he has made worse by having his death take place in her arms, and then he tries to revise his own end by reflecting on his distant past, the image of which he then employs to revise his immediate state:

> The miserable change now at my end
> Lament nor sorrow at; but please your thoughts
> In feeding them with those my former fortunes
> Wherein I liv'd, the greatest prince o' th' world,
> The noblest; and do now not basely die,
> Not cowardly put off my helmet to
> My countryman—a Roman by a Roman
> Valiantly vanquish'd.
>
> (4.14.51–57)

That he could expect this speech to find a sympathetic ear in the woman who said of herself "Mine honor was not yielded, / But conquer'd merely" (3.13.61–62) shows that Antony still does not know Cleopatra. That he could glorify his own botched suicide with the word "valiantly," shows that he still does not know himself. Cleopatra sees him for what he is, not "the greatest prince o' th' world, / The noblest," but her "Noblest of men" (57), whose death leaves no "odds" and nothing "remarkable" upon the Earth. In fact, Cleopatra dies the death Antony would like to think he is dying, dies it for him both in her desire to be with him and in her ultimate political manipulation of Roman politics: for Antony's death may have been pitiful, but she represents it as something glorious, glorious in the "high Roman fashion." When Mardian first tells

Antony of Cleopatra's supposed death, he projects Roman values upon her action: "she which by her death our Caesar tells / 'I am conqueror of my self'" (4.13.61–62). Cleopatra's act-5 speech, however, focuses more upon that which she will gain by death; only in relation to Roman Caesar does she speak of that which she leaves behind, and those words spring from amused contempt rather than from metaphors of empire. Caesar, of course, does not recognize what he sees, being to quick to dismiss Cleopatra as being brave, royal, and beautiful—he spoke of Antony, however briefly, as "my mate in empire" (5.1.43)—but not a force to be recognized except insofar as she can be used to diminish Antony. That Antony never knows any of this, that the truly victorious death we see in act 5 is the Egyptian queen's not the Roman general's, raises a fascinating question: does Cleopatra assume Antony's identity or has she come to exist—to be represented—primarily in relation to his Roman values? Neither, I would suggest. On the contrary, if we untangle this tight knot of identity, we find that Antony exists within this play almost entirely in relation to Cleopatra. That he cannot know her is further evidence that he does not know himself. Cleopatra knows Antony; Caesar knows Antony; first and finally Enobarbus knows Antony. But Antony does not know himself. Of all the characters in the play, only Cleopatra is given a sense of self that is not merely reactive—as Antony knows himself to be unworthy of Enobarbus' loyalty or Enobarbus knows himself to have made the wrong decision. This is not to say that Cleopatra's interior self is represented as complexly as is Britomart or Eve's, but given the limitations of the genre and the contrast with the other characters, we can say that Cleopatra knows she has a self to know. It is left to the audience, however, to acknowledge this dramatic interiority.

In this play Shakespeare presents the audience with a perspective portrait far more complex than the one to which Cleopatra makes reference. When we look at the play from one perspective, we see Cleopatra. When we look from another perspective we also see Cleopatra, now as the mirror on and from whose tain Antony is reflected. I have deferred my discussion of Cleopatra's interior selfhood for a reason. Shakespeare has constructed the entire play as a mirror designed to mediate our view of that self—the play as the shield of Perseus, if you will. I want to look carefully at the tain of that mirror, for it is here that we find Shakespeare's representation of Cleopatra's selfhood, constructed—like the play itself—as a reflecting surface. When we look at the very end of the play, we see the entire drama as a mirror (although a more problematic one than Hamlet suggests), a mirror which, like the burial of the two lovers, is ultimately in the hands of a powerful man and can be controlled by him to reflect whatever image he wishes to represent.

"WOULD I HAD NEVER SEEN HER!"

This is a play about ways of seeing a woman. Certainly this is not all that the play is about, but it is a crucial element of the drama. While this statement kicks open the door for a discussion of the woman as the object of the male gaze, I would argue that we should not be too quick to assume that this is all that is happening within the five acts during which various characters and the audience see Cleopatra variously. For one thing, none of the men who gaze at Cleopatra ever really knows her; but we might argue the same thing about the women in the play. The audience, too, is dared to know what they are seeing by that amazing line in act 5 when Cleopatra reminds them that they are looking at a boy-actor playing an Egyptian queen. Even today careful readers do not so much as blink when Cleopatra taunts them with the reality of her representation. Telling her waiting-women of the fate that really awaits her in Rome, she predicts that she would be forced to "see / Some squeaking Cleopatra boy my greatness / I' th' posture of a whore" (5.2.219–221). Shakespeare is very sure of his power here; for all that he plays with humor in Antony's death scene, there's no hint that he offers us Cleopatra's exit as the death of a drag queen.

So why raise the issue at all? Partly, I believe, Shakespeare is reminding us just how heavily our knowledge of Cleopatra depends upon sight—our sight of her, our sight of others seeing her, our sight of others' actions in reference to her. Poetry may indeed be a speaking picture, but drama offers speech more directly. The main Renaissance device for representing the interiority of a character is the soliloquy, a strategy Shakespeare does not employ for Cleopatra. Her speech always has an on-stage audience, an audience whose eyes mediate the effect of her words. How then can I possibly argue that this character constitutes the representation of an interior female self?

Well, I didn't exactly paint myself into that finite a corner. It's tempting, following the discussion of Britomart's allegorized struggle to gain some awareness or knowledge of an interior self, to look for the same sort of pattern in this play. But Cleopatra is not a young woman starting the journey of life in a quest for sexual and political identity. She is a mature woman who has enjoyed both for decades. We see the manifestation of her confident selfhood in her words and actions—a complex

meld of the public and the private—without the dichotomy of interior
and exterior that Spenser sets up in his epic. We see Cleopatra, but like
most of the characters in the play, we do not know what we are seeing.
Only in act 5, as she prepares for her death, do we see a careful representation of an female interiority and female power existing simultaneously. It's almost too much. We see queen, lover, wife, mother, fire, air,
and wit; petty emotions exist alongside immortal longings, and yet there
is no sense of contradiction. As a representation of the complex, Cleopatra's death scene is breathtaking.

Then, of course, she is gone. Her selfhood is articulated most clearly
as it is annihilated, and she performs both actions. That we are not left
with this dazzling display is a matter of more significance than can be
explained by the conventions of Renaissance tragedy that (almost) always
sacrifice a good curtain line for restored social order. Cleopatra's powerful female self, that image Shakespeare presents so clearly before the
halfline 313, vanishes on the breath that carries her last words. After
Cleopatra's death, we are once more at the mercy of others' perceptions
of her. The difference here is that the perception of Octavius is constructed by a playwright whose dramatic mirror is about to double as
the mirror of history. The most radical shift in the representation of
Cleopatra's identity takes place after her death. And here, as with Britomart, that powerful female identity is linked to the historical identity of
Elizabeth I.

"When such a spacious mirror's set before him He needs must see himself"

The historical/political uses of the mirror topos in the Renaissance,
from *A Mirror for Magistrates* and *The Steel Glass* to Hamlet's Mousetrap,
which holds a mirror up to nature, are invoked ultimately by Shakespeare in his presentation of Octavius Caesar's burial of Cleopatra,
queen of Egypt, a burial that in many ways mirrors the burial of Elizabeth, queen of England by James Stuart. When James VI of Scotland
became James I of England and Scotland in 1603, he faced the problem
of making a radical change seem like a natural sequence of events. He
was not the heir of Elizabeth's body; he was not English. From his coronation through the first decade of his reign, James set out to take advantage of the first fact and to revise the second. Without directly
disparaging the memory of Elizabeth, he set forth his gender, his heirs,
and the unity of his two countries as evidence of his destiny and of the

benefits England would reap from the fulfillment of that destiny. The coronation medal depicted James wearing a laurel wreath and had a Latin inscription proclaiming him Caesar Augustus of Britain, while many of the pageants commissioned for his initial progress through London incorporated the Augustus Novus theme. Soon after his coronation, he undertook a program of building designed to remind his new subjects of his blood claim to the Tudor throne. In the chapel of Henry VII in Westminster Abbey, James had Elizabeth moved from her original resting place in the central tomb of Henry VII, and—reserving that spot for himself—commissioned the construction of a tomb for Elizabeth that marginalized her importance and foregrounded her childless state. Elizabeth's tomb was completed in 1606, just as Shakespeare was working on *Antony and Cleopatra*. In that play we can see both of James's agendas, the idea of the unifying superruler and the demystification of the cult of his female predecessor, clearly represented—mirrored—in the last act.[21]

Sir Roy Strong, in *The Cult of Elizabeth*, provides us with a narrative, drawn from a variety of contemporary sources, of the Queen's funeral:

> on 28 April, a funeral procession of some fifteen hundred persons made its way to Westminster Abbey. Nothing quite like it had ever been seen before. "Her hearse (as it was borne) seemed to be an island swimming in water, for round it there rained showers of tears" wrote Thomas Dekker in his *Wonderful Year*. The streets were thronged with onlookers, the windows packed, even the rooftops were crowded with those who hoped for a glimpse of this spectacle. . . . When the royal chariot went by bearing the effigy of Elizabeth in crimson and ermine robes, crowned and clasping orb and sceptre, a sighing, groaning and weeping went up "as the like hath not been seen or known in the memory of man" [from Sir John Stowe's *Annales*].[22]

Elizabeth's death on 24 March at Richmond and her funeral on 28 April in London are both recorded in the diary of Lady Anne Clifford, the future countess of Pembroke, who was thirteen at the time and, on 24 March, living at Richmond, "sleeping on a pallet in the chamber of Lady Warwick, who was in charge of the arrangements."[23] Clifford writes:

> my Aunt Warwick's man, brought us word from his Lady, that the Queen died about 2/3 o'clock in the morning. . . . About 10 o'clock King James was proclaimed in Cheapside by all the Council with great joy and triumph. I went to see and hear. This peaceable coming-in of the King was unexpected to all sorts of people. Within two or three days we returned to Clerkenwell again. A little after this Queen Elizabeth's corpse came by night in a barge from

Richmond to Whitehall, my Mother and a great company of ladies attending it, where it continued a great while standing in the Drawing Chamber, where it was watched all night by several lords and ladies, my Mother sitting up with it two or three nights, but my Lady would not give me leave to watch, by reason I was held too young. . . . About this time my Lord Southampton was enlarged of his imprisonment out of the Tower. When the corpse of Queen Elizabeth had continued at Whitehall as the Council had thought fit, it was carried with great solemnity to Westminster, the lords and ladies going on foot to attend it, my Mother and my Aunt of Warwick being mourners, but I was not allowed to be one, because I was not high enough, which did much trouble to me then, yet I stood in the church at Westminster to see the solemnities performed.[24]

Clifford's reconstructed account of the death and funeral of Elizabeth has one advantage over contemporary narratives: she inserts things which—while seeming of no especial importance at the time—were later seen to be significant. So amid her lament that she was not tall enough (or old enough or noble enough?) to be a mourner and that the message of the queen's death "was delivered to my mother and me in the same chamber where afterwards I was married" we find the seemingly unrelated mention of Southampton's release from the Tower. Clifford, however, is not the only person to see this release as important.

We find an account of the way in which James spent 28 April in *The True Narration of the Entertainment of His Royal Majesty, from the time of his departure from Edinburgh till his receiving at London: with all, or the most special, Occurrences,* written by one Thomas Millington and printed in London in 1603.[25] Interestingly enough, the date 28 April is never written in this text. Millington begins his narrative of 27 April and runs it seamlessly—with pauses only to detail knightings, talk of hunting, and elaborate meals—right into 29 April. We can only speculate whether the omission of the precise date of Elizabeth's funeral in this narrative was in genuine deference to the sensibilities of those who were actively mourning her in London or whether it was to lessen (for those who might later read, remember, and resent) the contract between that public display of grief on 28 April and James's simultaneous hunting, wining, and dining. Other specific dates do go unmentioned, elided in the narrative, but very few; Millington is tediously detailed. One action James preformed on this unnamed April day, however, would have had particular significance for Shakespeare. As James approached the house of Master Oliver Cromwell [uncle of the future Protector], there "met him the Baliff of Huntingdon, who made a long oration to His Majesty, and there delivered him the Sword, which His Highness Gave to the new[ly] released [Henry Wriothesley] Earl of Southampton to bear before him"[26] Millington editorializes upon this event:

O Admirable work of mercy! confirming the hearts of all true subjects in the good opinion of His Majesty's royal compassion: not alone to deliver from the captivity such high Nobility, but to use . . . with great favors not only him, but also the children of his late honourable fellow in distress (ie. of Robert Devereux, Earl of Essex). Well, GOD have glory, that can send friends in the hour he best pleaseth, to help them that trust in him. . . . [So] His Majesty passed, in state, the Earl of Southampton bearing the Sword before him.[27]

When Clifford records her memories of the king's entry into London she also stresses the honor he pays Southampton and the heir of Essex. Both Clifford and Millington reflect on what seems to have been popular opinion, for in the diary of John Manningham we find a similar statement; on the day of Elizabeth's death Manningham writes: "One wishes the E[arl] of Southampton and others were pardoned, and at liberty."[28] The restoration of his sometime patron would certainly have been a matter of concern to Shakespeare. Whether or not it fully explains his 1603 silence amid the chorus of poetic grief prompted by Elizabeth's death, we can conclude that not only Shakespeare, but court figures as diverse as Lady Anne Clifford and Thomas Millington saw Southampton's release as a wrong being righted by the new monarch. I would not go so far as to say that this establishes Shakespeare's resentment of Elizabeth and subsequent willingness to diminish her power through his posthumous diminishment of Cleopatra, but I would suggest that these facts coupled with his almost unique silence as an active London writer on the occasion of the queen's death, make an interesting case for this reading of the situation. There are, however, other and equally interesting factors linking the historical and dramatic deaths and burials of these two powerful queens and the rise of two newly defined male rulers which may shed light on the final scene of *Antony and Cleopatra*.

As soon as he entered London—an entry delayed, according to some, because James wished his mother's murderer underground or, according to others, because Robert Cecil advised the king that London could not do equal honor to both the queen's burial and the king's entrance[29]—James sounded the theme of dynastic continuity, not by foregrounding his (albeit distant) blood tie to the deceased Elizabeth, but by stressing his own direct descent from Henry VII. In his early speeches and in the iconography of his reign, James makes a statement in which his presence on the English throne owes little to Elizabeth and much to his royal ancestor Henry VII, whose policy he offers as a pat-

tern for his own desire to rule England and Scotland as one country.
Of the seven triumphal arches in James's formal entry into London
(delayed by almost a year because of the plague), two address this theme
directly. The first arch links the Stuarts to the Trojan line celebrated by
Virgil as the ancestors of Augustus Caesar. In *The Golden Age Restor'd*,
Graham Parry reminds us:

> The old legends of the Trojan foundation of Britain took on new vigour with
> the accession of James, for he was the first modern king to restore the soverign
> unity that the British Isles were fabled to have enjoyed in ancient times. The
> Tudors had professed descent from the Trojans . . . [and] since James's right
> to the English throne derived from Henry VII, he naturally appropriated the
> myth of the Trojan origin of the Tudors. It was a good deal easier for English
> poets to celebrate the new King as the descendant of the Trojan Brutus than
> to represent him as the son of England's Catholic foe, Mary Queen of Scots. . . .
> [The] Trojan legend also lay behind the claims of nascent imperialism that
> would be made several times in the course of the day's entertainment, for the
> Trojans were the source of empire in the West, as Virgil and incontrovertibly
> established, and Britain like Rome was settled from Troy.[30]

The second triumphal arch on James's progress had a "central paining
over the archway [that] emphasized the legitimacy of James's inheritance,
showing Henry VII giving him the sceptre as the true successor to the
Tudor line."[31] Elizabeth, on the other hand, was not directly depicted in
any of the arches, although her presence was figured forth by images
of Astrea and of the phoenix, both redesigned to represent James. Finally, as the "royal party left the City and rode down the Strand, they
encountered one final tailpiece thrown up by Jonson at the last moment. . . . A human comet, Electra, prophesies, like an ancient Sybil,
that the new reign shall be free [from] 'All. . . . That might perturbe the
musique of thy peace' and at the climactic moment James is hailed as
the new Augustus."[32]

James himself continued to stress the themes of his triumphal entry.
He makes these dual claims for historical and dynastic inevitability both
immediately and consistently, as in a speech to his first Parliament on
22 March 1604 he argues:

> First, by my descent lineally out of the loynes of Henry the seventh, is reunited
> and confirmed in mee the Vnion of the two Princely Roses of the two Houses
> of LANCASTER and YORKE, where of that King of happy memorie was the
> first Vniter, as he was also the first groundlayer of the other Peace. . . . But
> the Vnion of these two princely Houses, is nothing comparable to the Vnion
> of two ancient and famous kingdomes. . . .[33]

Not only does James thus parallel his reign with that of the first Tudor, but he manages to present the union as entirely his own achievement and in no measure that of the queen who named him as her successor.

In an 1985 article in *Shakespeare Studies,* H. Neville Davies suggests further ways in which James Stuart's political situation can be seen as paralleling Augustus/Octavius Caesar's when he assumes control of the power held by Antony and—in Shakespeare's play—by Cleopatra. For as James was heralded in London pageantry and by his own proclamation, as Augustus Novus, Davies reminds us: "a great age had recently passed with the death of Queen Elizabeth, and similarities have been observed between the behavior of Shakespeare's lass, supposedly unparalleled, and Elizabeth that may reveal the dramatist's perception of a comparable diminishment."[34] Arguing that James continued to rely upon the Roman paradigm of dynastic power and imperial unification, Davies continues:

> It is inconceivable that a dramatist late in 1606, the time when Shakespeare is usually supposed to have been writing or planning his play, could have failed to associate Caesar Augustus and the ruler whose propaganda was making just that connection. The coronation medal, for instance, minted for distribution to his new subjects, had depicted James wearing a laurel wreath, while a Latin inscription proclaimed him Caesar Augustus of Britain.[35]

The analogy, however, contained a serious flaw. James was not replacing a female ruler of another country, a woman who any good Roman might rightly consider to be the enemy; rather James was the foreigner, displacing a monarch who had always and ever stressed her Englishness. Indeed, the Lancaster-York references in this 1604 speech to Parliament were prompted by the resistance of the House of Commons to the idea of union.[36]

Nor did James's problems with the common people diminish as his reign progressed. There is some disagreement among scholars as to the earliest revival of Elizabeth's popularity after the construct of a male monarch with children had ceased to be in itself a cause for uncritical popular approval. Neville Davies and others place the revival of Elizabeth's popularity around 1607, while Sir Roy Strong tells us that—after the flurry of images generated in 1603—the 1620s marked the next "revival of interest shown in her as reflected in the engravings."[37]

> There was little or none before that date as the country was entranced with the phenomenon of a royal family replacing a virgin queen. That revival coincided with the decline in popularity of Stuart rule and the outbreak of the

Thirty Years War. Elizabeth then became a golden age ruler and the posthumous heroine of the Protestant cause.[38]

Davies, however, quotes Bishop Goodman's account of celebrations of Elizabeth's accession day, arguing that as early as 1607 there "is evidence . . . some of it in plays and poems that . . . the memory of Queen Elizabeth was being revived with affection."[39] Carole Levin, in her 1994 study of Elizabeth, has it both ways, suggesting that the initial popularity and "mood of thanksgiving" following James's coronation lasted only a few years. Levin explains:

> Jame's Scottishness, his favorites, his extravagances, his policies, especially peace with Spain, all led to dissatisfaction. Within two or three years of Elizabeth's death there began to be a nostalgia for "good Queen Bess" and the glories of her reign that swelled by the 1620's.[40]

James countered the rise of Elizabeth's posthumous popularity with a propaganda move that was a revision of his earlier self-fashioning and that was aimed directly at the veneration of Elizabeth's tomb. He had coins struck with the Latin legend "Henry [united] the roses, but James the kingdoms."[41] Here again we see James linking himself to Henry and his Tudor ancestry in a way that bypasses Elizabeth's life. James further bypassed the importance of Elizabeth in his plans for the royal tombs in Westminster, marginalizing Elizabeth in death by the design and placement of her tomb in Henry VII's chapel. As James himself drew the parallel between his actions and those of Octavius/Augustus Caesar, so does Shakespeare's representation of the dead Cleopatra mirror James's revision of the dead Elizabeth.

"NO GRAVE . . . SHALL CLIP . . . A PAIR SO FAMOUS": CLEOPATRA AND ELIZABETH

Elizabeth's burial took place before James entered London, and her body was placed, according to Millington, in the crypt beneath the altar, "in the Sepulchre of her grandfather,"[42] Henry VII, and where her father, Henry VIII, had initially planned his own tomb.[43] William Camden confirms the original placement of Elizabeth's body in his 1603 edition of *Reges, Reginoe, Nobiles, . . .* stating that she was buried in "eadem crypta cum Henrico 7,"[44] and a 1606 treasury account sheet in Westminster Abbey lists a line item for more funding toward "removing

Queen Elizabeths Body."[45] It was James who gave the orders for Elizabeth's memorial as we see it today and the results make interesting reading. Elizabeth's monument is now in the north aisle of Henry VII's chapel in Westminster. She has thus been distanced from the central monument of Henry VII and is buried instead with her sister and rival, Mary Tudor. Even if we had no other evidence of the revisionist nature of Elizabeth's tomb, it is clearly unthinkable that in 1603 she would have been placed in the neglected grave of Mary Tudor.

In the south aisle of the chapel James ordered built a tomb for his mother, Mary Stuart, originally buried in Peterborough Cathedral, but brought by Royal Warrant to Westminster "that the 'like honor might be done to the body of his dearest mother and the like monument extant to her that had been done to others and to his dear sister the late Queen Elizabeth."[46] "Like" does not here mean "same." Elizabeth's tomb is, in the conservative words of the guidebook, "plainer and less sumptuous than that of Mary Queen of Scots."[47] The latter's, being very much larger, took much longer to complete and was much more expensive. The last recorded figure is an estimate of work yet to be done costing two thousand pounds.

In addition to size and cost, the placement of the tombs is invested with meaning, not just for us as twentieth-century readers, but for James himself who ordered his own remains entombed with those of Henry VII, thus claiming pride of place and stressing his link to the first Tudor through his great-grandmother, Henry's daughter. As Jonathan Goldberg says of James's agenda in family portraits, here the "family image functions as an ideological construct."[48] Goldberg argues that James consistently presented himself as

Head, husband, father. In these metaphors, James mystified and politicized the body. With the language of the family, James made powerful assertions . . . [resting] his claims to the throne in his succession and based Divine Right politics there as well. . . . [But] unlike his Tudor predecessor, James located his power in a royal line that proceeded from him.[49]

We can see this in the architecture of Westminster as clearly as in the portraits. Mary Stuart's tomb is next in line behind that of Lady Margaret Beaufort, Henry VII's mother, and buried in the vault beneath Mary's monument is an impressive collection of Stuart heirs, including Prince Henry and Elizabeth of Bohemia.[50] James was placing his own mother in a line of fruitful dynasty, while Elizabeth and her equally childless sister are isolated from the line of inherited power, having only generic "Reformation martyrs" and two infant female Stuarts near their joint tomb. By his placement of his own mother, Mary Stuart, in line with Henry VII's mother Margaret Beaufort, James foregrounds the claim of the queen of Scots to the throne upon which Elizabeth sat. Mary Stuart was the unquestionably legitimate great-granddaughter of Henry VII; Elizabeth had at one time been declared illegitimate by her own father and was always considered illegitimate by all Catholics. Even as he builds a tomb honoring the Virgin Queen, James reminds the public of this historical and biologic fact: virgins do not found or further the greatness of dynasties. As we example Shakespeare's *Antony and Cleopatra*, we find evidence that the playwright not only noticed James's representation of Elizabeth, but actively supported that revisionist political statement by mirroring it in his play.

Before we turn back to the play, however, one question must be asked: how did Shakespeare become aware of these agendas of James I? I cannot answer this question with hard evidence, since "hard evidence" would have to consist of a letter or other document saying something to the effect of "Dear Will, take a look at what I've done to Elizabeth and write me a play celebrating it." Court conventions aside, since the key to the success of James's revisionist strategy was subtlety, I am not, therefore, dismayed by the absence of such unprecedented evidence. There is, however, considerable circumstantial evidence to support my argument. The first circumstance is that this example of revisionist history through funerary monuments could, of course, have been seen by Shakespeare at any time; but, as H. Neville Davies persuasively argues, it was almost certainly brought to his attention in the summer of 1606 when James's brother-in-law, Christian IV of Denmark, paid a state visit to England. Among the many festivities planned to honor the visitor was a sightseeing tour of London. Davies suggests that since in many of the state processions, records indicate that "all our Kings Groomes and Messengers of the Chamber" marched along, "Shakespeare, as one of the King's Men (and therefore ranked as a groom extraordinary of the King's chamber) can be assumed to have been present."[51] Since one of the sights James showed to Christian was the royal tombs in Westminster,[52] it would be interesting, in this context, to "prove" that the playwright saw the tombs with the kings. While it is logical that James would have taken his brother-in-law to see the tombs—Princess Sophia, who was born and who died only weeks before Christian's visit, had just been buried there, and Queen Anne was unable to participate in many of the visits celebrations because of her health and her grief[53]—I am less convinced than Davies that Shakespeare might have been present for the sightseeing tours than for other royal entertainments; but he would certainly have been aware of the tour. And, whether or not he accompanied James and Christian to Westminster, he would certainly have heard about, and could have seen at another time, the relative size and grandeur of the two monuments. The play he wrote in 1606—the year of Christian's visit and the year in which Elizabeth's tomb was completed is, I believe, the best argument for Shakespeare's awareness of the tombs and for the statement of dynastic power they represent. It is here that we find our evidence, as Shakespeare revises the historical source to fit the history he sees being (re)made in London in 1606.

In the final scene of Shakespeare's *Antony and Cleopatra*, Shakespeare departs from Plutarch—the source to which he was so faithful—by having Cleopatra carried from her own queenly monument and buried elsewhere as Antony's lover. Octavius (soon to be Augustus) Caesar orders that Cleopatra be buried "by her Antony." Caesar goes on to speak the uncharacteristically romantic lines about the grave that shall hold so famous a pair of lovers, rhetoric that masks the overtly political motives of the immediately preceding lines: "Take up her bed, / And bear her women from the monument" (5.2.356–57). Cleopatra will not be given the burial of a monarch of Egypt, in her own monument long prepared for that purpose; her burial with Antony, a defeated and disgraced Roman, assures that she will be remembered not as a queen but as a lover. Critics have recently acknowledged the influence on this play— particularly the so-called sympathetic presentation of Caesar in act 5— of James I's presentation of himself, in his coronation pageants and later on coins, as "the new Augustus." This self-fashioning by James fits well with Shakespeare's portrait of an Octavius who resents the existence of Caesarion, whom "they call my father's son" (3.6.5). James had no illegitimate offspring of Elizabeth to contend with, but—like Octavius— neither was he the heir to the body of the great ruler. A male ruler whose presence on the throne accomplished the unification of England and Scotland, James felt the need of both acknowledging and distancing himself from the female ruler whose death and spoken will made his new power possible. As Sir Roy Strong points out, Shakespeare was one of the very few English writers who did not feel the need or desire to write a tribute to Elizabeth at her death in 1603. We have no explicit way of knowing, therefore, how the playwright might have viewed the subsequent apotheosizing of Elizabeth, having nothing but Cranmer's fulsome prophecy of her greatness when she appears as a baby in the final scene of *Henry VIII*, written (although possibly not by Shakespeare) in 1613. I suggest that we should read the final scene of *Antony and*

Cleopatra as a much more realistic representation of Shakespeare's views on the death and burial of powerful female rulers, especially since the date of the play's first production provides another link between the interpretation of Roman history and Jacobean politics.

Like Elizabeth, Cleopatra's body is placed in a tomb chosen by the man who is taking over her kingdom. And, like James, Shakespeare's Octavius Caesar is concerned with making a statement about that dead queen. Shakespeare engages in a double revision at the end of his play: he has Caesar revise the long-set burial plans for Cleopatra, and while accomplishing this he undertakes a radical revision of Cleopatra's burial as it appears in his primary source, Plutarch's *Lives*.[54]

In act 5, Shakespeare comes as close as he ever does in his plays to apotheosizing a female character; almost simultaneously, however, he diminishes her importance. The elevation is primarily in the private sphere, the identity of Cleopatra the woman, while the identity of Cleopatra the female ruler is foregrounded only so that it may be disempowered. The duality is Shakespeare's invention, for Plutarch offers him the opportunity to present a Cleopatra who is diminished in both aspects.[55] According to Plutarch, Cleopatra defaces her own body after the death of Antony: "she has plucked her hair from her head, as also for that she had martyred all her face with her nails, and besides, her voice was small and trembling, her eyes sunk into her head with continual blubbering: and moreover they might see the most part of her stomach torn in sunder."[56] Shakespeare, on the other hand, gives us a beautiful Cleopatra as he gives the queen all of act 5 to herself for one of his most impressive death scenes; her last actions and speech are based on Plutarch's narrative, but her appearance is not only unblemished but raised to an almost supernatural beauty, her speech and action elevated to the highest reaches of Shakespeare's art. As Carol Thomas Neely observes of act 5, scene 2:

> Cleopatra is allowed the fullest expression of her sexuality in the play. The elegant staging and ecstatic eroticism of the scene detach death from its connections with decay, corruption, pain, and lifelessness; the affirmation of future union mitigates its finality. Sexuality mystifies death, and death renders female sexuality benign. Its frank expression can be accommodated by the play and its audience because female sexuality here is tender, not violent; because it is autoerotic, expressed in the absence of men; because it is associated with conventional female roles; and because Cleopatra is dying of it, in it, for it.[57]

All of this is true up until the moment her last word is spoken. In the speeches and actions that follow her death, however, Cleopatra is transformed from a monarch who loves greatly to a girl who was a great lover. She is metamorphosed from a woman whose sense of interiority is at least acknowledged by the playwright to a queen whose identity resides entirely in her external qualities, including the final externalization of that identity by a funeral monument. As Neely points out, both Antony and Cleopatra's deaths "are framed and distanced by Caesar, whose commentary reduces the lovers' story from myth to stereotype and exploits it to enhance his power";[58] but Caesar is not the first to reduce the impact of Cleopatra's last scene. Shakespeare has Charmian begin this process of displacement, looking at Cleopatra and seeing "A lass unparallel'd" with eyelashes that are "Downy windows" (5.2.316), and speaks of her as but a "princess / Decended of so many royal kings" (326–27). Granted, that last line was lifted straight from Plutarch, but—as we shall see—the Greek historian allows Cleopatra more nobility in death than does the English playwright. After Charmian's death, Shakespeare's Caesar continues the diminishment of monarchy, seeing Cleopatra as a beauty and as a lover, but not as a powerful ruler who was also a beautiful lover. In Caesar's speech, Cleopatra's "strong toil of grace" is not the royal grace of the monarch, but that of the enchantress, and it is thus that he wishes her to be remembered, planning her burial not in her own royal monument but in Antony's eternal bed. Taking her from her monument is Shakespeare's invention, his revision of Plutarch that enables Caesar's revision of Cleopatra's identity.

In Plutarch we are never told that Cleopatra is taken from her monument. Antony is brought to her in her monument, he dies here, and Plutarch tells us: "Many Princes, great kings, and Captains did crave Antonius' body of Octavius Caesar, to give him honourable burial, but Caesar would never take it from Cleopatra, who did sumptuously and royally bury him with her own hands."[59] Later Plutarch describes Cleopatra being carried to Antony's grave where she speaks a long and emotional lament.[60] There is nothing to suggest, however, that this grave is not within Cleopatra's monument; indeed, she seems never to have left the monument, for when she writes to Caesar just before her death, she sends the message, according to Plutarch, "written and sealed unto Caesar, and commanded them all [those who dined with her] to go out of the tombs where she was, but [for] the two women: then she shut the door."[61] Therefore, when Plutarch later states: "Now Caesar, though he was marvellous sorry for the death of Cleopatra, yet he wondered at her noble mind and courage, and therefore commanded she should be nobly buried, and laid by Antonius,"[62] we can only infer that this burial took place within her own monument. We must also note that this version of

Caesar's admiration for Cleopatra is a far cry from Shakespeare's Caesar who speaks not of her "noble mind and courage" but of grace and beauty and charm and who orders: "Take up her bed, / And bear her women from the monument" (5.2.356–57), clearly implying that this grave that will clip in it a pair unsurpassed is elsewhere.

How does an ambitious male ruler deal with a dead but popular (popular with London crowds who see tombs or with London audiences who see plays) female monarch? Not by direct criticism, clearly. But, while the good may or may not be interred with their bones, the monuments men (and women) build live on long after everyone involved. Both Elizabeth and Shakespeare's Cleopatra were powerful female rulers made less powerful in death by the way in which the males who buried them chose to construct their monuments. The tomb internalizes whatever degree of personal identity may have existed; the psychological self obviously departs with death, but the tomb removes from the public gaze the individual body that had been linked to that interior self. In the absence of a self linked to the individual, the maker of the tomb is able to inscribe an external identity that may or may not be consistent with that which the tomb contains.[63] As the last Tudor monarch, Elizabeth planned her final statement of identity in relation to that of the first Tudor. James Stuart rewrote that identity by constructing another tomb, one by which Elizabeth was distanced from the first Tudor, placed with her childless sister in a monument smaller than the one James constructed for his mother, who was placed in the line of those who had both ruled and produced royal children. Shakespeare revised the source to which he was so faithful, giving us a Cleopatra ultimately, if not immediately, diminished by Caesar's description of her and by his burial of her body in the grave of her Roman lover, somewhere outside her own royal monument. The political climate of London in 1606, when James was trying to add to his image as the Augustus Caesar of Britain by returning to his Tudor roots through association with Henry VII, could not have gone unnoticed by Shakespeare, even if he were not already waiting for an appropriate opportunity to make his own statement about the dead queen. Certainly the royal tombs in Westminster offered a paradigm of posthumous empowerment and disempowerment that could have influenced the closing lines of *Antony and Cleopatra*. Marble— whatever Shakespeare may suggest in sonnet 55—can speak louder than words.

In Shakespeare's play we find a number of James Stuart's concerns and goals foregrounded by the Roman conquest of Cleopatra. While it is true that Cleopatra was not ruling a country independent of the Roman

Republic, it is also true that James was not the conqueror of the queen he succeeded. Finally we see that in both the play and the politics this hegemonic concept of male-defined dynastic continuity is both literally and metaphorically built upon the space created by the marginalization of a dead woman ruler. Nevertheless, we find the play mirroring the politics that constructed the paradigm of displaced female power linked to male pseudodynastic empire building—"pseudo—" because James's thrice-removed Tudor blood was at least as problematic as Octavius/Augustus' indirect relationship to Julius Caesar; in both the play and the politics we find the paradigm of political self-fashioning employed to give the illusion of historical inevitability. The play, therefore, becomes a mirror twice over: not only does Shakespeare accomplish representation and diminishment of Cleopatra through a complexly structured drama that relies heavily upon images of reflection and reversal, but he also reflects the comparable disempowerment of Elizabeth as enacted by James Stuart.

"THAT I SHOULD NOT / BE NOBLE TO MYSELF"

Cleopatra speaks of Caesar when she says to Charmian and Iras: "He words me, girls, he words me, that I should not / Be noble to myself" (5.2.191–92). As I began this chapter, I spoke of the danger of conflating the historical Cleopatra with Shakespeare's character. And yet we are tempted to this vision by the playwright himself. As the audience, but even more powerfully as the readers, we begin to separate the figure of Cleopatra not only from the men around her, but also from the man who created her. As he does in the line reminding the audience that they are watching a young man portray a mature, sexually active woman, Shakespeare here dares us to realize that while Caesar "words" Cleopatra in one way, he as playwright "words" her entirely. If we fail to see that, if we see Cleopatra as a powerful creation somehow able to escape the confines of the stage or the page, the powerful playwright has scored a victory over our suspended disbelief. I am reminded of a student in a class I taught more than a decade ago. In the midst of a discussion over the play's "real hero," he burst out with more passion than literary precision: "Cleopatra not only seduced Antony, she's even seduced Dr. Walker and most of this class; but worst of all, she seduced Shakespeare into giving her all of Act Five to die in!"

As Linda Woodbridge has observed, this critical cri de coeur is not limited to undergraduates. Many Shakespeare scholars react to Cleopatra as if she were a real woman who had somehow wandered—uncontrolled and almost uninvited—onto one of Shakespeare's stages. While I do not endorse such readings, I would suggest that they are largely generated by the element of selfhood we sense within Shakespeare's construct of Cleopatra. We see this selfhood tacitly acknowledged in Cleopatra's speech and actions, but we do not see it complexly represented, as we see Britomart's. Nevertheless, it is Shakespeare's acknowledgment of the existence of a self more interior than either words or actions that controls his representation of her female power. We do not see her in moments of introspective doubt, as we see Antony. On the other hand, Antony is in the process of coming to know the elements of interiority that his Roman self has always dismissed. Shakespeare presents this model of interiority well because he recognizes it in the context of a male life of public power and private emotion; this is not a new paradigm. With Cleopatra there is no such recognition for the male writer, nor are there many (if any) models. Dido's struggle with her public duty and her private desires is represented by Virgil in relation to her oath to her dead husband and to the external intervention of the gods. Neither has much to do with Dido as a powerful woman, for her power is presented in relation to her unproblematic abdication of her sexuality. The struggle we see represented in the figure of Dido arises from an artificial conflict imposed upon an artificial construction of the female in an epic about male dynasty. Shakespeare goes far beyond this, but that element of recognition that we find in his representation of Antony is still absent. Still, he gives us a character in which this public / private dichotomy is unproblematic, a character who differs radically from Antony in this respect: a powerful woman. We do not see her examine the interior selfhood that contains both female sexuality and female control of male-defined political power, but we see an identity built upon the assumption of such a self.

If conflating the historical Cleopatra and Shakespeare's Cleopatra is seductively dangerous, far worse would be the conflation of Shakespeare's queen with Elizabeth I. When I argue for the parallels between Cleopatra's burial and James's reburial of Elizabeth, I do not mean to imply that we are suddenly meant to reread Shakespeare's character as an Elizabeth figure. Once again, what was true for Britomart does not apply here. Spenser is using Britomart to represent the problems of gender and power and self-knowledge he saw as irreconcilable. Britomart's exploration of her interior self results in a rejection of interior female selfhood in favor of the exterior self of an icon of female power. The power Shakespeare represents and celebrates in the last lines of his play is the power of the male ruler assuming the rule of the dead queen even as he refashions her sexual and political power in relation to traditional representations of woman: lover, wife, mother. Cleopatra's interior self is represented only as a lack of conflict over her multivalent roles of mother, monarch, wife, ruler, lover, queen, and woman. As the identities of Antony, Enobarbus, and Octavius are in flux, they are reflected off the tain of the constant mirror that is Cleopatra. As they gaze at her, they see each other and themselves differently; they use those reflections for self-definition and to define each other. They do not really see the tain that reflects their changing images. But she is not without power, for while she lives, Cleopatra can return the gaze of Antony or Enobarbus or Octavius with various results. Only in death does she fall completely into the power of a male character's representation. Octavius can use her burial with Antony to diminish both his rival's powerful reputation and Cleopatra's power as a woman ruler. As long as she is alive, Cleopatra has the power to know herself; she can "be noble to myself," however rudimentary Shakespeare's representation of her interior selfhood might be. After her death, when her eyes are finally closed, Octavius decides how she will be known. Shakespeare, in effect, takes the place of Athena and places the tain of representation in Octavius' hand so that he can control the power of the uncontrolled woman, although the playwright does grant that woman the power to kill herself. That Shakespeare uses her finally as a mirror of history is ironic, as her displaced identity serves to mirror the re-presented identity of Elizabeth I. By now, of course, any sense of selfhood is gone. In death Cleopatra is metamorphosed by Octavius; in death Elizabeth is metamorphosed by James. In his play, Shakespeare gives us a sense of the female self as an interior reality, but it is an elusive construct that is easily lost in the more traditional search for male identity and power.

5

Eve: the first reflection

GENDERING THE GEOGRAPHY OF EDEN

WHEN Eve looks into the mirror of the lake in book 4 of *Paradise Lost,* she looks into a mirror created as part of a carefully gendered representation of Genesis 1 and 2. The cosmic creation narrative in *Paradise Lost* does not appear until book 7, but in book 4 we are given Eve's version of her own creation and are first shown the landscape of Eden through the eyes of Satan. This reordering of the Genesis chronology can be read as an epic poet's attempt to impose the principle of in medias res upon the narrative of creation, but I will argue that it has less to do with poetic tradition than with the identity Milton is establishing for his representations of Eve and Adam. Within his representation of the first two people, Milton can articulate a theory of hierarchies of power and gender and identity, a theory much more complex (if even more sinister) than suggested by the oft-quoted phrase "he for God only, she for God in him." While that construction of Eve locates any sense of selfhood she has firmly within the construct of Adam, the representation of Eve within the expanding narrative of Milton's epic does develop for her the concept of interiority, but that very conceptual interiority is linked to the doom of humankind. Within this nexus of identities Milton makes a gesture toward representing the interior self of Eve, a self as distinct from Adam's male self; in so doing, he represents Eve's sense of her own selfhood as a central problem in the narrative of man's first disobedience. But the construction of an interior self for his Eve would have to be seen as one of Milton's greatest failures—would have to be seen, I say, because I will argue that he introduces the necessity of female selfhood only as an imaginative space that cannot be filled. Avoiding the chimera of intentionality and looking firmly at the text, we see the problem of Eve's selfhood foregrounded; and yet that self is never represented. More clearly than either of the other texts we have examined, Milton's epic presents us with the problem of female selfhood as one of cognition and recognition. Milton's failure to present any elements of female interiority can be read as his own failure to recognize those elements of woman's identity.

As I have suggested elsewhere, Milton writes of women as though they were texts to be translated, not as half of humankind. That he fails in his attempt to represent the female self is not a point that needs to be argued—the text gives us that failure, a failure the poet implicitly acknowledges. We see strategy after strategy employed as the poet tries to avoid his own pejorative, a heretic in the truth, one who accepts knowledge without making it his own. Eve's identity is central to Milton's Genesis narrative, but that identity depends upon a sense of selfhood that is absent. Ultimately I believe this absence to be deliberate, as Milton makes his failure Eve's failure and then Adam's. In this chapter, I want to examine the strategies Milton constructs in his attempt to suggest the necessity of that which he does not represent. For, however necessary Eve's selfhood may have been to Milton's poetic vision, his failure to imagine or to represent it does not prevent him from writing the poem. Indeed, his failure of imaginative vision becomes central to the representation of woman within *Paradise Lost*. What this gives us is a fascinating variety of strategies of representation, all lacking the actual presence of a coherent construction of interior female identity. Obviously the paradigm of the reflective mirror appears in a number of these strategies, but Milton pushes it to limits unknown by Ovid as he constructs a cosmos to mirror a face that is never there.

In book 4, 205–355 we find the initial description of Eden, a description that is amplified throughout books 4 and 5, culminating in the description of Eve harvesting the fruits that "Earth all-bearing Mother yields" (5.338). The relationship between Eve's identity and the gendered cosmos in which Milton places her is so problematic as to seem contradictory. Genesis 3:23 ("the Lord God sent him forth from the garden of Eden, to till the ground from which he was taken") stresses the link between Adam and the ground of Eden, continuing the "man of dust from the ground" image of generation of Genesis 2:7. But in Milton's Paradise the correspondences are not that simple, for Eden itself, we learn in book 4, is feminine. Satan comes to the border of Eden "where delicious Paradise, / Now nearer, Crowns with her enclosure green" (4.132–33); and fewer than one hundred lines later we are told that "*Eden* stretch'd her Line / . . . Eastward" (4.210–11).[1] God set the boundaries of Eden, so Milton presents a feminine geography circumscribed by a masculine maker, the feminine Earth being the raw material for that maker's masculine creation—an interesting reversal of the paradigm of human creation in Genesis 2 and privileged by Milton in book 8.

And yet the geographic features of Eden are gendered both male and female, and gendered with less attention to poetic tradition and etymology than we generally expect to find in Milton's poetry. In *The Politics of Landscape*, James Turner reminds us that "Genesis insisted on the prominence of the rivers"[2] in Eden, and indeed, one of the first-mentioned topographical features of the Garden is "a River large," which "went" "southward" "Nor chang'ed his course" and "which from his darksome passage now appears" (4.223, 224, 232). There seems to be, initially, no reason for the river being given a masculine pronoun; the Lethe in book 2 and the "river of blis" in book 3 are both feminine and the Nile in book 12 is ungendered.[3] Other features of the Garden—trees, glades, sands, hills, dales—are here left genderless, even if they are gendered elsewhere in the poem; and Nature (elsewhere consistently feminine), Art, and Earth (although all capitalized) are here neither masculine nor feminine. Paradoxically, both the very inconsistency of Milton's gendering and the lack of logic with which he assigns genders make the reader more aware of the problematic relationship between gender and identity in this poem.

We find the most interesting group of gendered Edenic pronouns in the genesis of Eve's lake: "The flow'ry lap / Of some irriguous Valley spreads her store" (255–56), "the mantling Vine / Lays forth her purple Grape, and gently creeps / Luxuriant" (258–60), and "a Lake, / That to the fringed Bank with Myrtle crown'd, / Her crystal mirror holds" (261–63). If Eden is feminine (as it is elsewhere in the poem), the ground of Eden logically—if not etymologically—might also be expected to be feminine, so the Valley's flowery lap is both consistent and iconographically suggestive with the masculine river running through the indentations in the feminine earth. Furthermore, as we will find in book 7, this paradigm is a reversal of the initial relationship between waters and dry land described in Genesis 1 and amplified by Milton.

Presenting the mirroring Lake as a feminine product of the masculine River sets up a paradigm of gender identities for Eve's cognition scene, which follows one hundred eighty lines later, but it also raises a problem. God set the boundaries of Eden; Eden's valleys set the course of the river; the river creates the lake in the "lap" of a valley. Or does the widening of the valley into a plain create the lake? The former appears to be the case, at least syntactically, for the river is always mentioned as the source of the lake. But without the "lap" of the feminine valley, there would be no space for a lake to exist. At what point does water of the lake, made from the river, cease to be masculine and become feminine? At the point where the waters from the river "unite their streams" (1.263) and after they have fallen down "the slope hills dispersed" (1.261), the poet-narrator arbitrarily assigns the pronoun "her" to the lake, replacing the "his" of the river. I will argue that within the tightly wrapped nexus of Eden's gendered geography we find the central paradigm of Eve's identity within this epic. Milton gives us an elementally feminine universe, but a universe where those elemental feminine forces are circumscribed by masculine principles.

We are forced to recognize the significance of Milton's gendered geography when we realize that the most available scholarly explanation—the gendering of these nouns being consistent with their genders in Hebrew or Latin or even Greek—does not begin to account for what we find.[4] If etymology fails us as we try to puzzle out the connections between geography and gender in Milton's epic, we can turn to the logical source of literary precedent and find in Ovid, if not a neat correspondence of gendered nouns, an imaginative conflation of persona and geography which is in many ways a mirror image of Milton's gendering in his epic. In Ovid's *Metamorphoses,* we find story after story in which a human becomes some feature of the landscape; in Milton's *Paradise Lost* we find a landscape gendered to provide a subliminal subtext for the poet's version of the Adam and Eve story. In Ovid's epic, features of geography and landscape have their genesis in human or semidivine figures: laurel tree or reed, mountain or body of water, the pattern of transformation—with a few notable exceptions—is from human to thing. In Genesis 2 Milton is given another pattern, with Adam being created from dust and Eve from Adam's rib. Milton's amplification of Genesis 2, however, may owe as much to Ovidian metamorphosis as to biblical creation, for in books 4, 5, and 7 Milton creates a predominantly feminine geography and landscape he uses to generate the identity—if not the physical being—of Eve. This external identity is interiorized by Eve's perceptions; but this is not the same thing as a constructed interior self, for there is no sense of self-recognition. As the feminine lake is formed from the masculine river in the lap of a feminine valley, so is Eve's identity formed from the masculine Adam as he lies on the feminine ground of Eden. Eve's image on the surface of the lake is displaced in her creation story by the masculine body of Adam, the feminine identity being circumscribed by two male voices and two male hands, God's and Adam's. To stress the importance of these gender hierarchies, Milton paints the same pattern on the larger canvas of cosmic creation. In his initial description of Eden, Milton calls our attention to gendered

geography; in his description of the creation of the cosmos that gendering assumes even greater significance. As Turner points out, "*Paradise
Lost* is unique among heroic poems in that the description of paradise
is not peripheral."[5] The physical geography—the gendered geography—of Eden is indeed important, but when we consider it in relation
to the gendering of the cosmos, we find an even more complex paradigm
of power and gender and identity.

GENDER AND THE ARTICULATION OF THE COSMOS

Raphael's narrative of creation in book 7 is remarkable both for its
fidelity to Genesis and for its departures from that source—amplifica-
tions that almost exclusively involve the gendering of the universe. Along
with the questions raised by these changes arises the question of authority. In whose words does Raphael speak? Not his own, at least not entirely,
for he tells Adam in Genesis 8.229 that on the day of man's creation "I
that day was absent."[6] Even as he invokes the authority of biblical narrative by following the ordering of creation found in Genesis 1, Milton
usurps some of that authority for his poet/narrator by presenting a
creation in which all first things—light, water, earth—are feminine.

As Mary Nyquist observes, "in spite of the existence of scholarly studies of the history of Genesis in its exegetical traditions, the view that
the relationship of *Paradise Lost* to Genesis is basically direct or at least
unproblematically mediated continues to flourish."[7] On the face of it,
this sounds hardly surprising; but while "the view . . . continues to
flourish" and, indeed, to be articulated in lecture halls and classrooms,
the implied connections between biblical narrative and this epic are far
from simple to establish. Teasing out the lines of connection and mediation is a task made enormously difficult by the multiple and various
versions of the creation story we find both within Genesis and within
Milton's poem. As have the Priestly and Yahwehist [hereafter P and J]
creation stories, the ordering of Milton's narratives of first things has
been much discussed.[8] The ordering of those narratives and their relation to their sources in Genesis present many problems, and so, too,
does the way in which Milton invokes authority for these narratives. In
the opening lines of his epic, Milton asks the "Heav'nly Muse" for inspi-
ration comparable to that of Moses on Sinai when he "first taught the
chosen Seed, / In the Beginning how the Heav'ns and Earth / Rose
out of Chaos" (1.7–9). This is a revealing choice of model for divine
transmission, given Milton's views on Moses as a writer with an agenda.

Regina M. Schwartz calls our attention to this, pointing out that in *De Doctrina Christiana* Milton "indulges in his own composition history, imagining some editorial patchwork by Moses in order to stress—up front, in Genesis, rather than later in the Law—the commemorative function of the sabbath."[9] The tradition of Milton scholarship cites Exodus 19–20 as the locus of Moses's sanctioned speech, a passage that shows that speech to be much closer to revision than to "patchwork," for here Moses—however scrupulous about reading stone tablets—engages in some substantive remaking of God's remarks. When God tells Moses that the children of Israel should prepare for his revelation, he says:

> Go to the people and consecrate them today and tomorrow and let them wash their garments, and be ready by the third day; for on the third day the Lord will come down upon the Mount Sinai in the sight of all the people. And you shall set bounds for the people round about, saying "Take heed that you do not go up into the mountain or touch the border of it; whoever touches the mountain shall be put to death; no hand shall touch him, but he shall be stoned or shot; whether beast or man he shall not live." When the trumpet sounds a long blast, they shall come up to the mountain. (Exod. 19:10–13)[10]

This is not, however, exactly the message Moses conveys: "So Moses went down from the mountain to the people, and consecrated the people; and they washed their garments. And he said to the people, 'Be ready by the third day; do not go near a woman'" (Exod. 19:14–15).

Moses's second injunction both explicates and alters God's message: the "he" and the phrase "whether beast or man" are made unambiguously to refer to male "people"; and the mountain is replaced by the woman as the thing that must not be touched. Two principles of this passage—revisionist transmission and the confusion or conflation of women and geography—are enacted in Milton's poem only seven lines after he invokes the authority of Moses:

> And chiefly Thou O Spirit, that dost prefer
> Before all Temples th' upright heart and pure,
> Instruct me, for Thou know'st; Thou from the first
> Wast present, and with mighty wings outspread
> Dove-like satst brooding on the vast Abyss
> And mad'st it pregnant.
>
> (1.17–22)

Both the metaphoric possibility of birdlike flight and the stance of "satst brooding" are Milton's revisionist transmission of "and the Spirit of God was moving over the face of the waters" (Genesis 1.2), while the gendering of the "vast Abyss" into female matter that can be impregnated is Milton's own act of creation. This creative amplification, however, is not without scholarly context.

Discussing the degree of relationship between the P narrative in Genesis 1 and a Mesopotamian creation myth (in which a male maker, Marduk, forms the universe from the body of the just-defeated Tiamat, "mother of all the gods and associated, at the epic's beginning, with the primeval salt waters"[11]), Mary Nyquist suggests that, although biblical scholars have long attempted to separate the Genesis narrative from the Mesopotamian myth, the watery "deep" of the Genesis 1 still "bears some faint, residual traces of its female character."[12] Citing the Greek philosophical tradition, "which has in one way or another informed commentaries on Genesis since Philo," Nyquist reminds us:

> Formless, dependent matter, which passively awaits and receives the form actively bestowed upon it by its maker, is, in this tradition, of course a feminine as opposed to a masculine principle. In Plato's Timaeus, one of the main texts used to assimilate Greek and Judeo-Christian traditions, the unformed chaos ordered by the Demiurge is unambiguously feminine.[13]

"Unambiguously feminine" is a good description of the universe in the first three days of Raphael's creation story.

> Light . . . first of things. . . .
> Sprung from the Deep and from her Native East.
>
> (7.243–245)

Light, always given priority in Hebrew and Christian references to creation, as well as in the classical tradition, is here described in its purest form as purely feminine. The Earth has been "Mother" since Ovid's sources were fresh-minted, but light—from classical mythology and philosophy to the opening lines of John's Gospel—is both implicitly and explicitly associated with the masculine. When this feminine light is reduced to forms, the sun and moon, the greatest planet is gendered masculine while the lesser moon becomes

> His mirror, with full free face borrowing her Light
> From him, for other light she needed none.
>
> (7.377–78)

Although this paradigm of priority obviously mirrors the creation of Adam and Eve, the initial creation of light as a formless feminine force problematizes Milton's central creation narrative.

The complicated paradigm of a male voice generating feminine light that will eventually emanate from a masculine sun is rendered even more complex by the creations of the second and third days. On the second day "God made / The Firmament" (263–64) and that is a blend of "liquid" and "Elemental Air" dividing water from water, but dividing concentrically, not laterally. The "Firmament" is a "partition firm and sure, / The Waters underneath from those above / Dividing" (267–69).

> The earth was form'd, but in the Womb as yet
> Of Waters, Embryon immature involv'd,
> Appear'd not: over all the face of Earth
> Main Ocean flow'd, not idle, but with warm
> Prolific humor soft'ning all her Globe,
> Fermented the great Mother to conceive.
>
> (7.243–45, 276–81)

This division is of circles within circles, resulting in a "womb of waters," the Earth, which in turn (as the great Mother) is made "to conceive" in a sort of double, female-generated conception.[14] Feminine light, feminine waters, a womb for the feminine Earth that conceives not directly from the action of the masculine word but by the action of the possessive feminine ocean all give us a cosmos which, in its initial and most elemental state, is gendered entirely female. The male logos generates and the male voice narrates, but the creation—both cosmic and poetic—is female. But it is a female power which itself can generate, can create first things.

The totality of this feminine cosmos is almost shocking when we consider that it is a fundamental revision of that ultimately privileged text, Genesis 1. Suggesting that feminist scholars should turn away from arguing about the implications of the J narrative in Genesis 2—however much that version is beloved of Pauline and patristic writers—Nyquist points beyond the androgynous, archetypal implications of Genesis 1:27 to the more subtle significance of the narrative:

For it is there that we find—or do not find—the absent or repressed maternal body, which has been unveiled by modern critical methods but still assigned a place apart from the sacred text itself. And the absence of this "old ancient ancestor" would seem to be the condition for a discourse associating the potency of the divine father's word with a historically and theologically motivated mastery of meaning, a mastery that seems easily to translate itself into more speculatively logocentric discursive statements.[15]

If Raphael's account in book 7 gives us a logocentric creation that questions the necessity for the repression of the feminine as a "condition for a discourse associating the potency of the divine father's word with a historically and theologically motivated mastery of meaning," Adam's account of first things in book 8 provides a textbook example of such repression. For all that he shifts from the P account to the J account for the creation of Adam and Eve both in Raphael's narrative in book 7 and Adam's account in book 8, Milton subverts the hierarchy of Genesis 2 by placing Eve's creation story first in his epic.

ENGENDER IN AND BY THE POOL

In books 4 and 5, Eden is gendered feminine and given an identity inextricably linked with Eve's. As Eve's face is bounded by the edge of the mirroring lake, so is the question of gender identity and self-knowledge framed by the gendered geography of Eden. Eve neither recognizes nor names herself. Eve's ultimate act in her book 4 creation narrative is to yield, not to learn. She submits to the arbitrary gender displacement, coming to see Adam as at once the generative image of and better than herself, but thus learning—or accepting—that she can know herself only in herself only in relation to Adam. There is no place for interiority in this construction of selfhood. Milton presents Eve to herself and to the reader only in relation to Adam and to the gendered universe of which she and Eden are each a part. As the relationships among the valley and the river and the lake are not perfectly separable, neither can the identities of Eden, Eve, and Adam be neatly categorized, although the latter will be given an interior self. Milton reiterates at many points his gendering of the Earth as feminine, but Adam seems to have no sense that it is from this feminine Earth from which he was formed. He draws his self-identity solely from his maker and not from matter, but expects Eve to privilege his absent rib above any other aspect of her being.

At what point does Eve cease to be a part of Adam, becoming not his rib but her self?

Never.

At what point does Eve cease to seek for self-knowledge from her reflection?

Never.

Can a narrative act of gender displacement generate a representation of self-knowledge—even in its most simple form, physical self-recognition—sufficient to stand as self-identity, the sort of simple self-identity Adam exhibits when he peruses his own body, calling it *Myself* (8.267)?

No.

Does she ever see Adam, "hee whose image thou art," as her own image?

She does not.

Literally, then, Eve never *re*cognizes anything; she does not "know again"; she simply accepts the cognition given to her by the voice and hand of God and by the voice and hand of Adam. In the gendered geography of Eden—the geography of the river, the valley, and the lake—Milton presents his readers with a pattern of displacement, a paradigm of arbitrarily gendered causality, which he immediately repeats in human terms in Eve's cognition scene. Milton does not here rely on mere conjunction. By using the first displacement as the generative locus for the second, by having Eve turn without recognition of her identity in the re-gendered mirror of the lake's water, Milton emphasizes the necessity of reading one reinscription through and by the other, thus calling attention to the arbitrary nature of both types of gendering and to their inextricable relation.

With the scene at the lake we are given a second geographical subtext for Eve's identity, the pool of Narcissus in Ovid's *Metamorphoses*. Not only does "Eve's interaction with her own image in the water . . . [raise] the specter of narcissism,"[16] as Marshall Grossman puts it, but this subtext invades and becomes part of the text with stunning effect. Critics from James Holly Hanford to Stanley Fish speak of Eve and of "the mirror of the pool,"[17] of Eve "at the pool."[18] Yet nowhere in Eve's description or in the narrator's framing of it does the word "pool" occur; it is always "lake," always. The reader supplies "pool" just as the reader—cued by Milton's visual allusion—supplies the subtext of Ovid's Narcissus. But Eve's narrative is properly both an invocation and a rejection of Ovid's story. Eve is not only herself pleased with what she sees in the pool, as is Narcissus, but she identifies pleasure and admiration (this she does *re*cognize) when she describes this Other as also pleased: "Pleas'd it return'd as soon with answering looks / Of sympathy and love" (464–65). Eve, like Narcissus, is unknowingly, "unwittingly" self-absorbed. Milton reminds us of this, as the Voice of God both informs and warns Eve:

> What thou seest,
> What there thou seest fair Creature is thyself,

With thee it came and goes: but follow me,
And I will bring thee where no shadow stays
Thy coming.

(4.467–71)

those phrases echo almost exactly the words with which Ovid's narrator
tries to warn Narcissus:

quod petis, est nusquam; quod amas, avertere, perdes!
ista repercussae, quam cernis, imaginis umbra est:
nil habet ista sui; tecum venitque manetque;
tecum discedet, si tu discedere possis!

(2.433–36)

(What you seek is nowhere; but turn yourself away, and the object of your love
will be no more. That which you behold is but the shadow of a reflected form
and has no substance of its own. With you it comes, with you it stays, and it
will go with you—if you can go.)[19]

Richard J. DuRocher, in his discussion of these two passages, acknowledges that the "correspondences between the passages reside in syntax
. . . and in diction," but argues that "the distinct tonal qualities of these
two voices—Ovid's taunting, condescending; Milton's gracious, magnani-
mous—register widely divergent evaluations of the situations of Narcissus and Eve."[20] DuRocher goes on to take issue with Arnold Stein's
distinction between the two passages, discussing thematic issues at some
length.[21] But, surprisingly, neither of these critics focuses on the most
concrete difference between Narcissus and Eve: Narcissus eventually
recognizes that he is gazing at himself; Eve never recognizes that image
as herself.[22] When she sees herself in the water, she does not know that
"it"—literally and grammatically neuter—is herself that she sees. She is
soon told by the voice of God, but is never allowed to see the image while
knowing that she gazes at herself. Tradition, particularly the medieval
tradition of moral allegory, links vanity and self-absorption to the Narcissus story, but Ovid's story offers a less judgmental account of the fair
young man, Ovid's narrator expressing regret at the youth's initial inability to recognize himself and pity at his subsequent grief. In Ovid's narrative we find no hint of self-gratification—quite the reverse. In the
tradition of moral allegory Narcissus becomes an icon of destructive
self-love, but this is not the tradition invoked by Milton's syntactical parallel; he quotes Ovid, but we hear the narrative of Vanity from the *Romance
of the Rose*.[23] And yet we should not be too quick to convict ourselves of

careless reading, for Eve's phrase "with vain desire" (however strongly "vain" may be glossed as "fruitless") makes our misreading almost inevitable.

Not only is Eve's initial encounter with Eden rendered problematic by Milton's invocation of the Narcissus story, but as a narrative it lacks the specificity of Adam's in many ways. Not the least important is her omission of any gendered pronouns. Even though this narrative is presented as memory, memory that we might expect to be embellished by subsequent knowledge,[24] Eve's speech does not gender. She quotes the "voice" who will take her to "hee / Whose image thou art, him thou shalt enjoy." That voice gives her two names, Eve and Mother, but these names are not gendered by the voice of God or by Eve, only by our fallen knowledge.[25] Eve also quotes Adam's odd third-person identification of himself, "whom thou fli'st, of him thou art, / His flesh, his bone," but she uses no other gendered pronouns in this narrative. Neither Eve nor God's voice nor Adam genders her. She is drawn to the feminine lake; the mirror of that lake gives her the first vision she has of another human form; but she is not allowed to identify herself with that vision, nor indeed does she identify by gender anything that she sees. She speaks of "it"; she is first told of and then shown "he," and she quotes God and Adam's use of the masculine pronoun; but there are no feminine pronouns in this narrative. Only the reader's knowledge of the feminine lake and of fallen sexuality gender Eve's identity. Eve herself genders nothing and the voices she hears speak only of maleness, leaving her otherness unnamed. How, then, can she identify herself as physically different and individual from either Adam or her surroundings? She cannot know herself as separate and particular, as an individual entity unique in the cosmos, as Adam knows himself. As she is allowed to know her image only in relation to Adam, so can she know her function only in relation to the fruitful earth with which she is associated, not seeing herself as a unique Other—which explains why, in book 9, she worries that Adam might enjoy "another Eve" (9.827). As the poem progresses, Eve's sense of self becomes important in its absence. Milton gives us a more extreme version of Britomart's negative description of what she sees in the mirror, for Eve is never allowed to know what she is supposed to see.

As Eve "yields" to Adam's voice in book 4, satisfying his need for her, so does the Earth on which they live yield to them that which will satisfy their other needs. To honor Raphael's arrival in book 5, Adam sends Eve out to find the fruits of the Earth, and the narrative of his order,

Eve's activities, and Raphael's response further tie Eve to the fruitful,
yielding, feminine earth. Adam orders:

> But go with speed,
> And what thy stores contain, bring forth and pour . . . well we may afford
> Our givers thir own gifts, and large bestow
> From large bestow'd, where Nature multiplies
> Her fertile growth.
>
> (5.314–15, 316–19)

Eve goes forth to gather "Whatever Earth all-bearing Mother yields"
(5.338). Earth, gendered female, "yields" as did Eve in her book-4 narrative, and the fruit of that yielding is both implicitly feminine and explicitly under the control of Eve as "She gathers . . . and. . . . Heaps with
unsparing hand," "She crushes," and "She tempers" the moist and
creamy fruits for the feast. Fifty lines later Raphael greets Eve: "Hail
Mother of Mankind, whose fruitful Womb / Shall fill the World" (5.388–
89). Because Eve "yields" to the voice of God and to the voice of Adam
in book 4, she will ultimately yield, as does the earth, the fruit of her
womb to "fill the World." In the context of epic gender roles, this passage
of book 5 offers a most interesting set of allusions in relation to Eve's
identity. Eve goes to gather the feminine fruits of the feminine Earth,
fruits that the "all-bearing mother" also yields on "the Punic coast, or
where / Alcinöus reigned" (340–41); the narrator's specific geographical
and patriarchal allusions thus link Eve—at least superficially—to Dido
and Naussica. Although Eve is called (oddly) "the fairest of her daughters" (4.324), those daughters of Eve that Milton actually associates with
her are usually at least as ominous as fair: Pandora (4.714), Aphrodite
at the choice of Paris (5.381–82), Dalilah (9.1061). While it's true that
less than fifty lines after invoking Dido and Naussica Raphael gives Eve
the greeting of Mary, I would suggest that this seemingly positive identification is made problematic by the prior references to two other women
who nurtured epic heroes and who were subsequently left behind in
the narrative wake of male destiny, their own female identities left unde-
veloped and ultimately submerged. The words of Adam and of the narrator and of Raphael all associate Eve with the feminine identity of
Nature and with the womb of the world, an association that confirms—
or foretells, if we speak of narrative rather than chronological order—
not simply Mary but the feminine cosmos Raphael describes in book 7.

THE FACE OF GOD AND THE FACE OF EVE

Narcissus fell in love with his image taking it to be another.

Jack falls in love with Jill's image of Jack, taking it to be himself. She must not die, because then he would lose himself. He is jealous in case any one else's image is reflected in her mirror.

Jill is a distorting mirror to herself. Jill has to distort herself to appear undistorted to herself. To undistort herself, she finds Jack to distort her distorted image in his distorting mirror She hopes that his distortion of her distortion may undistort her image without her having to distort herself.

One is afraid of the self that is afraid of the self that is afraid of the self that is afraid One may perhaps speak of reflections.

R. D. Laing[26]

When we finally reach Adam's narrative in book 8, we are forced to compare it with four canonical narratives: those of Genesis, Eve, and Raphael, as well as the poet-narrator's gendering of Eden. But although Adam's narrative comes last, his presence as auditor of Eve and Raphael's narratives shaped those versions, and her quotation of his plea fills eight of the fifty lines of Eve's own story. The placement of Eve's speech four books before Adam's is the only example we find in the poem—unless we count the eating of the fruit—of the trope of reversed order so important in Hebrew Scripture from Abel in Genesis 4 through David in 1 Samuel Patricia Parker makes this point very forcefully:

> In the rest of the Genesis text—in a reversal given its theological statement in Exodus 4:22—the second-born in the order of nature (Jacob, famously, in relation to the first-born Esau) has spiritual priority over the first. But in the misogynist tradition which grew out of the second Genesis account, the sequence which has woman similarly born second in the order of time, and after man, only makes her secondary to man.[27]

Order of placement in the poem does not necessarily constitute priority, however, for Adam's detailed narrative and privileged discourse with God cast Eve's memory in deep shadow, in turn reversing in priority the temporal reversal of placement within the poem.

In contrast to Eve's, Adam's description of the garden into which he awakens is gendered by his sense of self, bathed in a balmy sweat that

is both generated and devoured by the masculine sun with which he feels
some connection, the sun, to which he speaks and that he genders male:

> As new wak't from soundest sleep
> Soft on the flow'ry herb I found me laid
> In Balmy Sweat, which with his Beams the Sun
> Soon dri'd, and on the reeking moisture fed.

(8.252–55)

By the streams of Eden dwell all the creatures of Eden, but not the
"great Maker," whom Adam also independently genders male: "Tell
me," he asks the sun, "how may I know *him*" (280). Adam "knows" that
God is male, but this is a knowledge that allows no alternative, a knowledge of an exclusively male universe. Unlike Eve, who in her creation
narrative displays no knowledge of herself or any gender, Adam speaks
of "Myself" and his speech does gender—but exclusively in the masculine. There are no female pronouns in Adam's speech before the creation of Eve. As he describes the naming of the animals, he speaks in
plurals ("they") or in masculine pronouns,"each Bird stoop'd on his
wing" (351). Even when he speaks of pairs of gendered nouns, the pronouns avoid the feminine: "Each with thir kind, Lion with Lioness"
(393). Lioness is here a name merely; it conveys no awareness of the
inherently gendered female. As Grossman observes about Eve being
called "Mother" in book 4, the name "is delivered as a style, a title."[28]
When God responds to Adam request to meet his Maker, God's speech—
as remembered by Adam—likewise acknowledges only the male. In lines
316–33 the pronouns are "I," "they," "thou," "thee," and "thine." In lines
339–40 God tells Adam: "To thee and to thy Race I give; as Lords /
Possess" Eden. God had allowed Adam to name the creatures of the
earth and in line 472, in his sleep of abstract Fancy, Adam also names
the first female with the first female pronoun; in his own act of creation
he names this image as image; as object, not subject, he names "her."

The great majority of feminine pronouns in Adam's eighty-five-line
narrative about Eve are either in the objective or genitive case.[29] Moving
beyond the obvious implications of subject/object, Patricia Parker points
out the more sinister implications of the genitive, which "is always possessed by something it depends upon."[30] This constitutes a remarkably
good description of Eve's position in book 8: Eve is returned to Adam
"Led by her Heav'nly Maker" with Grace in "her steps" and "Heav'n in
her Eye" (485, 488). "The genitive," Parker continues, "(despite or perhaps because of its associations with both gender and the generative) is
always grammatically related to another,"[31] as is Eve. Adam sees Eve as

object, first an object to which he has given life, then an object of desire. With only one major exception, Eve exists here as an object or as a pronoun in the genitive case, that allows her to possess attributes in "her steps," "her Eye," "her Name," "her worth," "Her loveliness," and "her presence," but most significantly of all, in the possibility of "Her loss," all of which make her more pleasing as an object of desire. Eve attains the status of subject only in relation to her disappearance. "Shee disappear'd," then back "she came, / Led,"; after Adam speaks to her—"She heard me thus"—Eve turns away, but, responding to Adam's pleas, once again "she turn'd" (478, 484, 500, 507). Only the first subject pronoun, marked by the alternate spelling "Shee," denotes an Eve acting not in response to Adam or to God, and even there, all Adam has to do is "to deplore / Her loss" and she returns, led by God. Eve's actions are subordinated to those of Adam and of God with a determined consistency we dare not ignore. Her power lies in Adam's response to her, not in her own speech or actions. Even if it were represented for the reader, Eve's sense of self could not be recognized by Adam because he cannot imagine her—let alone know her—as separate from his own sense of self.

As Adam's narrative continues, we quickly see that the passive power of Eve's objective case begins to draw to her in an ever-increasing flow all of the power of Adam's created world, until

> All higher knowledge *in her* presence falls
> Degraded, Wisdom in discourse *with her*
> Loses discount'nanc't, *and* like folly shows;
> Authority and Reason *on her* wait,
> As one intended first, not after made
> Occasionally; and to consummate all,
> Greatness of mind and nobleness thir seat
> Build *in her* loveliest, and create an awe
> *About her,* as a guard Angelic plac't.
>
> (551–60, emphasis mine)

The one exception is Adam's narrative of Eve's flight from him. Here, in a single main clause (500–7) Eve becomes "she," is given the power of the subject, is briefly empowered so that she may become more dramatically an object. Milton allows his reader to see how thoroughly Adam is remaking the identity of Eve when he gives us Adam's revision of Eve's reason for flight. Although we (and Adam, for that matter) have heard Eve say that she turns from Adam because she finds him less fair than the image in the lake, Adam tells Raphael that coy modesty is the cause of Eve's flight. We are meant to recognize Adam's speech as revision, but as revision that goes essentially uncorrected. Furthermore, this revision generates a fictive self for Eve, an interior self where coy modesty reigns. Adam's construction of this fictive self is in direct conflict with the little we have been allowed to know about Eve's thoughts,[32] but that contradiction passes unremarked in the narrative. Any true recognition will be the reader's, not Adam's or Eve's or the narrator's.

Adam has here "created" Eve, not as an independent or even separate being, but rather as the object of his gaze, as doubly his own image— the female form God has told him will be made in his, Adam's, image and the reflection of himself that he sees in her eyes:

> I now see
> Bone of my Bone, Flesh of my Flesh, *my Self*
> *Before me.*
>
> (8.494–96, emphasis mine)[33]

Here the nuances of the Narcissus narrative resurface, along with echoes of that other Ovidian mirror narrative, the Medusa story. As Adam gazes at Eve he is doubly metamorphosed: he becomes that Medieval Narcissus figure transfixed by the image of his beautiful self and he loses sight of God. If we consider the way in which Adam perceives Eve—as the image of his own face reflected in her eyes and as a beautiful body in which that reflection is located—we see both Ovidian mirror stories as subtexts. As Hazel E. Barnes remarks of Sartre and Laing's various uses of the Medusa paradigm: "one could, I believe, say that the individual has made himself into a Medusa and destroyed himself by his own Look. Medusa proves to be the first cousin to Narcissus."[34]

Adam begins his speech on line 491 by recounting the words he spoke to God in thanks for Eve. But this same speech separates him from God: "for this cause shall [man] forgo / Father and mother, and to his wife adhere" (497–98). What can "Father and mother" to him mean in the context of prelapsarian Eden? Adam's speech shifts from speaking to God to speaking of man to speaking to woman as man's possession and other self. After he recounts this speech to Raphael, Adam neglects to recount God's response; he says instead that Eve "heard me thus" (500). Adam's sight of Eve has caused him to lose sight of God; Adam's speech to God is important only as it is overheard by Eve. Adam's focus on his vision of Eve excludes her maker just as his version of his memory of that first sight ignores her own book-4 narrative.

Nor does Adam stop his revision—his metamorphosing—here, for he continues to revise Eve's association with the Earth and all that it contains. There is an element of circularity in this portion of the narrative, for this association of Eve and the Earth, so carefully established by the gendering of Eden and of creation and yet so totally out of Eve's own control, is what prepares us for the radical revisionism of Adam's reaction at his first sight of Eve:

> what seem'd fair in all the World, seem'd now
> Mean, or in her summ'd up, in her contain'd. . . .
> Shee disappear'd, and left me dark, I wak'd
> To find her, or for ever to deplore
> Her loss, and other pleasures all abjure.
>
> (8.472–73, 478–80)

Adam first awoke in the light of the masculine sun, while Eve awoke in the shade; Adam knew himself and knew of God, while Eve knew nothing; yet in this speech Adam implicitly acknowledges the gendered powers of Raphael's narrative where the first elements of light, water, and Earth are feminine. As he names Eve with his first feminine pronoun, he shifts the focus of his vision to give centrality to this initial feminine priority. What he does not consider is that although the universe began with feminine abstractions, when these elements were made discrete, they often became masculine: the light becomes the masculine sun that the feminine moon can only reflect; the water becomes a masculine river that forms a less forceful feminine lake. Between Adam's failure to see Eve as one woman, not the feminine cosmos, and his inability to separate her image from his own, he articulates a series of perceptions and representations—generated by Milton's own manipulations and innovations upon the Genesis narratives—which are, in the context of the story of the fall of man, fatally flawed. If Adam's flaw resides in his inability to see Eve as separate from his own self, Eve's absent sense of selfhood—potentially a force more powerful than all of Raphael's words—is represented as an even greater flaw.

But Man, says Milton's God, is both created sufficient to have stood and further prepared by the teaching of Raphael. Yet, as with his explanation of cosmic order at the beginning of book 8, we find Raphael's response "Accuse not nature, she hath done her part" (8.561) not only to be inadequate, but something of a non sequitur. There was no word for "nature" in biblical Hebrew. In Raphael's remarkably unsuccessful rebuke, which Adam's narrative of identity and perception calls forth, we recognize—as we do in all of Adam's speech after his declaration of marriage—Milton's own creation of a postcreation story. But what we are seeing here is not merely gloss or amplification, but rather profound revision. Nowhere is this more evident than in the shift in focus between

Adam's outpouring of adoration for Eve and Raphael's rebuke. Adam's speech is pronounced officially and significantly wrong; but the poem offers us no revised reading of his narrative of knowing the feminine as opposed to the female. Furthermore, the shift in emphasis from Adam's view of Eve as the (re)organizing principle of his world to Raphael's pronouncement that "Nature" stands accused of some inadequacy from which she must be defended goes unchallenged in the text. The angel's first line seems an inappropriate response to Adam's speech, especially since Adam did say "well I understand in the prime end / Of Nature her [Eve] th' inferior" (540–41). As Raphael goes on to pick up *Wisdom* and *Reason* from Adam's lines, we can be lulled (wrongly) into accepting his use of these terms as perfectly referential. But Raphael doesn't hear, doesn't understand what Adam is saying. If he did he would never fuel the flames of Adam's love of his own image with a remark such as "Oft-times nothing profits more / Than self-esteem" (471–72). Adam's self-esteem in relation to Eve is the source of his misperceptions in book 8, but Raphael cannot grasp this and leaves those misperceptions uncorrected. Ironically, if Raphael's remark about self-esteem were directed at Eve, the angel would be moving toward a solution to the problem of self-knowledge. Instead, he further confuses the issue of identity.

This is a crucial moment in the poem, one that calls into question Adam's sufficiency, because Adam's flawed narrative—ineffectively rebuked by Raphael—is the creation narrative that leads us directly to the narrative of the fall. Since Raphael's reproving remarks have more to do with Adam's perception of Eve than with the identity of Eve herself, Raphael's speech simply expands the scope of Adam's flawed narrative, as Adam, too, is focused on his reaction to Eve rather than upon the reality of the woman as an entity in her own right. And as in Adam's narrative, Eve attains the status of subject in Raphael's speech only so that she may subject her self to Adam: "the more thou know'st, / The more she will acknowledge thee her Head" (573–74).

Adam's image of Eve is his own image, an image of all the best that the natural world can offer, the feminine principle turned into a cosmic mirror for his own image.[35] Even Raphael's words link Eve more closely to that feminine force than to God who created her. Of course Raphael already knows the end of the story, knows that Adam will say, when rejecting the possibility of life without Eve, "no, no I feel / The Link of Nature draw me" (9.913–14). In Raphael's response to Adam's description of Eve we therefore hear something closer to a commentary on the reason for the fall than a dramatic rebuttal meant to prevent the fall. Even if we accept as unproblematic God's statement in book 3 that man

was created "sufficient to have stood," the Adam we see at the end of
book 8 has assumed a new identity, a sense of self not sufficient, but
linked to the presence of Eve, a sufficiency no longer intrinsic to Adam
but extrinsic, as Raphael's arbitrarily ordered imperatives that close
book 8 remain extrinsic to the drama of the narrative.

Adam's perception of Eve follows the pattern set up by the gendering
of first things in Raphael's creation narrative. Light, water, and earth are
all initially feminine, although when they become separate and discrete
entities—sun, moon, river, lake, mountain, valley—they can be gendered
male and female, with the masculine coming first and being held superior, just as Adam and Eve are gendered from the abstract image of
God. Yet that subtext of cosmic femininity remains, reappearing in the
poem when Adam speaks of Eve's genitive possession of all the universe
around them. Are we to see Adam's response to Eve as Raphael sees it
or as an unconscious acknowledgment of, a response to the power of that
feminine cosmos detailed in book 7? We can question Adam's priorities,
critique Raphael's rebuke, but we cannot ignore the pattern of gender
identity that Milton places at the very heart of the creation of his poetic
cosmos. This privileged paradigm of gendering allows Milton to move
from the too-immediate problems of man-and-woman offered by the
Genesis narratives and their traditional interpretations to the creation
of almost mystical cosmic forms, allows him to play off of Ovid's stories
of metamorphosed identities, and ultimately allows for the possibility
that our fallen perceptions of gender identity and selfhood, not "the
ways of God," are in need of justification.

THE SECOND FACE OF MEDUSA

Although it has become a critical commonplace to cite Ovid's Narcissus
story—particularly with a sort of medieval spin on the dangers of self-
love as rendered in *The Romance of the Rose* (lines 1425–1615)—as a subtext for Eve's narrative of her creation in book 4 of *Paradise Lost*, the two
(or three if you count the *Romance of the Rose*) paradigms of gazer, mirror,
and reflection have less than commonplace correspondences. We are, of
course, meant to make the connections, but the allusion does not hold
up, not even to the end of Eve's narrative; we as readers must realize
this, even though—or especially because—Milton has so suggestively
planted the image of Narcissus before us. While both the first part of
Ovid's narrative and the medieval retelling of the story do have some
relation to Eve's narrative, too loose a definition of "relation" can be

dangerously misleading. By developing the implications of the phrase "dangerously misleading," I want to suggest ways in which the less obvious, but equally available, subtext of the Medusa story can better inform our reading of what Milton is actually up to in book 4 and subsequently in books 8, 9, and 10. For it seems to me that at the crux of our reading of the poem must be not Eve's perception of herself, but Adam's perception of Eve and Eve's lack of self-perception. If Adam's sufficiency to stand may be compromised by his inability to separate Eve's image from his own sense of self, Eve, on the other hand, seems to have no clear image of self, either individual or in relation to Adam. Here the Medusa story—in both Ovid's epic and in the interpolation in the *Romance of the Rose*—offers much more subtle and provocative paradigms of the power of the gaze as a way of knowing. The Narcissus story, especially in this famous medieval manifestation, thus constitutes a trap for reader of Milton's epic, one of the many traps he sets for us so that we may ourselves fall because of our own pride in and quest for knowledge.

Without digressing into the sort of source study that Rosemond Tuve called "the next to last infirmity of noble minds," I must raise the issue of Milton's knowledge of the *Romance of the Rose*. Reading critics on this topic makes for an interesting stroll down the serpentine paths of rhetorical ambiguity. Such canonical luminaries as A. Bartlett Giamatti[36] and John V. Fleming[37] speak of the poem's influence on Milton's epic, but they speak in sentences that never quite step over the line between the subjunctive and the declarative. They assume; they do not assert. In an essay in *Milton and the Middle Ages,* Edward Sichi Jr. puts his finger on the problem: "In discounting the dependence of *Paradise Lost* on the *Roman* we can cite differences in time, place, and language, Milton's antipathy to things French, and the decidedly different tone of the two works. However," Sichi continues correctly if a trifle hopefully, "the two authors do share a common background."[38] Then Sichi goes on to point out that Milton does mention Chaucer's incomplete translation in his *Commonplace Book.*

This is not a point I feel the need to argue. In fact, I would be more excited to "prove" that Milton never laid eyes on the complete French *Romance of the Rose,* with or without Medusa interpolation, as this would strengthen my initial argument about the subconscious desire of a patriarchal society's imagination to conflate the issues of mirrors, interior identity, power, and gender. I am not arguing for the direct influence of either *Romance of the Rose* or the Medusa interpolation on Milton's poem as I argue for the influence of Ovid's poem, but I want to use the French narrative as an example of the degree of complexity to be found in medieval representations of Ovidian narratives. To discuss the sort of intertextual generation of meaning I think Milton is employing in *Paradise Lost,* I want to use as my principle of analysis an observation made by John Freccero about Dante's use of the Medusa image in *Inferno* 9: Freccero speaks of "a generic recall to a moral code exterior to the text" reminding us that "this passage, like all of the addresses to the reader, is exterior to the fiction, but central to the text."[39] This is exactly what I believe we find with the Narcissus and Medusa images in *Paradise Lost;* the references are of course "exterior to the fiction" of the epic, for they are postlapsarian stories; but Milton is playing on his readers' fallen knowledge to mediate our understanding of the Genesis narrative.

Milton deliberately lets his reader fall into the medieval tradition of moralizing the Narcissus story, a fatal but all too easy error for the reader of *Paradise Lost.* Tradition links vanity and self-absorption to the Narcissus story, particularly the medieval tradition of moral allegory, but as Ovid's story offers a less judgmental account of the fair young man, so Ovid's narrator expresses both regret at the youth's initial inability to recognize himself and pity at his subsequent grief. In Ovid's narrative we find no hint of self-gratification—quite the reverse. In the tradition of moral allegory Narcissus becomes an icon of destructive self-love, but this is not the tradition invoked by Milton's syntactical parallel; as I have suggested, he quotes Ovid, but we hear the Narcissus narrative from the *Romance of the Rose.* And yet we should not be too quick to convict ourselves of careless reading, for not only Eve's phrase "with vain desire," but also the presence of a warning voice that speaks directly to the gazer, as Reason does to the Lover in the *Romance of the Rose,* make our misreading almost inevitable. Here the argument for intertextuality is on firm ground, for this version of the Narcissus story, coming so early in the *Romance of the Rose,* appears in Chaucer's translation.

And yet for this very reason, we must read still more carefully, for Guillaume de Lorris does not present the Narcissus story as we find it in Ovid. Yes, the emphasis here is that medieval moralizing on the dangers of vanity, of self-love, but here is a more significant change—as least in the context of this argument: there is no flower beside the Perilous Fountain in the *Romance of the Rose,* only a stone plaque telling of the death of Narcissus. Milton will use both the imagery of self-love and the transformation from flesh to stone in his narrative of the fall of our first parents, but it is of Adam he speaks, not Eve.

Sylvia Huot, in an essay on the Medusa interpolation in the *Romance of the Rose,* makes a connection between four major Ovidian narratives that are reworked in the medieval text.[40] Speaking of "mythographic

program and Ovidian intertext," Huot points to the stories of Narcissus
and Echo, of Deucalion and Pyrrha, and of Pygmalion and Galatea as
paradigms of flesh-and-stone used by the *Romance of the Rose* poets, arguing that the Medusa interpolation "responds to the thematic nexus of
Narcissus, Deucalion, and Pygmalion as a program within the conjoined
Rose."[41] In the *Romance of the Rose*, all that remains of Narcissus is a stone
plaque (and Huot reminds us of the images of stone and bone in Ovid's
narrative); Deucalion correctly interprets the instructions of the oracle
and, with his wife, generates bodies out of stones; Pygmalion makes a
woman out of stone, stone that comes to life. As Huot observes: "For a
reader whose understanding of the *Rose* was informed by a knowledge
of the *Metamorphoses*, the progression from Narcissus through Deucalion
to Pygmalion could be graphically envisioned as a progression from
human to stone or marble statue and death, countered by one from
stone to marble or ivory statue and so back to human."[42] Additionally,
Huot reminds us, in the text of the *Romance of the Rose*, each of these
transformations is in answer to a prayer—Echo's prayer that Narcissus
be cursed, the prayer of the two flood survivors to the oracle, Pygmalion's
prayer to Venus—concluding that "The story of Medusa participates
explicitly in this network of imagery. . . . By inserting the Medusa passage as a prelude to the story of Pygmalion, the anonymous redactor
calls attention to the imagery of petrifaction and sterility, while also
stressing that the Lover has escaped these dangers."[43]

Huot's phrases "thematic nexus" or participation in a "network of
imagery" can of course be used to discuss almost any aspect of *Paradise
Lost*, but the Ovidian context—or subtext—is one that particularly informs the identities and actions of Eve and Adam. Milton allows us to
read Eve's creation narrative through Ovid's story of Narcissus and
then—if we are careful readers—forces us to unread, to reject the image
of the youth whose tragedy is that he finally recognizes himself. But the
story resurfaces in Milton's epic with another recognition scene. In book
8 Adam tells Raphael how he first awoke and explored his new existence,
saying "Myself I then perus'd" (8.267)—something Eve never does, her
knowledge of "self" being exterior and limited to a memory of a neuter
image; Adam has heard Eve's narrative, including her reason for turning
back toward that image; and yet Milton has Adam remake both his own
identity and that of Eve in his book-8 creation narrative.

When Adam declares:

> I now see
> Bone of my Bone, Flesh of my Flesh, *my Self*
> *Before me.*
>
> (8.494–96, emphasis mine)

Here the nuances of the Narcissus narrative resurface—for in remaking the image of Eve, Adam is redefining himself. "Myself" of two hundred lines before is no longer Adam, but the face of Eve, Eve who was given to Adam at his own request—Milton's version of the Ovidian prayers to which Huot makes reference—and with this ominous introduction from Milton's God:

> What next I bring shall please thee, be assur'd,
> Thy likeness, thy fit help, thy other self,
> Thy wish, exactly to thy heart's desire.
>
> (8.449–51)

As Adam stands transfixed—although certainly not silent—before this new vision of himself, "weak / Against the charm of Beauty's powerful glance" (533), we hear the echoes of that other Ovidian mirror narrative, the Medusa story.

In the *Romance of the Rose*, the Medusa story appears in a fifty-two-line interpolation, added within twenty or thirty years of Jean de Meun's completion of the poem.[44] It appears very late in the poem—line 20,800—just before the Pygmalion story. First the redactor summarizes the Medusa story from Ovid, although not in the narrative order in which the Ovid presents it, and with the first twenty-eight lines being more about Perseus' use of and treasuring of—love for is really not too strong a phrase—the powerful head of the dead Medusa. This in itself is a good introduction to the Pygmalion story, but the last twenty-four lines are even better. Here the fleshly Medusa of Ovid is compared to the image on the tower described in Jean de Meun's narrative. In the interpolation this image is the face of Medusa, but the stone face has the reverse effect of Ovid's fleshly head:

> There has never been such an image on any other tower;
> More miracles surround it
> Than ever surrounded Medusa.
> But this image [the one on the tower] has a much better use [than Medusa's]
> Nothing lasted around Medusa
> For into rock she transfigured
> All those who looked upon her,
> So many evil deeds did she do
> By means of her criminal locks.
> By no device could anyone protect himself from this,
> Except Perseus, the son of Jove
> Who by means of his shield saw her [face],
> He saved himself by means of this shield
> Which his sister, Pallas, had given him,
> [He took off her head] by means of the shield
> He carried it with him for all his days;

It was valuable to him, he trusted in it;
In many combats he put it to work, to good use.
Strong enemies he killed with it
Others he killed with his sword.
But he never looked at the head except [reflected] in the shield
For otherwise he could not have lived;
His shield was a mirror for him,
For such was the power of the head, that
If he had looked at it straight on,
He would have turned into rock right on the spot.
But the image I'm telling you about
Surpasses Medusa's powers
For it doesn't serve to kill people
Nor to make them change into rock.
This one changes them back from rock,
Brings them back to their original form
In truth to be better than they had been before
And better than they could ever have been.
Medusa's image harms, but this image I'm talking about here benefits
That one snuffs out life, this one resuscitates,
That one harms the mighty
This one relieves the hurt;
For whoever comes near to this one
And sees it all and touches it all
If ever he had been turned into rock,
Or taken out if his senses,
No longer could the rock hold him,
He would come back to his right senses,
Thus he was cured forever
Of all evils and all perils.
So help me God, if I could
Willingly I would look upon it more closely
In truth by God, I would touch it everywhere,
If I could get so close to it.
But it is worthy and virtuous
Such is she precious by her beauty.[45]

Here we see the tradition of the beautiful Medusa found in Boccaccio, even to the phrase "precious beauty," a Medusa based on Ovid's implication that, as Huot observes, "what is dangerous is neither feminine desire and its effects on men, nor male desire as such, but rather the lack of desire in a woman who refuses to yield."[46] This is a more sophisticated analysis than that of John Freccero who begins his discussion of the beautiful Medusa by observing that she "was said to be powerless against women . . . [but that she] represented a sensual / fascination, a *pulchritudo* so excessive that it turned men to stone."[47] Huot's insight should certainly remind us both Adam's first and second sight of Eve and of the separation quarrel at the beginning of book 9, while Freccero's comment prepares us to recognize the way in which Milton ultimately will use this icon of deadly female beauty—female charm—to a far different end than does either Dante or the Medusa redactor. As Huot explains:

The author of the Medusa passage inserted his work at a crucial point in the differentiation of the Lover from Narcissus. . . . [Both] Genius and Pygmalion, in different ways, outline the requirements for a love that will not lead to narcissistic death: it must rest on a desire for a real and obtainable other, and it must lead to the perpetuation of life. The Medusa passage reiterates that the Lover has indeed chosen a love object that contributes to the perpetuation of life, and it further suggests that even if he had fallen victim to the errors of Narcissus, the sight of this image would be sufficient to cure him."[48]

Eve is created in response to Adam's request that he have a mate as do all the other creatures of Eden. God's first naming of Eve in book 4 links her to regeneration: Mother. Surely, then, Eve in herself is presented in the same iconic paradigm as the life-giving Medusa in the *Rose* redaction. The difference is that Adam does not need to be put "back into his right senses"; rather, this figure that is made exactly to his heart's desire causes him to privilege his physical senses and to lose his knowledge of God. Eve's effect upon Adam, its purpose never clearly articulated in the poem, is presented as a conflation of the worst of the two Ovidian mirror stories. Eve herself is as innocent as the young maiden raped in the temple of Athena, but her effect upon Adam is at once both that of the image of Narcissus in the pool and of the face of the transformed Medusa. The transformation, however, has its genesis not in Eve's face but in Adam's gaze. As Freccero points out about the danger of the beautiful Medusa:

Its threat is the threat of idolatry. In terms of mythological *exempla*, petrifica-tion by the Medusa is the real consequence of Pygmalion's folly.
The point is worth stressing. Ever since Augustine, the Middle Ages insisted upon the link between Eros and language, between the reaching out in desire for what mortals can never possess and the reaching out of language toward the significance of silence.[49]

To return to Huot's observation about the danger of "the lack of desire in a woman who refuses to yield," let us add one other Medusa paradigm to this palimpsest. In the closing lines of the final poem in the *Rime sparse*, Petrarch turns from the image of Laura to the image of the Virgin Mary, justifying himself to the Virgin with an image that conflates both Ovidian mirror stories: "Medusa et l'error mio m'àn fatto un sasso / d'umor vano stillante" ["Medusa and my error have made me a stone dripping vain moisture."][50] Surely if there is a construct in Western literature that gives us a quick fix on the unattainable object of female desire, it is Petrarch's Laura. As the poet-narrator speaks of her with contempt, we see the "danger" of which Huot speaks.

With this nexus of Medusa imagery in mind, let us explore Adam's response to Eve's narrative of eating the fruit: lines 856 and following in book 9. Eve's twenty-nine-line speech to Adam—in addition to using the pronoun "I" seven times—includes the phrases "the pain of absence from thy sight," "To open Eyes," and "opener of eyes," all stressing the relation between "I" and "eye." "Thus Eve with Count'nace blithe told her story" the narrator concludes. Faced with this sight of Eve and the words of her narrative, Adam

> *Astonied* stood, and blank, while horror chill
> Ran through his veins, and all his joints relaxed.
> From his slack hand the garland wreathed for Eve
> Down dropt, and all the faded roses shed.
> Speechless he stood and pale.
>
> (890–94, emphasis mine)

After he regains the powers of speech and motion, it takes him all of eleven lines to respond "for with thee Certain my resolution is to die" and he goes on to repeat the "Flesh of Flesh, Bone of my Bone" identification he makes at his first sight of Eve.

Here Milton conjoins two external fictions about reflected identity to generate a third. The Narcissus imagery of books 4 and 8 is still present as is the Medusa subtext of book 8, both represented here by Adam's reaction to Eve's countenance: he is astonied, turned to stone as are those who gaze at Medusa; but he is also weak and wasted as is Narcissus beside the pool. The OED gives the etymology of "astonied" as deriving from astunned or astonished, but comments parenthetically that "Various writers have apparently fancied this word to be a derivative of 'stony' and used it as petrified." Since this is the *only* time Milton uses the word in his poetry, we can place considerable weight on the availability of the reference to stone, especially if it was traditional in the works of "Various writers." Adam sees Eve's face, is turned to stone, becomes weak, then chooses death. But it is the beauty of that face, not the horror, which transforms him, just as it is the beauty of her image as "myself before me" that causes him to lose sight of God in book 8. This complex invocation of the Medusa narrative forces the reader to participate in a comparison of Ovid's tale *and* the medieval versions (even if not in the specific usage of the Interpolation or *Inferno*) of a beautiful Medusa *and* the Genesis story.

The nexus of self-love and fear and female beauty—fatal or fruitful—

which we find among the external narratives of the Narcissus and Medusa stories are, in Freccero's words, elements that are "external to the
fiction, but central to the text" most especially to the text of line 999 that
tells us that Adam fell "fondly overcome with female charm."

So what am I suggesting here? That Milton saw the pattern Freccero
illuminates in *Inferno* or that which Huot points out for us in the *Romance
of the Rose*? No. But I am suggesting that such a paradigm of intertextual
meaning is being employed here to suggest to our fallen eyes the ways
in which fallen narratives may retrospectively illuminate first acts. The
tactic employed by the Medusa redactor in introducing the story of
Pygmalion with a reidentified stone Medusa, the pattern of mythic authority that Guillaume de Lorris and Jean de Meun weave in this hor-
rifically canonical medieval text, is a pattern we should not fail to seek
in Milton's epic where two Ovidian mirror stories are fragmented to
reflect the fallen knowledge of the reader in and from the textual mirror
of *Paradise Lost*. That Milton, after his complex manipulations of the
Narcissus paradgim, constructs Eve as a Medusa figure speaks directly
to the issue of Adam's sufficiency. Here, unlike Dante's *Inferno*, there is
no one to cover the protagonist's eyes at the crucial moment (although
it can be argued that Raphael tried in book 8). As Adam looks upon
the metamorphosed Eve and becomes himself "astonied," we see Milton
participating in the imaginative construction of the Medusa narrative—
the story of a woman who has no power of her own, but to whom the
gaze of men is drawn with powerful consequences. Medusa is at once a
powerless object and the generative locus of a power over which she has
no control. First the object of male desire, then a monster, then a weapon,
Medusa provides a telling paradigm for Milton's construction of Eve in
his narrative that justifies the ways of God to men.

THE FACE OF EVE AND THE FACE OF GOD

The search for the self which is the quest of the poet can only be accomplished
through the mediation of the imagination, the Narcissus image which is at
once an image of the self and all that the self is not. For a Medieval poet
steeped in the Augustinian tradition, the search for the self in the mirror of
creatures, the beloved, ends with a false image of the self which is either
rejected in favor of God, the light which casts the reflection, or accepted as a
true image, an image which is totally other. Seeing the self in otherness and
accepting the vision as true reduces the spirit to something totally alienated
from itself, like a rock or a tree, totally deprived of consciousness. Like language itself, the image can only represent by pointing beyond itself, by

beckoning the beholder to pierce through it to its ultimate significance. Idolatry in this context is a refusal to go beyond, a self-petrification.[51]

As Freccero speaks about the dangers of reading Dante's Medusa, we hear a shrewd summary of Adam's error in books 8 and 9. Adam, however, manages to make both mistakes: he see "a false image of the self" but does not reject it "in favor of God, the light which casts the reflection"; neither does he accept it as "an image which is totally other." He sees and is told that Eve is a reflection of himself, his image made from his desires; if she is his reflection, when he looks at her he sees himself. And, in the mirror of her eyes—the charm of beauty's powerful glance— he literally sees himself. His identification of Eve with himself is so immediate, so powerful, and so resistant to reason that he never views this self-identification as a deliberate act, as something that could have been avoided or that could be undone. He cannot imagine himself as he was before the creation of Eve ("'How can I live without thee?'" 9.908), even though he narrates this solitary vision of himself to Raphael. He does not realize that his first sight of Eve returning to him is his last sight of God. He speaks of the morning-of-the-world garden state of his first awareness as "'these wild woods forlorn'" (9.910) and declares: "'to lose thee were to lose myself'" (9.959). Eve's power, so variously represented by the narrative of causality in Genesis 2, by the rantings of Paul, by the brushes of artists who give the serpent the face of Eve, and by Milton's own phrase "fondly overcome with female charm," is actually represented as the power of Adam's idolatrous transformation described in book 8 and enacted in book 9. The pool of Narcissus, the shield of Perseus here become the mirror of Eve and of Eve's eye as Adam gazes at her and sees himself in a woman's body. The voice of God foregrounds Adam's error in book 10:

> Was she thy God, that her thou didst obey
> Before his voice? or was she made thy guide,
> Superiour, or but equal, that to her
> Thou didst resign thy manhood, and the place
> Wherein God set thee above her, made of thee
> And for thee, whose perfection far excelled
> Hers in all real dignity?

Since God realizes that Adam's answer—or the answer tacitly supplied by his actions—to all of these questions has been "Yes," the voice goes on to critique the error of Adam's perception:

> Adorned
> She was indeed, and lovely, to attract
> Thy love, not thy subjection; and her gifts
> Were such as under government well seemed—
> Unseemly to bear rule; which was thy part
> And person, hadst thou known thyself aright.
>
> (145–56)

Ah, now this is the crux of Adam's failure in Milton's narrative: he did not know himself aright. Had he known himself "aright," he would also have known Eve. He would also have known God. In Milton's poem, Eve's power is reduced to the reflection of Adam's lack of self-knowledge. Like the Ovidian Medusa, Eve is ultimately blamed then punished then shunned and feared because of a series of actions performed upon her by a male gaze and male actions. Eve's association with the powerfully gendered female cosmos is detailed seemingly to no end, until we realize that it is detailed so that it may be dismissed. In Milton's poem, her female power—her beauty, her grace, her charm—is power only when it is perceived by a male, a power at once mediated and generated by the process of reflection.

What does Eve see? Not herself. Not God. Not Adam as "her image" remembered from the lake. Milton's narrative of Eve, like Ovid's narrative of Medusa, presents female power only as the object of the actions of a god or the gaze of a man. The figure that supposedly generates the reflection is, in Milton's text, curiously absent. Her fictive presence and her physical attributes are necessary for the narrative, but the narrative itself is Adam's, is God's, is Milton's. Eve, in *Paradise Lost,* is the reflection of the perceptions of these men, not of herself.

Eve's sense of self ultimately cannot be represented in this text because Milton, in his imaginative creation narrative, does not recognize the feminine. That female power exists he cannot deny, but he constructs that power as an absence of self. If the eyes of Medusa were open as Perseus approached, she would see him, either directly or as a reflection in the shield. Like Eve, Medusa never sees herself. In his epic of first actions, Milton constructs Eve as the first reflection; but the reflection of Eve is Adam.

6

the mirrors of Medusa

[Women] are being turned all the time into objects of display, to be looked at and gazed at and stared at by men. Yet, in a real sense, women are not there at all. The parade has nothing to do with woman, everything to do with man. . . . Women are simply the scenery on to which men project their narcissistic fantasies.
—Laura Mulvey, "You Don't Know What Is Happening, Do You, Mr. Jones"

THAT Laura Mulvey wrote those words about late twentieth-century pornographic films does not, I believe, limit the acuteness of her insights to the products of our modern culture. The paradigm she critiques is older than Ovid. The same can be said of the works of Susanne Kappeler, Andrea Dworkin, and Susan Griffin. I cannot stop myself from wondering if any of these feminist critics of gender relations and representations in our society have read the texts I discuss in this study. Certainly their insights into the nature of pornography could—if we decontextualize them from that shocking (and technically anachronistic) noun—just as easily form part of the critical debate over these representations of Britomart/Elizabeth, Cleopatra, and Eve. Let us for a monument willingly suspend our cultural and chronological disbelief and hear the echoes generated by old, old voices telling ancient stories. When we hear Eve speaking her creation narrative, let us also hear the commentary of Susanne Kappeler:

The assumption of the female point of view and narrative voice—the assumption of linguistic and narrative female "subjectivity"—in no way lessens . . . the fundamental elision of the woman as subject. On the contrary, it goes one step further in the total objectification of woman. It is indeed one of the well-tried pornographic devices to fake the female's, the victim's, point of view. . . . The so-called female point of view is a male construction of the passive victim in

188

his own scenario, the necessary counterpart to his active aggressor: whether "she" resists her own violation, whether she enjoys it in involuntary bodily response and against her own will, or whether she is voluntarily and infinitely available to his impositions—all available alternatives serve to enhance . . . the active subjectivity of the male, his feeling of life.[1]

When we recall the power that Shakespeare grants Cleopatra over Antony, let us note, with Andrea Dworkin, that essential to the gratification felt by the audience in a pornographic film is the "illusion that the women are not controlled by men but are acting freely."[2] And when we see Britomart metamorphosed from an allegorical representation of a woman into the allegorical representation of a virtue, we can consider Susan Griffin's argument:

> The pornographer reduces a woman to a mere thing, to an entirely material object without a soul, who can only be "loved" physically. But the church, and the Judeo-Christian culture, give us the same ethos. For we read in church doctrine that the man is the head and the wife the body, or that the woman is known, whereas man is the knower.[3]

No. No, I am not trying to argue that Milton and Shakespeare and Spenser were writing *pornography* nor would I suggest that we should anteriorize that term to discuss their texts.[4] But yes, I would and do argue that we should stop and pay attention to the commonalities between the paradigm of pornography and the paradigm of gender and power and the interior self found in these Renaissance texts. Both sets of relationships ostensibly hold women up as objects of desire and admiration, and both promote the fiction that this status gives the women power over men. But both sets of relationships empower men as they disempower women. As Dworkin observes: "Male sexual power is the substance of culture. It resonates everywhere. The celebration of rape in story, song, and science is the paradigmatic articulation of male sexual power as a cultural absolute."[5] The three Renaissance texts, of course, are not rape stories. But the Medusa story is an archetypal rape narrative, and the paradigm of reflected power and identity it generates is ultimately inseparable from the act of rape. Rape is not primarily a sexual act; it is an act of power: the rapist is empowered by disempowering the victim. It is also, as figured in the Bible, an act of knowing; again, the man is the knower, the woman the known object. The discourse of rape—whether we find it in Genesis or Chaucer or Senate confirmation hearings—simply mirrors the act. The discourse is generated by a narrator or a defense attorney or Orrin Hatch just as the act is generated by the rapist. In both paradigms, the woman is the object being controlled.[6]

All three of the Renaissance texts in this study show us women being controlled by men. While we could hardly expect this to be otherwise insofar as all of the authors are male, the degree to which each woman is constructed as having a sense of self is ironically a measure of how impossible she finds the task of self-recognition within the textual worlds created by these writers. Britomart is controlled by Spenser, of course, but also by the cultural fear of a woman ruler. Cleopatra's dead body in the control of Octavius Caesar grants that male ruler the power to diminish not only the queen herself, but also his most powerful enemy, Antony; and Shakespeare grants him that power, having first constructed a woman strong enough to be used as a powerful political force. Eve is controlled by God and Adam as well as by Milton, as the poet's epic offers us a more complex construction of Eve than we find elsewhere in the canon; but that constructed complexity weighs more heavily on her as she fails to know herself. Only in the first text is the freedom of a free woman left undamaged within in the text—undamaged, at least by others; because of the culture in which she finds herself, Britomart must be made to take herself out of the active paradigm, so that she may appear in the text as simple allegory. But of the three representations of woman, Britomart is the most limited; not only is she limited by the structures of allegory but, more importantly, by her relationship to the reality of Elizabeth I. As daring as Spenser's "third mirror" of representation may be, he could not script an ending for his Elizabeth figure that is other than allegorical. Britomart may be actively saved by the construct of Isis, but Isis is a statue; we must not turn from the fact that Britomart's power in Isis Church leads her directly to active combat with, and mutilation of, a living female ruler. Mercilla is Spenser's version of the "Rainbow portrait" (all the more impressive because he never saw the painting), the cult of youth of the last years of Elizabeth's reign, representing an eternally ageless royal virgin fictively in control of both her cosmos and her own sexuality—fictively in control of both public and private, but able to live as a woman in neither.

Shakespeare's Cleopatra mirrors the identity of the men around her and mirrors the reality of Elizabeth only in her diminishment at the hands of the ruler who buries her. The character of the Egyptian does represent a real historical figure, but one who lived in another country and who, besides, is long dead. Unlike Spenser, Shakespeare offers a woman who has been represented and re-represented in art and literature, providing a sense of recognition for his audience, albeit a superficial sort of re-knowing.

First and last we find Eve. Looking at Milton's representation of the first woman—linked by patriarchal Christianity to all her daughters, the first woman and all women—we realize that there is little basis for an argument about the increasingly powerful position of women in canonical Renaissance texts. By linking Eve to the female landscape, Milton overgoes God's charge in Genesis 1 (a command given, ironically, to both Adam and Eve): fill the earth and subdue it. The void of Eve's identity is filled by Adam with a reflection of his own, and every element of the poem conspires to subdue Eve. And yet there is within the text a sense of something missing. Milton's invocation of Narcissus and Medusa may constitute a sort of metaphoric negation of Eve's identity: she is not Narcissus, because she leaves the pool; she is not Medusa because there is no figure to fill the role of Perseus. But this leaves us with no face in the mirror. Adam's sense of self is roughly constructed. He claims "who I was, or where, or from what cause, / Knew not" (5.270–71) and that "I . . . feel that I am happier than I know" (281–82). And yet he knows much as "Pensive I sat me down" (287), and he is about to learn more through the classical convention of the dream vision. His psychomachia in books 10 and 11 is closer to interior selfhood than any other passages in the poem. The contrast with Eve's creation narrative is stark. Milton does not represent any sense of interior self for Eve until after the fall, and even then it is still a self defining its being in relation to Adam.

Nevertheless, we are given a sense of something that is absent; Milton represents a lack, Eve's lack of a developed interior self. Shakespeare, on the other hand, gives us selfhood by implication. Cleopatra is presented as complete, even though that completeness is not represented in detail. In this woman we are given a sense of undefinable presence rather than undefinable absence. Why then does the earlier poet, the poet writing in the supposedly simpler form of allegory, give us the clearest picture of an interior female self? Well, part of the answer, of course, is that allegory allows for modes of representation unavailable to the dramatist and the less mimetic epic poet. The overt symbolism of Britomart's bleeding "ulcer" would seem too crude in a nonallegorical work, for all that it is a fairly sophisticated rendering of physiological and psychological female interiority. I wish I could proclaim that Spenser and Shakespeare and Milton were striving to construct female figures with developed interior selves, but that they merely lacked models of representation. I wish I could, but I can't. What I must acknowledge is that the main focus of these male poets is still men. With their male characters, Shakespeare and Milton give us a sense of an interior self, something at once more complex and less concrete than Greenblatt's definition of "self-fashioning." But as they develop the strategies with which to develop the interior selves of their male characters, they make gestures toward the construction of a female self. Spenser's gesture seems the most complete, but it is so generated by the extratextual reality of Elizabeth and so colored by the art of allegory that the immediacy may be deceptive.

What I hope to have established here is that the female self is represented by the male poets with differing strategies and to differing ends than is the male self. Perhaps representation is too strong a word. The interior female self is *acknowledged* in these texts, and is acknowledged variously. The similarities lie in the consequences of that acknowledgment. However problematic the representations of male interiority may be, they lack the common ground we see in Spenser's and Shakespeare's and Milton's constructions of the female. Each of these women figures suffers a metamorphosis disempowering in direct proportion to the degree to which her interior selfhood is acknowledged. The metamorphosis of Britomart is the most radical: from an allegory of a flesh and blood young woman to an icon. Cleopatra's selfhood survives as long as does the Egyptian queen, but that selfhood is not clearly represented, and her public self is translated after death. Eve's self is best described by the old jargon of the absent presence. So too does her diminishment seem less radical, for there is less to lose.

In his study of male self-fashioning, Stephen Greenblatt suggests that in the sixteenth century "there appears to be an increased self-consciousness about the fashioning of human identity as a manipulable, artful process. Such self-consciousness had been widespread among the elite in the classical world, but Christianity brought a growing suspicion of man's power to shape identity."[7] Seeing Spenser and Shakespeare, among others, as writers who would challenge the patristic and medieval concepts of identity, Greenblatt continues:

> We should note in the circumstances of the sixteenth-century figures on whom this study focuses a common factor that may help to explain their sensitivity as writers to the construction of identity: they all embody, in one form or another, a profound mobility.[8]

Greenblatt identifies this mobility as primarily social and economic.[9] (Although Greenblatt's arguments apply directly to Spenser and Shakespeare, the phrase "a profound mobility" and all that it implies about cultural context can, with very little significant alteration, also be applied to Milton, living as he did through a series of profound restructurings of the social order.) What limits Greenblatt's insights and those of the band of brothers who follow in his train, is his focus on male self-fashioning. While willing to discuss Elizabeth as an historical construct, he is less interested even than Spenser in her possible representation as a woman: "She was a living representation of the immutable within time, a fiction of permanence."[10] Aside from Elizabeth as a political construct, these historicist studies of the 1980s expend very little ink on representations of powerful women. Nor does that definition of the "profound mobility" of social structures of the period take into account the changing role of women. Not only was there a queen on the throne, but there were women writers on the streets. None of these three authors could have been completely unaware of the functioning literary imaginations of their female contemporaries, and we can only speculate about the extent to which this awareness prompted them to ponder the self-fashioning of women even as they were engaged in male self-fashioning.

As I point out in the first chapter, I am hardly the first to notice the gendered limitiations of historicist criticism—Carol Thomas Neely is perhaps its shrewdest metacritic[11]—and I make this observation largely because I feel that my own study has moved only a little beyond the charmed circle of male critics discussing male poets who self-fashioned male representations. Nor do I invoke Greenblatt only to make a self-fashioned straw-text of his work. Rather, I want to adopt the the Virgilian strategy of invoking a similarity to show a difference. The male representations fashioned by More and Wyatt, by Spenser and Shakespeare were products of the aspirations of those writers. The representations of woman fashioned in the three texts I discuss in this study are far otherwise. The power of the female self is represented—acknowledged—so that it may be controlled rather than fostered by the male poet's vision. Work currently being done on Amelia Lanyer, Mary Wroth, and other women writers of the Renaissance may soon give us the other half of that world, but this study lies somewhere in between. These representations of women fashioned by male poets also contain radical revisions of patristic and medieval visions of the female; but none of the three women is presented as an unproblematically powerful woman with a developed sense of an interior self. And yet the possibility of selfhood is acknowledged in all three texts. Acknowledged and then subdued. The element of reversal, the chiasmus of reflection turns the image on the mirror of the text so that, however powerful the image of woman's selfhood may seem as the epic or play unfolds, the ultimate image is of a disempowered figure. That the process of reflection is central to each of these representations is both significant and unsurprising. The paradigm of metamorphosis by the mediation of mirrors is deeply rooted in the Western imagination. That it is a paradigm that can diminish the identity of the reflected figure, that the diminished figure is so often simply or by conflation female, tells us less about the imaginations of the individual writers in this study than about assumptions of the culture from which they grew and in which they participated. If Medusa's face deprives those who view it of life, so does its reflection kill her. As the shield of Perseus—Medusa's mirror—allows us to gaze at the face of the Gorgon, so does it empower him to destroy her.

> *Two kinds of blindness are arguing over the monopoly on conception.* For the optics of Truth in its credibility no doubt, its unconditional certainty, its passion for Reason, has veiled or else destroyed the gaze that remained mortal. With the result that it can no longer see anything of what had been before its conversion to the Father's law. That everything foreign, other, outside its present certainties no longer appears to the gaze. It can perceive nothing more of them. Except—perhaps? sometimes?—the pain of being blinded in this way, of being no longer able to make out, imagine, feel, what is going on *behind* the screen of those/his ideal projections, divine knowledge. Which cut him off from his relations with the earth, the mother, and any other (female), by that ascent toward an all-powerful intelligibility. Alone, then, in the closed circle of his "soul," that theatre for the re-presentation of likeness, that vertigo of a god that recognizes nothing but himself now. And who, *if it were suggested he identify a (female) other,* would no doubt come up with the confession that he can't see it very well—anymore? That he needs time to evaluate, to take the measure of, what and whom he's dealing with. Time to accustom his eyes to what is in front of him? Or to bring this "object" into his own perspective?
>
> The duplication figured by the shadow is now supported by all that *mimics* him, by those specularizations of him that fill, to the incommensurable limit, his horizon. His "Universe" indeed: his double full of doubles. All more or less close to the reproduction of Sameness. More or less appropriate. Specular reflections exposed in full daylight? Except that their paradigm is never visible. The concentration of light informs the gaze by a *shadow hole* that makes a screen across the sight of the other side. The ideal always holds itself *behind* the circle that limits the field of prospection. Behind the mirror? Concealing the inversion?[12]

What can I say to link this angry critique offered by Irigaray to the often frustrating task of discussing female interiority?

Pay no attention to that little man behind the mirror?

If the paradigm of interior female selfhood is not actually invisible in these Renaissance texts, we may say with some fairness of each writer that "he can't see it very well." Writing in the canonical Western tradition, which has so consistently constructed women as creatures apart from men, these early modern writers do indeed need "time to evaluate, to take the measure of, what and whom [they are] dealing with. Time to accustom [their] eyes to what is in front of [them]" as something they might know as they know themselves. What we mark in these three early modern texts is, perhaps, the beginnings of that necessary recognition.

Notes

INTRODUCTION: THE METAMORPHOSIS OF TERMINOLOGY

1. Katharine Eisaman Maus, "Proof and Consequences: Inwardness and Its Exposure in the English Renaissance," *Representations* 34 (1991): 29–52. See also, Maus's study *Inwardness and Theatre in the English Renaissance* (Chicago: University of Chicago Press, 1995.) This book was published after my study was completed, so I was unable to take advantage of Maus's developed insights.

2. Ibid., 30.

CHAPTER 1. THE CONSTRUCTION AND RECOGNITION OF A FEMALE SELF

1. Katharine Eisaman Maus, "Proof and Consequences: Inwardness and Its Exposure in the English Renaissance," *Representations* 34 (1991): 38.

2. Ibid.

3. This statement will naturally raise the question: and what about the constructions of male interiority by women writers? I hope this question will be answered in this decade, but it lies beyond the scope of this study.

4. Stephen Greenblatt, "Psychoanalysis and Renaissance Culture," in *Literary Theory/Renaissance Texts*, eds. Patricia Parker and David Quint (Baltimore: Johns Hopkins University Press, 1986), 210–24. So many people have refuted this essay that I will content myself by observing that—in addition to building his house on the double sands of a set of historical documents rather than on a Renaissance text and citing an essay on the medieval sense of intellectual property to validate his premise (216)—Greenblatt's assumption that psychoanalytic critics necessarily insist that "the self is at its core a stable point of reference . . . a fixed value of identity" that can be studied "only by repressing history" (217) is, to put it mildly, self-fashioned. When, in his closing paragraphs, he finally confronts a Renaissance text, he speaks only of Red Cross, that paragon of simple allegory, evincing a degree of textual selectivity that is unfortunately characteristic of both sides of this debate—hardly a surprising failing when the focus becomes the theory of discourse rather than the texts themselves.

5. This talk was published the next year in a more diplomatic, if less entertaining, form: Carol Thomas Neely, "Constructing the Subject: Feminist Practice and the New Renaissance Discourses," *English Literary Renaissance* 18 (1988): 5–18. Speaking of the new historicists and of their mostly British cousins, the cultural materialists, as "cult-historicists," Neely argues that by their choice of texts and topics, these critics "seem to produce, or to reproduce patriarchy . . . [to] represent, and by representing, reproduce in their *new* history of ideas, a world which is heirarchical, authoritarian, hegemonic, unsubvertable" (12).

Whether or not it was the intention of Greenblatt and his followers, the "effect of the new theoretical discourse has been to suppress the memory of the vigorous and radicalizing feminist criticism of the seventies" (14).

Furthermore, I would suggest, the elision of *feminist* and *psychoanalytic* as terms defining schools of scholarly endeavor has allowed the (pejorative) critics of the latter to simultaneously dismiss the former.

6. *New Literary History* 21 (spring 1990). See Richard Levin, "Unthinkable Thoughts in the New Historicizing of English Renaissance Drama," 433–47; Catherine Belsey, "Richard Levin and In-different Reading," 449–56; Jonathan Goldberg, "Making Sense," 457–62; "Reply to Catherine Belsey and Jonathan Goldberg," 463–70; and Jonathan Dollimore's semireferential piece of self-fashioning: "Shakespeare, Cultural Materialism, Feminism, and Marxist Humanism," 471–93.

7. *Modern Language Quarterly* 54 (March 1993). See particularly: Meredith Anne Skura, "Understanding the Living and Talking to the Dead: The Historicity of Psychoanalysis," 77–89 [hereafter referred to as "Understanding"]; Peter Stallybrass, "Editing as Cultural Formation: The Sexing of Shakespeare's Sonnets," 91–103; and Walter Benn Michaels, "The Victims of the New Historicism," 111–20.

8. For two examples of essays that successfully combine elements of psychoanalytic and historicist scholarship, see Skura, "Discourse and the Individual: The Case of Colonialism in *The Tempest*," *Shakespeare Quarterly* 40 (1989): 42–69; and Linda Gregerson, "Narcissus Interrupted: Specularity and the Subject of the Tudor State," *Criticism* 35 (1993): 1–38.

Lee Patterson has carried the argument back to the Middle Ages in his Introduction to *Chaucer and the Subject of History* (Madison: University of Wisconsin Press, 1991), 7 ff. He observes: "Since at least the time of Petrarch in the mid-fourteenth century the Middle Ages has functioned as an all-purpose alternative to whatever quality the present has wished to ascribe to itself. The claim that selfhood becomes problematic only in the Renaissance is a prime instance of this impulse" (8).

9. Elizabeth J. Bellamy, *Translations of Power: Narcissism and the Unconscious in Epic History* (Ithaca: Cornell University Press, 1992), 2–3.

10. Ibid., 5.

11. Ibid.

12. Ibid., 3.

13. Skura,"Understanding," 77.

14. Ibid., 78.

15. Ibid., 83.

"Anthony Easthope has suggested a similarly inclusive approach to the interpretation of literary texts: 'Although the conceptual frameworks of historical materialism and psychoanalysis will remain distinct, resisting a synthesis we have no right to demand, the literary text always produces ideological and phantasy meanings in a simultaneity and both must be considered together as social phantasy: *nec tecum nec sine te* (neither with you nor without you). Any attempt to discuss a poetic text only with attention to one side is reductive and inadequate" [*Poetry and Phantasy* (Cambridge: Cambridge University Press, 1989), 43]. The socially and psychologically produced readings resist the 'synthesis we have no right to demand,' and their relationship will vary from text to text, let alone from period to period. But we can learn from the variability" (ibid., 86).

16. Skura, "Understanding," 89.

17. Ibid., 79.

18. Ibid., 80.

19. Catherine Belsey, "A Future for Materialist Feminist Criticism?" in *The Matter of Difference: Materialist Feminist Criticism of Shakespeare*, ed. Valerie Wayne (Ithaca: Cornell University Press, 1991), 257.

20. Leo Spitzer, "Notes on the Empirical and Poetic 'I' in Medieval Authors," *Traditio* 4 (1946): 414–22.

21. Greenblatt, "Psychoanalysis and Renaissance Culture," 216.

22. Maus, "Proof and Consequences," 34.

23. Ibid.

24. Ibid., 47.

25. Ibid.

26. Ibid.

27. Ibid.

28. Actually, this is not a very good example, as the Queen in *Richard II* is such a minor figure that we see nothing of herself. I bring up this example only to forestall the objection that the distinction I am making is merely generic— the difference between a history play and one that is not taken from history. So, for the sake of argument, if Richard's Queen had been developed in such a way that we might have discussed her concept of selfhood, I would argue that this construction of the female self is significantly different from one representing an historical woman in an imaginative work.

29. *The Complete Poetry of John Donne*, ed. John T. Shawcross (Garden City, N.Y: Anchor, 1967). All quotations from Donne's poems cite this edition.

30. Ibid., 249 n 1.

31. This figure's interiority is arguably the best represented of the personae in "The Canonization," but that is only a relative best. I would love to argue that the observer-figure constitutes an attempt to represent the self, but I think "The Extasie" makes that argument impossible, as the focus is clearly on the two active personae. The observer-figure is a convention of Mannerist art that Donne adapts in a number of his poems.

32. Much of the following discussion appears in my essay, "Anne More Donne: A Name Not Written," in *John Donne's "Desire of More": The Subject of Anne More in His Poetry*, ed. M. Thomas Hester (Delaware: University of Delaware Press, 1996), 89–105.

33. "Donne's Words Taught in Numbers," *Studies in Philology* 84, no. 1 (1987): 44–60; "The Visual Paradigm of 'The Good-Morrow': Donne's Cosmographical Glasse," *The Review of English Studies*, new Ser. 37, 145 (1986): 61–65; "'Here You See Mee': Donne's Autographed Valediction," *The John Donne Journal* 4 (1985): 29–33; "John Donne's 'The Extasie' as an Alchemical Process," *English Language Notes* 20 (1982): 1–8.

34. See John Carey, *John Donne: Life, Mind and Art* (New York: Oxford University Press, 1981); and Thomas Docherty, *John Donne, Undone* (London: Methuen, 1986) to name but two examples.

35. Dennis Flynn, "Donne and a *Female* Coterie," *LIT: Literature and Interpretation Theory* 1 (1989): 127–36.

36. Ibid., 127.

37. Carey, *John Donne*, 74 passim.

38. Arthur Marotti, *John Donne, Coterie Poet* (Madison: University of Wisconsin Press, 1986).

39. Flynn, "Donne and a Female Coterie," 129.

40. Ibid.

41. Joan Kelly, "Early Feminist Theory and the *Querelle des femmes*, 1400–1789," *Signs* 8 (1982): 8.

42. Susan Groag Bell, "Medieval Women Book Owners: Arbiters of Lay Piety and Ambassadors of Culture," in *Women and Power in the Middle Ages*, eds. Mary Erler and Maryanne Kowaleski (Athens: University of Georgia Press, 1988), 166.

43. Antony Grafton and Lisa Jardine, *From Humanism to the Humanities* (Cambridge: Harvard University Press, 1986), 57.

44. Izaak Walton, *The Lives of John Donne, Sir Henry Wotton, Richard Hooker, George Herbert, & Robert Sanderson* (New York: Oxford University Press, 1956), 31.

45. Janet E. Halley, "Textual Intercourse: Anne Donne, John Donne, and the Sexual Poetics of Textual Exchange," in *Seeking the Woman in Late Medieval and Renaissance Writings: Essays in Feminist Contextual Criticism*, ed. Sheila Fisher and Janet E. Halley (Knoxville: University of Tennessee Press, 1989), 187–206.

46. R. C. Bald, *John Donne: A Life* (New York: Oxford University Press, 1970).

47. Halley, "Textual Intercourse," 190.

48. Ibid.

49. Ibid., 196.

50. Ibid., 193.

51. Ibid., 191.

52. Most of the argument about numerology in "A Valediction of My Name, in the Window" appears in my article "'Here You See Me,'" 28–33.

53. Vincent F. Hopper, *Medieval Number Symbolism* (New York: Columbia University Press, 1938), 66.

54. See Julia M. Walker, "John Donne's 'The Extasie' as an Alchemical Process," *English Language Notes* 20 (1982): 1–8; and "Donne's Words Taught in Numbers," *Studies in Philology* 84, no. 1 (1987): 44–60. For Renaissance poets, numbers were a natural repository of concrete meanings and patterns of order from which they could draw isolated references and with which they could frame whole discussions. Numbers, with their constant values, must have seemed particularly reliable points of reference in an age of such great intellectual flux. The fact that numbers could be manipulated in meaningful numerological processes—thus being both constant and in a state of flux, having one value and many values—would have added to their appeal for a poet such as Donne, a poet fascinated by paradoxes and "imagin'd corners" where seemingly disparate bodies of knowledge meet and merge.

55. John Skelton, *Poems*, ed. Richard Hughes (London: William Heinemann, 1924), 178 n.

56. Shawcross, *Complete Poetry of John Donne*, 401 n 49.

57. Alastair Fowler, *Triumphal Forms* (Cambridge: Cambridge University Press, 1970), 3.

58. For an exhaustive study of the significance of 64 in Renaissance poetry, see the following work by Thomas P. Roche Jr.: *Petrarch and the English Sonnet Sequences* (New York: AMS Press, 1989).

59. A. Kent Hieatt, *Short Time's Endless Monument* (New York: Columbia University Press, 1960), 4.

60. This is the favorite point of attack of critics who would disallow any use of numerology because of the impossibility of "proving" which system the poet might be privileging. These critics, in whose rebuttals words and phrases such as

"arbitrary" and "apples and oranges" occur with the predictability of repeating decimals, thus ironically deny in Donne's use of numerological analogues the very qualities of his verse they celebrate in discussions of this other images. Although Dr. Johnson's pejorative "heterogeneous ideas . . . yoked by violence together" has long ceased to be anything by a critical strawman, its condemnation echoes in the lines of those scholars who would limit Donne's metaphysical vision to angels and fleas, compasses and kings. And yet Donne's mixing of numerological systems was less a poetic vision than an intellectual necessity because of the multiple and virtually inseparably intertwining nature of Renaissance numerological doctrines (Walker, "Donne's Words," 47–48 n 5).

61. John Donne, *Catalogus Librorum*, 14, cited by Charles Monroe Coffin, in *John Donne and the New Philosophy* (New York: Humanities Press, 1958), 248.

62. The use of Anne MORE and the mention of rivals in stanza 8 combine to suggest an earlier date for the poem than it is usually assigned (see Shawcross, *Complete Poetry of John Donne*, 413).

CHAPTER 2. THE CHIASMUS OF PERCEPTION

1. Many versions of the Medusa story exist. See Robert Graves, *The Greek Myths* (New York: Penguin, 1957), in which the author collects Medusa references in which the skin of Medusa is made into the aegis of Athene (45); in which her name means "cunning one" (129); in which her blood could raise the dead (175); in which her face had "huge teeth, protruding tongue, and [was] altogether . . . ugly" (239); in which she "was a beautiful daughter of Phorcys, who had offended Athene, and lead the Libyans of Lake Tritonis in battle" (242); and in which "the Gorgon-head is a prophylactic mask, work by . . . priestesses [of the Moon-goddess] to scare away the uninitiated" (244).

In Lucan's *Civil War*, Medusa is never transformed into a monster, but seems to have been one from birth. Furthermore, the snakes on her head are not the source of her horrible power: "These snakes are the only part of ill-fated Medusa that all men may look upon and live. For who ever felt fear of the monster's face and open mouth? Who that looked her straight in the face was suffered by Medusa to die? . . . she had power to threaten sky and sea with strange paralysis, and clothe the world with stone. . . . No living creature could endure to look on her, and even her serpents bent backward to escape her face" (Book 9, lines 634 ff., trans. J. D. Duff, Loeb Classical Library [Cambridge: Harvard University Press, 1962]).

Fulgentius, in his sixth-(?) century *Mythologies*, cites Ovid and Lucan, but provides of gloss rooted in the Christian trinity: "But let me explain what the Greeks, inclined as they are to embroider, would signify by this finely spun fabrication. They intended three Gorgons, that is, the three kinds of terror: the first terror is indeed that which weakens the mind; the second, that which fills the mind with terror; the third, that which not only enforces its purpose upon the mind but also its gloom upon the face," in *Fulgentius The Mythographer*, trans. Leslie George Whitbread (Columbus: Ohio University Press, 1971), 62.

In *Concerning Famous Women*, Giovanni Boccaccio uses Hyginus' *Fabularum Liber* as a source to refute the horrific tale of Ovid, and presents Medusa as a beautiful woman whose only problem was her success:

Her hair was golden and abundant, her face was of special beauty, and her body properly tall and straight. Among other things, her eyes had such great and pleasant force that if she looked kindly at someone, he remained almost motionless and beside himself . . . she not only preserved her wealth with marvelous shrewdness but greatly augmented it, so that those who knew her believed that she surpassed all the western kings in wealth. . . . Her fame reached Greece, where Perseus, the most excellent among the young men of Achaea, heard these reports and became desirous of seeing that beautiful woman and taking her treasure (trans. Guido A. Guarino [New Brunswick: Rutgers University Press, 1963], 43).

In the English Renaissance, Ovid's version in *Metamorphoses* (translated by Golding in the 1560s) was the most influential, and—although I will discuss the idea of a beautiful Medusa in the Eve chapter—it is Ovid's version to which I make primary reference in this study. I am grateful to my former research assistant, Sarah Pagano (SUNY-Geneseo class of 1991), for the excellent work she did on this topic.

See also: Hazel E. Barnes "The Look of the Gorgon" in *The Meddling Gods: four essays on classical themes* (Lincoln: University of Nebraska Press, 1974) 1–51. Barnes summarizes modern uses of Medusa story by Freud, Sçndor Ferenczi, Jean-Paul Sartre, R. D. Laing, Willa Cather, and John Barth in addition to citing a number of works by scholars of the classics, such as Jane Harrison's *Prolegomena to the Study of Greek Religion* (New York: Meridian Books, 1955), 187–97. Barnes tells us that "Harrison concludes that the Gorgon is the incarnation of the Evil Eye" but counters that argument with one of her own: "It is not accurate to identify the Gorgon and the Evil Eye. The latter is more inclusive. . . . Medusa represents its oldest and purest form. She is the spiteful stare incarnate. We might say that the fear of her is the inverse side of wish fulfillment. 'If looks could kill . . .' we often hear. Medusa's could," 7.

See also: Thalia Feldman, "Gorgon and the Origins of Fear," *Arion* 4 no. 3 (Autumn 1965) 484–93, in which the author connects the Gorgon to the martriarchal period of Greek mythic culture.

See also: Marina Warner, *Monuments and Maidens: The Allegory of the Female Form* (New York: Atheneum, 1985) 108–14. She summaries the classical sources and analyzes some modern commentaries, pointing out that: "Medusa is filled with ambiguous potency: she is both death-dealing [the freezing stare] and capable of bringing forth miraculously [the birth of Pegasus]," 112. Warner locates the development of this duality in Euripides' drama *Ion*, "where Creusa the heroine had inherited from her ancestor . . . two drops of Gorgon blood, one that kills and one that heals," 113.

    2. Ludovico Ariosto, *Orlando Furioso*, vol. 2, canto 35, stanza 28, lines 1–2, 4–5, trans. Barbara Reynolds (New York: Penguin, 1987.) All quotations from the poem cite this edition.

    3. Francis Quarles, *Emblemes* (London, 1635), in *An Index of Icons in English Emblem Books 1500–1700*, ed. Huston Diehl (Oklahoma: Oklahoma University Press, 1986), 84. The entire emblem reads as follows:

MOTTO. "Sic decipit orbis."
ICON. Cupid looks into a glass which is the shape of the world and which reflects his image; Divine Love, behind the mirror, looks into a small glass.
EPIGRAM. The glass of the world deceives, making a man look larger and fairer than he is; the grace of God, however, shrinks men's shadows.

4. Virgil, *The Aeneid of Virgil*, trans. Allen Mandelbaum (New York: Bantam, 1985), lines 491–92, p. 93.

5. Publius Ovidius Naso, *Metamorphoses*, ed. and trans. Frank Justice Miller for the Loeb Classical Library (Cambridge: Harvard University Press, 1984). All quotations and translations of this text cite this edition.

6. Marina Warner develops this paradox by teasing out the complex symbolism of the serpents.

> The transformation potency of the dead Gorgon originates with Athena in part: if it was Athena who set the snakes, symbols of regeneration, on Medusa's head, then when Athena clamps the dread mask on her breast, she takes back a power she herself bestowed. But the combined figure Athena/Medusa also represents a solution to the fundamental theme of origins, a reply to the eternal question that much exercised the Greeks: who is more important, the mother or the father? With regard to lineage, Medusa stands to mothers as Athena stands to fathers, and Medusa's subordination to the Athenian goddess signals a predominant bias to accept that purity of descent can be more reliably traced through a male than a female line. . . . Medusa's head represents the womb as patrimony (113–14).

7. Graves, *Greek Myths*, 127.

8. As limited and limiting as I find Freud's brief essay on Medusa, it needs to be mentioned here because he does fall into the same paradigm of representation as does Ovid: his analysis is that of the male gazer discussing the effects of the male gazing at the female object. In " The Medusa's Head," in *The Standard Edition of the Complete Psychological Works of Sigmund Freud*, vol. 18, ed. and trans. James Strachey et al. (London: Hogarth Press, 1955), Freud makes the following observations:

> The terror of Medusa is thus a terror of castration that is linked to the sight of something . . . it occurs when a boy, who has hitherto been unwilling to believe the threat of castration, catches sight of the female genitals, probably those of an adult, surrounded by hair, and essentially those of his mother.
>
> The hair upon Medusa's head is frequently represented in works of art in the form of snakes, and these once again are derived from the castration complex. It is a remarkable fact that, however frightening they may be in themselves, they nevertheless serve actually as a mitigation of the horror, for they replace the penis, the absence of which is the cause of the horror. This is a confirmation of the technical rule according to which a multiplication of penis symbols signifies castration.
>
> The sight of Medusa's head makes the spectator stiff with terror, turns him to stone . . . becoming stiff means an erection. Thus, in the original situation it offers consolation to the spectator: he is still in possession of a penis, and the stiffening reassures him of the fact.
>
> This symbol of horror is worn upon her dress by the virgin goddess Athene. And rightly so, for thus she becomes a woman who is unapproachable and repels all sexual desires—since she displays the terrifying genitals of the Mother. Since the Greeks were in the main strongly homosexual, it was inevitable that we should find among them a representation of woman as a being who frightens and repels because she is castrated (273–74).

9. The medieval tradition of the beautiful Medusa, which I will discuss later, is both a rationalization and a romantization of the Ovidian paradigm. As John Freccero observes in an essay on Dante's use of the Medusa story: "In mythology, the Medusa was said to be powerless against women, for it was her feminine *beauty* that constituted the mortal threat to her admirers. From the ancient *Phys-*

iologus through the mythographers to Boccaccio, the Medusa represented a sensual/fascination, a *pulchritudo* so excessive that it turned men to stone." "Medusa: The Letter and the Spirit," *Yearbook of Italian Studies* 2 (1972) 7–8.

10. Erwin R. Goodenough, *Jewish Symbols in the Greco-Roman Period,* vol. 8 (Bollingen Foundation, 1958), 224 ff. See also vol. 7, 61–63 passim.

11. Tobin Siebers, *The Mirror of Medusa* (Berkeley: University of California Press, 1983), 24.

12. Freud, "Medusa's Head," 273–74.

13. The canonical answer to that question seems to be "Yes." See Graves's notes: "J. E. Harrison rightly described the story of Athene's birth from Zeus's head as 'a desperate theological expedient to rid her of her matriarchal conditions'" ("Greek Myths," 46).

14. Siebers, *Mirror of Medusa,* 26.

15. The best example I've found of this complex nexus of priorities is James Maxwell's *Queen Elizabeth's Looking-glass of Grace and Glory* (1612). Addressed to Princess Elizabeth, daughter of James I, and nominally lauding her father's predecessor, Maxwell's text is actually dedicated to the glorification of Queen Mary Stuart. See the notes of the Cleopatra essay for more details.

In *Orlando Furioso,* Ariosto is less cautious.

Canto 35

25

> Aeneas was not so pious, nor so strong
> Achilles was, as they are famed to be;
> Hector was less ferocious; and a throng
> Of Heroes could surpass them, but we see
> Their valour and their deeds enhanced in song
> For their descendants had so lavishly
> Rewarded poets for their eulogies
> With gifts of villas, farm-lands, palaces.

26

> Not so beneficent Augustus was
> As Virgil's epic clarioun proclaimed.
> His taste in poetry must be the cause
> Why his proscriptions were left uncondemned.
> No one would know of Nero's unjust laws,
> Nor would he for his cruelties be famed
> (Though he had been by Heaven and earth reviled)
> If writers he had wooed and reconciled.

27

> Homer makes Agamemnon win the war;
> The Trojans cowardly and weak he show.
> Although the suitors so persistent are,
> Penelope is faithful to her spouse.
> But if for truth you are particular,
> Like this, quite in reverse, the story goes:
> The Greeks defeated, Troy victorious,
> And chaste Penelope notorious.

28

> Consider Dido; she, whose heart was pure,
> Was faithful to Sichaeus to the end;
> But she is thought by all to be a whore,
> Because Vergillius was not her friend.
> And do not be amazed that I deplore

The fate of writers and on them expend
So many words: I love them, and I do
But pay my debt: I was a writer too

29

Reward above all others I have won,
Which neither Time nor Death can take from me,
Which I was justly granted by the Son
Whom I so praised, as was my destiny
And now I grieve for those whose course is run
In times ungenerous, when Courtesy
Has shut the door, and writers, lean and pale,
Beat on it night and day, to no avail.

30

And so there is no cause to be amazed
If poets and if scholars now are few;
For where there is no pasture to be grazed,
Nor shelter, such as a terrain beasts eschew.
As the Disciple spoke, his eyes so blazed,
That like two fires of righteous wrath they grew.
Then with a smile he turned towards the duke.
Serene, no longer troubled, was his look.

Ariosto could hardly expect Alfonso or Ippolito d'Este to find that passage amusing, set as it is in the context of an dynastic epic supposedly glorifying their family. Perhaps, as one of my students suggested, he did not expect them to read to canto 35.

16. "You only have to look at the Medusa straight on to see her. And she's not deadly. She's beautiful and she's laughing" (Hélène Cixous, "The Laugh of the Medusa," *Signs* 1 [1976]: 885).

17. Tin was used in both the early mirrors of polished metal and in the looking glasses of the Renaissance. In *The Mirror and Man* (Charlottesville: University Press of Virginia, 1985) Benjamin Goldberg tells us that the "Romans used a white bronze alloy richer in tin than Etruscans or Greeks. They added a hard, silvery-white reflecting surface by hot-tinning the bronze surface. This consisted of laying a very thin sheet of tin over the face of the bronze mirror and heating the combination by fire to diffuse the tin directly into the underlying surface of bronze and form a bright reflecting surface" (108). He goes on the explain the more complicated process of making glass mirrors, recounting the early success of mirror-craft in Venice:

This came about in 1507 when Andrea and Domenico d'Anzolo del Gallo, who knew or perhaps discovered for themselves the tin amalgam process and combined it with the new Venetian glass to produce mirrors far better than those ever seen before [*sic*]. . . . The success of the marriage of crystalline glass to the tin amalgam process was enormous. . . . The success of the tin amalgam process, also known as mirror foiling, which dominated the manufacture of mirrors for over three-hundred years, lies in its ability to be applied to glass of almost any size. And, more important, it could be produced and applied without heat (140).

Goldberg goes on to detail the process.

18. Ritamary Bradley, "Backgrounds of the Title *Speculum* in Medieaval Literature," *Speculum* 29 (1954): 100. See also Herbert Grabes's exhaustive study of mirror-titles, *The Mutable Glass* (Cambridge: Cambridge University Press, 1982).

19. See Jenijoy LaBelle, *Herself Beheld: The Literature of the Looking Glass* (Ith-

aca: Cornell University Press, 1988) in which the author, overlooking the gender
of Narcissus, argues: "What women do with mirrors is clearly distinct from and
physically more important than what men do with mirrors in their pursuit of
generally utilitarian goals. . . . Men look at their faces and their bodies, but
what they *are* is another matter entirely—ultimately a transcendental concept of
self. . . . [but] women explore the reaches of the mirror for what they really are,"
(9). LaBelle states early on that her theories of mirror-gazing as "a key to some
of the distinctions, social and psychological, between men and women" is "particularly . . . portrayed in the literature of the last one hundred and fifty years"
(2). Herein lies the weakness of her argument, for to speak of the representations
of masculine and feminine selfhood "which underlie a great deal of Western
thought" by considering closely the only works of the last century and a half is
to build one's house on very brittle foundations. In her brief discussions of
Renaissance texts, LaBelle consistently misreads both Milton (68, passim) and
Shakespeare (179). Her readings of her self-defined area of expertise are acute,
but can hardly be seen as a study of the foundations of Western thought.

For a more astute evaluation of the importance of the mirror in Western
thought, see Theodore Ziolkowski, *Disenchanted Images: A Literary Iconology*
(Princeton: Princeton University Press, 1977); see also Goldberg, *Mirror and
Man,* an interesting history of mirrors, divided into two sections: the mirror
turned toward man, touching his psyche and contributing to his superstitions,
and the mirror turned away from man as an "impersonal implement of science
and technology" (xii). Goldberg, however, is even weaker in his knowledge of
Renaissance texts than is LaBelle (e.g., he states that Spenser's Merlin gives a
magic mirror to King Arthur who is Britomart's father [10]). For a study of the
mirror as a literary device in Renaissance poetry, see Louis R. Zocca, *Elizabethan
Narrative Poetry* (New Brunswick: Rutgers University Press, 1950).

20. Graves, in his summary of the legend, says that Narcissus "had a stubborn
pride in his own beauty" ("Greek Myths," 286).

21. Guillaume de Loris and Jean de Meun, *The Romance of the Rose,* trans.
Charles Dahlberg (Hanover: University Press of New England, 1983), 50. All
quotations from this poem cite this edition.

22. William D. Reynolds, "Sources, Nature, and Influence of the *Ovidius Moralizatus* of Pierre Bersuire," in *The Mythographic Art: Classical Fable and the Rise of
the Vernacular in Early France and England,* ed. Jane Chance (Gainesville: University of Florida Press, 1990), 85.

23. *Three Ovidian Tales of Love,* trans. and ed. Raymond Cormier, vol. 26, ser.
A, Garland Library of Medieval Literature (New York: Garland Publishing,
1986), 135.

24. Jeanne A. Nightingale, "From Mirror to Metamorphosis: Echos of Ovid's
Narcissus in Chrétien's *Erec et Enide,*" in *Mythographic Art,* 47–82. Nightingale,
however, takes a much more benign view of these revisions than I am arguing.
Citing Edward Kennard Rand's 1924 study *Ovid and his influence* (reprint, New
York: Longmans, Green, 1928), she downplays the specific influence of Chris-
tian/Pauline morality on these revisions:

"Chrétien shared with Ovid a belief in the underlying universality of myth and the duty
of each successive generation of poets to adapt its antiquated forms to the idiom of
their own times, and to revive and transmit its eternal message. As Rand expressed it,
'The past is plastic in the author's hands. It is the same process that ran rigorous course
in the Hellenistic age of Greek literature and culminated in Ovid himself. He was the
first of the medieval romancers. He would have enjoyed seeing his stories . . . extracted

from their context and retold in what to the Medieval author seemed a modern way'
(125).

I think that both Nightingale and Rand are skirting the issue of substantive
revision representing polemical poetics. To say that Ovid revised the Greeks and
that the medieval writers revised Ovid is a long way from making the case for
Ovid as the"first of the medieval romancers" who would have "enjoyed" what
Franciscans and other wandering moralizers did with his textual authority.

Nightingale continues: "In an age when the inner life of the individual was
being subjected to scrutiny both inside and outside the monastery, the experience of Narcissus stood as the paradigm of the problematic quest for self-
knowledge through love" (52). No argument here, but I would push on to suggest that the Narcissus tale was more often used in this context to argue for the
dangers inherent in the recognition of the individual and even more specifically
against the recognition of the individual in relation to woman than to make any
other point.

25. Nightingale, "From Mirror to Metamorphosis," 57.

26. Ibid., 59–60.

27. Ibid., 65–66.

28. Philippa Berry, *Of Chastity and Power: Elizabethan Literature and the Unmarried Queen* (London: Routledge, 1989), 2.

29. In Ovid, even Echo does not die because of Narcissus. Before she ever
sees him she has been transformed by the wrath of Saturnia into one who cannot
initiate speech. After the death of Narcissus, she loses human form but still
remains an echoing voice. I'm certainly not arguing that she is unaffected by
her love for Narcissus, but the cause and effect relationship is far from that of
a gaze turning the gazer into instant stone.

30. Ziolkowski argues that man's "perennial fascination with mirrors had produced at least three familiar metaphors that are culturally significant but not
magic in our sense of the word: the mirror of art, the mirror of God, and the
mirror of man" (*Disenchanted Images*, 150). In relation to the first, "the mirror
remains a simile, or, at most, a metaphor; it has no real existence as an image
but exists only as a figure of speech. Shakespeare's dramas are in no literal sense
a mirror, anymore than Stendhal's novels or the creations of Plato's artist. These
creations may be like a mirror, for better or worse; but they are not mirrors"
(152). He continues: "A second important mirror-metaphor in Western thought
descends from Plato and the Bible by way of Christian Platonism. This syncretic
analogy, which was first publicized by Augustine and his commentators, is based
principally on two passages in the New Testament [1 Cor. 13:12 and James
1:23–24]. Relying principally on these two texts, which they combined with ideas
loosely adapted from Platonism, medieval Christian theologians developed the
mirror-analogy into three rhetorical topoi. Man's soul is a mirror in which God
is reflected; Holy Scripture is a mirror that reflects the truth of God; and,
negatively, man's mind is a mirror that reflects the illusory world of these
senses" (152).

31. World folklore, Ziolkowski points out, "is full of mirrors that are conspicu-
ously magical." According to Ziolkowski, folklorists "divide magic mirrors into
two categories: cognizant . . . and causative" (*Disenchanted Images*, 162). "A quick
glance at the *Motif-Index of Folk-Literature* (Bloomington: Indiana University
Press, 1955) reveals dozens of legends concerning clairvoyant mirrors and transforming mirrors, mirrors that render the viewer invisible or that rejuvenate him,

mirrors that cause blindness or in which the devil appears, mirrors that answer questions and that make wishes come true, mirrors that turn black or that reveal hidden treasures" (158).

32. Ziolkowski, *Disenchanted Images,* 162–63. "Whereas the catoptromantic mirror tends to remain at the level of a minor motif, the doubling and the penetrable mirror easily develop into symbolic images: of the self and of an alternative world-model" (ibid., 163). He continues: "Evidence suggests that the belief in magic mirrors was quite extensive during the Middle Ages. The medieval passion for order, which systematized all existing knowledge into encyclopedias, also applied itself to magic, including the so-called *magia specularia*. In his *Polycraticus* (1159), for instance, John of Salisbury described the various techniques of the *specularii*, those who practice divination by means of reflecting surfaces. Any competent sorcerer was expected to be able to make a magic mirror, and every really important ruler was reputed to own one" (ibid.).

Citing a variety of examples from modern literature (from Hawthorne to Wagner to "Beauty and the Beast"), he concludes: "In all these representative cases the catoptromantic mirror of folklore has been appropriated as a requisite for literary purposes, but it seems to have no deeper meaning: its function, in the works that accept magic as a convention, is simply to reveal certain information. In the other cases it supplies little but atmosphere" (ibid., 168). While I find Ziolkowski's categories and definitions useful, I profoundly disagree with this conclusion.

33. We find this both in the Medusa interpolation in the *Romance of the Rose* and in the final lyrics of Petrarch's *Rime Sparse*. I will discuss this tradition in the chapter on Eve.

34. *Alcibiades,* in *The Dialogues of Plato,* vol. 1, trans. B. Jowett (Oxford: Oxford University Press, 1964), 670.

35. Ibid., 671.

36. Neil Hertz, "Medusa's Head: Male Hysteria under Political Pressure," *Representations* 4 (fall 1983): 27.

37. Ibid.

38. Ibid., 40.

39. Joel Fineman, "More about 'Medusa's Head'," *Representations* 4 (fall 1983): 55–72.

40. Madelon Gohlke. "'I wooed the with my sword': Shakespeare's Tragic Paradigms," in *Representing Shakespeare: New Psychoanalytic Essays,* ed. Murray M. Schwartz and Coppélia Kahn (Baltimore: Johns Hopkins University Press, 1980), 170.

CHAPTER 3. ELIZABETH IS BRITOMART IS ELIZABETH:
THIS SEX WHICH IS NOT WON

1. Ibid., 91.

2. Ibid., 96.

3. Much of the material in this essay appears in my essay "Spenser's Elizabeth Portrait and the Fiction of Dynastic Epic," *Modern Philology* 90, no. 2 (1992): 172–99.

4. Sir Roy Strong, *Gloriana: The Portraits of Queen Elizabeth I* (German Democratic Republic: Thames and Hudson, 1987), 11. This is a revised edition of

Strong's 1963 *Portraits of Queen Elizabeth I* and constitutes the single most exhaustive study of the topic. See also Strong's valuable study *The Cult of Elizabeth: Elizabethan Portraiture and Pageantry* (Berkeley: University of California Press, 1977); on the same topic, see Robin Headlam Wells's synthesis of received opinion: *Spenser's Faerie Queene and the Cult of Elizabeth* (Totowa, N.J.: Barnes & Noble, 1983). See also Jonathan Goldberg's discussions of several Elizabeth portraits in *Endlesse Worke: Spenser and the Structures of Discourse* (Baltimore: Johns Hopkins University Press, 1981), and the sometimes imaginative essay of Andrew Belsey and Catherine Belsey: "Icons of Divinity: Portraits of Elizabeth I," in *Renaissance Bodies: The Human Figure in English Culture c. 1540–1660*, ed. Lucy Gent and Nigel Llewellyn (London: Reaktion Books, 1990), 11–35. Belsey uses "The Allegory of the Tudor Succession" as a set piece for her argument in "Richard Levin and Indifferent Reading" in that cluster of essays in *New Literary History* 21 (spring 1990): 449–56. There is a fine selection of color plates of the Elizabeth portraits in Elizabeth W. Pomeroy's semiotic gloss on the work of Strong and Frances Yates: *Reading the Portraits of Queen Elizabeth I* (Hamden, Conn.: Archon Books, 1989). For an excellent study of the cultural context of the portraits, see Clark Hulse, *The Rule of Art: Literature and Painting in the Renaissance* (Chicago: University of Chicago Press, 1990) especially 115–56. Lowell Gallagher, in *Medusa's Gaze: Casuistry and Conscience in the Renaissance* (Stanford: Stanford University Press, 1991) uses the Siena/Sieve portrait in relation to the Faerie Queene to illustrate his complex argument about public and private conscience in Elizabethan politics, 126 ff.

Four studies that concentrate on the ideology underlying the various representations of Elizabeth are Philippa Berry's *Of Chastity and Power: Elizabethan Literature and the Unmarried Queen* (London: Routledge, 1989); Susan Frye's *Elizabeth I: The Competition for Representation* (Oxford: Oxford University Press, 1993); Carole Levin's *Heart and Stomach of a King: Elizabeth I and the Politics of Sex and Power* (Philadelphia: University of Pennsylvania Press, 1994); and Helen Hackett's *Virgin Mother, Maiden Queen: Elizabeth I and the Cult of the Virgin Mary* (New York: St. Martin's, 1995).

5. Constance Jordan, "Representing Political Androgyny: More on the Siena Portrait of Queen Elizabeth I," in *The Renaissance Englishwoman in Print: Counterbalancing the Canon*, ed. Anne M. Haselkorn and Betty S. Travitsky (Amherst: University of Massachusetts Press, 1990), 157–76. At the 1988 meeting of the Shakespeare Association of America, Joel Fineman discussed the "Rainbow" portrait, arguing that Elizabeth's dress is covered not only with eyes and ears but with vaginas. Roy Strong discusses both portraits in *Gloriana*. See also Marina Warner, "The Sieve of Tuccia," in *Monuments and Maidens: The Allegory of the Female Form* (New York: Atheneum, 1985) especially 244.

6. Edmund Spenser, *The Faerie Queene*, ed. A. C. Hamilton (New York: Longman, 1977); all quotations from the poem cite this edition.

7. David Lee Miller, *The Poem's Two Bodies: The Poetics of the 1590 Faerie Queene* (Princeton: Princeton University Press, 1988), 151. See 147–53 for an excellent discussion of the etymology of "portrait" in Spenser's representation of Gloriana and Elizabeth.

8. In the *Diary of John Manningham of the Middle Temple, and of Braddbourne, Kent, Barrister-at-Law, 1603–1608*, edited from the original manuscript by John Bruce, Esq., and presented to the Camden Society by William Tite, Esq., M.P., F.R.S., F.S.A., president of the society, (Westminster: Printed by J. B. Nichols and Sons, 1868). The entry is for 12 February 1602, which seems odd as Hatton

died in 1591; but there is no explanation, nor does he record which representation Elizabeth preferred.

9. Louis Adrian Montrose, "The Elizabethan Subject and the Spenserian Text," in *Literary Theory/Renaissance Texts*, eds. Patricia Parker and David Quint (Baltimore: Johns Hopkins University Press, 1986), 325. In relation to this problem of representation, Stephen Greenblatt argues: "It is art whose status is questioned by Spenser, not ideology; indeed, art is questioned precisely to spare ideology that internal distantiation it undergoes in the work of Shakespeare or Marlowe. In *The Faerie Queene* reality as given by ideology always lies safely outside the bounds of art, in a different realm, distant, infinitely powerful, perfectly good" (*Renaissance Self-Fashioning: From More to Shakespeare* [Chicago: University of Chicago Press, 1980], 192).

10. See Sheila T. Cavanagh's *Wanton Eyes and Chaste Desires: Female Sexuality in The Faerie Queene* (Bloomington: Indiana University Press, 1994) in which she expands upon this point: "Like the queen she partially figures, Britomart symbolizes many qualities which she only tangentially manifests and which defy realization by ordinary women. . . . Like Elizabeth, Britomart is an improbable woman illustrating an improbable role" (140). Cavanagh concludes, however, by acknowledging that "real women could not emulate Britomart any more than they could model themselves after Elizabeth does not matter in the long run" (152).

11. The distinction I am making here is set forth in more detail in Gerard Genette's *Narrative Discourse* (Ithaca: Cornell University Press, 1980). I am indebted to Mary Nyquist's use of this distinction in her excellent article "The Genesis of Gendered Subjectivity in the Divorce Tracts and in *Paradise Lost*," in *Re-Membering Milton*, ed. Nyquist and Margaret W. Ferguson (New York: Methuen, 1987), 99–127.

12. See Frances Yates, *Astraea: The Imperial Theme in the Sixteenth Century* (London: Routledge and Kegan Paul, 1975). In her analysis of the "Sieve" portrait of Elizabeth, Yates points out that of a series of ten medallions on a column in the picture's background, one "shows an imperial crown" while the other nine "tell the story of Dido and Aeneas in little scenes" (115). After summarizing the scenes depicted in the medallions, Yates connects the Roman story with the English queen.

> The column thus tells the story of Pious Aeneas, the Trojan ancestor, through Brut, of the British imperial line of which Pious Elizabeth is the descendant. The little scenes on the medallions tell of his love for Dido, from which he extricated himself and sailed piously away, whilst she succumbed to the Triumph of Love and perished on the funeral pyre. The extraordinarily elaborate and ingenious allusion seems to be that, unlike Dido, the chaste descendant of Aeneas has achieved a Triumph of Chastity and wears the imperial crown of pure empire. She is Gloriana, the empress of the pure imperial reform, combined with Belphoebe, the chaste Petrarchan lady." (115)

See also Lucy Gent, *Picture and Poetry, 1560–1620: Relations between Literature and the Visual Arts in the English Renaissance* (Leamington Spa: James Hall, 1981). Gent argues that it

> is no surprise, therefore, that English poets, eager to assert themselves as peers of Continental artists, makers and creators such as Sidney described, imitated the fictive stand of painting in a variety of ways, whether they were writing sonnets, epic, or Ovidian narrative such as *Venus and Adonis*. *The Faerie Queene* is the embodiment of the

theory put forward by Sidney. Spenser uses the speaking picture of poesy to create feigned images of virtue, vices and so on, which give pleasure and at the same time, because they illuminate the "imaginative and judging power," are more profitable than the prosaic and even historically true examples of philosophy and history. He also constructs the whole poem, as many critics have pointed out, around contrasts of light and shade so that it is like a vast well-shadowed picture, for the contrasts attach to truly pictorial effects (like Una laying aside her stole). . . . Spenser's pictorial effects increase enormously the life and appeal of the poem, offering the reader a freedom of vision (and the necessity for choice) which would be denied him if the poet's visual language was only that of the emblem. It is rather ironic that Spenser, whose main subject is arguably the error of illusion, or delusion, should nevertheless display an art which depends considerably on illusion, though doubtless *The Faerie Queene* would be a closed book today if he had not done so. (46–47)

13. Elizabeth J. Bellamy, "The Vocative and the Vocational: The Unreadability of Elizabeth in *The Faerie Queene*," *ELH* 54 (1987): 1. Bellamy expands the statement: "Even as Arthur's search for Gloriana informs the structure of *The Faerie Queene*, we may surely go one step further and claim Spenser's parallel, and equally futile, search for Elizabeth as the epic's ultimate quest" (3). Bellamy is right to compare the two quests, and provides an excellent discussion of the strategies Spenser takes to avoid naming Elizabeth; I differ with her judgment that these devices constitute a series of "futile" failures.

14. In support of this argument, I would like, briefly, to examine one of the instances in which Britomart defers her fictive destiny as a dynastic mother and to examine it in relation to a poem, "On Monsieur's Departure," by Elizabeth. In book 4, canto 6, Britomart meets Artegall face-to-face and (although she has just acquitted herself honorably in anonymous battle) immediately begins to manifest symptoms of feminine weakness as significant as those in canto 2 of book 3. Not only does Britomart go all over girlish at the sight of Artegall, but when she "heard the name of *Artegall*, / Her hart did leape, and all her hartstrings tremble, / For sudden joy, and secret feare withall" (29.1–3). This "secret feare," when discussed at all, is generally read as fear of sex, an interpretation that I don't wish to discount, but rather to amplify by suggesting that it may also be fear of losing her male empowerment. Britomart's initial illness in book 3 was generated by the vision of the male "Other" that she wished to become but was not. Between her meeting with Merlin and this sight of Artegall, Britomart has be granted a gender reprieve, a space and time in which she can function as a man while seeking out her female destiny. Since her initial anxiety was not really assuaged, but merely displaced by the quest for Artegall, it's not surprising that it resurfaces here as "secret feare."

Now let us examine the first stanza of Elizabeth's poem.

> I grieve and dare not show my discontent.
> I love and yet am forced to seem to hate.
> I do, yet dare not say I ever meant.
> I seem stark mute but inwardly to prate.
>   I am and not, I freeze and yet am burned.
>   Since from myself another self I turned.

Much of the rhetoric—"love . . . hate," "mute . . . prate," "freeze . . . burn"—is standard Petrarchan posturing; but consider the last line of the stanza: "Since from myself another self I turned." Seeing the man who she turned away (notice she claims the active role) as "another self," Elizabeth acknowledges that a permanent alliance with a man would change "myself" into "another," into another of altered identity and possibly of altered power. What Elizabeth's line describes, Spenser's Britomart figures forth. When faced with Artegall, Britomart becomes another self: meek, humble, soft, fearful. But this diminishment, like her book 3 illness, is temporary. Britomart recovers, but never stabilizes. We see her, even in book 5, in a state of becoming, not of being.

15. This parallel of the Virgilian pattern extends to the content of the cantos, with III. ii of Spenser's poem mirroring the siege and fall of a city by presenting the collapse of Britomart and III. ii presenting an unresolved journey toward a new future.

16. When Britomart appears in III. i, the narrator describes the "secret power unseen" (7.8) of her spear, a weapon of which only the Palmer knows the "secret vertue" (10.5). Britomart—whose true identity is also a secret from all except the reader (via the narrator) and Glauce—does not acknowledge the secret power of her weapons; she took them from her father's church because they were "for her purpose fit" (III iii 60.9) but she never publicly explains their efficacy. The appearance of Florimel, whose story is at that point a secret from the reader, catapults Guyon and those who witness his defeat by Britomart into action and out of the immediate narrative. With all of the emphasis on various uses of the word "secret," I find it difficult to avoid thinking of the term in relation to the proem of book 3 where Britomart is offered as the unspoken—the secret—mirror of Elizabeth.

17. While, as we are later told, Britomart possesses a knowledge of Ovid that makes her failure to read the tapestries even more telling, it is worth noting that the Venus and Adonis story here is somewhat closer to Shakespeare's version than to Ovid's—certainly it is more overtly sexual. I would not, however, go as far as Elizabeth J. Bellamy's claim that "in a maternal display of erotic necrophilia. . . . Venus lovingly cleanses the wound of her Adonis" in the same way that Marinells' mother, Cymoenet, "almost erotically wipes 'the jelly blood ; From th' orifice' (4.440.6–7), less a tender image of maternal healing than an elaborate realization of male castration anxiety" (*Translations of Power: Narcissism and the Unconscious in Epic History* [Ithaca: Cornell University Press, 1992], 198).

18. Bellamy, *Translations of Power*, 197.

19. See John B. Bender's discussion of the narrative framing in this episode in *Spenser and Literary Pictorialism* (Princeton: Princeton University Press, 1972), 98–100.

20. See Kenneth Gross's illuminating discussion of the mirror and its relation to Arthur's shield in *Spenserian Poetics: Idolatry, Iconoclasm, and Magic* (Ithaca: Cornell University Press, 1985), 145 ff.

21. Bellamy, *Translations of Power*, 203.

22. See Ziolkowski's discussion of mirror traditions in the notes to the second chapter.

23. As I discuss in the introduction, I am not anteriorizing the vocabulary of modern theory, but merely giving credit for the awareness of the concept.

24. When Britomart sees this image of Artegall, an image that provides an external focus for her vague thoughts of marriage, the inscription linking him to Achilles seems out of place. Wouldn't the logical association be with Aeneas? No; Britomart herself will become an Aeneas figure. The allusion to the dead Achilles, moreover, suggests a pattern for reading Britomart's response to the vision. In book 11 of the *Odyssey* Odysseus learns from the shade of the dead Achilles that he should alter his goals and values. Achilles tells the crafty sailor

that, far from wanting to be the world's greatest hero, he should realize that it is better to be a slave and alive than to be the greatest of dead heroes. As this speech of Achilles changes the way Odysseus looks at the rest of his life, so does the vision of Artegall/Achilles change Britomart. That Turnus is called "a new Achilles" in book 6 of Virgil's *Aeneid* may also have some signifincance here; certainly it would explain Britomart's preception of Artegall as an enemy.

25. These intrusive parenthetical markers of discourse appear at interesting points in the poem—Una's first conversation with Arthur in book 1 and Britomart's first encounter with Arthegall in book 4, to name but two. They are not necessary, as the punctuation indicates the shift to dialogue, so I would suggest that Spenser uses them to call attention to the passages as exchanges too important to be delivered in third-person narration.

26. See the discussion of the puns on "dismayd" in the section on Isis Church.

27. See Pamela Joseph Benson, *The Invention of the Renaissance Woman: The Challenge of Female Independence in the Literature and Thought of Italy and England* (University Park: Pennsylvania State University Press, 1992) in which Benson places Britomart in the context of the defenses of women and of other epics. Although I differ with many of Benson's arguments, she points out that in Britomart we are given a more complex figure of woman than in the Italian epics: "Britomart does not get off so easily as Marfisa, who never has to face up to her physiological difference from men" (269). She further argues: "Although the ladies seem comparable, Britomart is not the same kind of woman as Bradamante; she is a refutation of her, of the case for women made in the Italian poem, and thus, of the Italian humanist notion of the equality (sameness), of the sexes" (257).

28. See Barbara J. Bono, *Literary Transvaluation: From Vergilian Epic to Shakespearean Tragicomedy* (Berkeley: University of California Press, 1984), 61–77 for a discussion of what she calls the Venus-within-Diana paradigm of Dido used by Spenser to represent Elizabeth. In his discussion of the Sieve portrait Jonathan Goldberg argues: "even though she [Elizabeth] is in the position of Dido in the painting, her destiny fulfills the model of Aeneas" (156).

29. Virgil, *The Aeneid*, eds. J. B. Greenough and G. L. Kittredge (Boston: Ginn and Company, 1895).

30. Bono seems to suggest that Glauce is a sort of failed Anna (*Literary Transvaluation*, 76). Since Bono begins with the Virgilian model and seeks to find remakings of it in Renaissance texts, she overlooks the more simple implications of analogy that the Britomart/Glauce/Dido/Anna paradigm offers to the reader.

31. For a discussion of Spenser's use of Virgil in connection with the Britomart narrative, see Mihoko Suzuki, "'Unfitly Yokt Together in One Term': Vergil and Ovid in *Faerie Queene*, III.ix," *ELR* 17 (1987): 172–85. See also Gross, *Spenserian Poetics*, 154.

32. Thomas Greene implies that Britomart's descent into the underworld may be more complicated than the act of simple imitation would allow. See *The Light in Troy* (New Haven: Yale University Press, 1983), 237. Bono takes quite a different view of the descent, however. "Britomart's feminine epic quest differs pervasively in tone from its Vergilian model. . . . One need only to contrast the amusingly archaic fairy-tale terrors that surround Merlin with the real horror of Aeneas's descent" (77). While Britomart's descent is not as horror-filled as that of Aeneas, I disagree with Bono about Spenser writing "tongue in cheek" (77).

33. Cavanagh, *Wanton Eyes and Chaste Desires*, 152.

34. This definition is from the publisher's notes to Luce Irigaray's *This Sex*

Which Is Not One, trans. Catherine Porter and Carolyn Burke (Ithaca: Cornell University Press, 1985), 220.

35. Benson's discussion of this passage places it in the humanist tradition of praising women, but acknowledges the problematic shift from ancient to modern (*Invention of the Renaissance Woman,* 288 ff.)

36. Ibid., 291.

37. Ibid., 261.

38. Edmund Spenser. *Poetical Works,* eds. J. C. Smith and E. de Selincourt (Oxford: Oxford University Press, 1975), 418.

39. Susan Frye, *Elizabeth I: The Competition for Representation* (Oxford: Oxford University Press, 1993), 115–16. Frye argues that "Amoret, too, is a figure for Elizabeth because she is the twin of the Amazon Belphoebe; Amoret, Belphoebe, and Britomart 'mirror' the queen's 'rare chastitee'" lauded in the poem of book 3 (123). While I find this conflation too simplistic as a general statement, I do agree with Frye that the confusion between Amoret and Britomart in the crucial action of canto 12 is deliberate: "The profusion of singular feminine pronouns referring one moment to Amoret and the next to Britomart seve to conflate them into a simgle unstable fiminine figure who, whether rescuer or rescued, is also an unwilling audience" (123).

40. Ibid., 124.

41. By avoiding a detailed reading of the House of Busirane, I place myself with those who argue that the episode has more to do with Amoret than with Britomart, for all that it falls at the end of her book. The most coherent reading of the episode is that of Thomas P. Roche Jr. in *The Kindly Flame* (Princeton, N.J.: Princeton University Press, 1964), 72–88, in which he argues that "the House of Busyrane is presented as if it were an objectification of Amoret's fear of sexual love in marriage" (77) which "explains why Scudamour cannot rescue her. . . . Britomart, on the other hand, can attack these fears on both the moral and physical grounds. As a woman she understands Amoret's attitude toward the physical side of love, and as the exemplar of chastity she is able to make the moral distinction between marriage and adulterous love" (83). The weakness of this reading is that it does not take into account Britomart's own confused gender identity. For a current summary of readings of the Busirane episode, see James W. Broaddus, "Renaissance Psychology and Britomart's Adventures in *Faerie Queene* III," *English Literary Renaissance* 17 (1987): 186–206. See also James Nohrnberg, *The Analogy of the Faerie Queene* (Princeton, N.J.: Princeton University Press, 1976), 471–91.

Although I single out Roche's reading of the episode, I must direct the reader to Lauren Silberman's *Transforming Desire: Erotic Knowledge in Books III and IV of The Faerie Queene* (Berkeley: University of California Press, 1995). This study came out after I completed my work, so I unfortunately have not been able to incorporate Silberman's arguments into this chapter.

42. For all that critics such as Mary Adelaide Grellner argue that "the Mask is to Britomart not only a summation of her psychological development thus far, but also a foreshadowing and cautionary prefiguration of emotional upsets yet to come" (40), the fact remains that she thinks about it not at all. When the masque ends, Britomart, who "saw both first and last, / Issewed forth, and went vnto the dore, To enter in" (xii. 27.5–6). We are given no thoughts, no "secret fear," only action.

43. Silberman, "The Hermaphrodite and the Metamorphosis of Spenserian Allegory," *English Literary Renaissance* 17 (1987): 221.

44. Frye, *Elizabeth I*, 131–32. Frye continues: "To a large extent, for both Spenser and Busirane, persuasion of the female is ultimately less important than her textualization. . . . The textualization of the female is one of the most effective means to belie the connection between poet and rapist, especially because the text so insistently asks us to separate Spenser and Busirane" (133). By the same token, the text insistently asks us to conflate Britomart and Elizabeth.

45. In discussion in a Spenser session at the 1987 Sixteenth Century Studies Conference in Tempe, Arizona.

46. Quoted in J. E. Neale, *Elizabeth I and Her Parliaments 1559–1581* (London: Jonathan Cape, 1957), 127.

47. Maureen Quilligan, *Milton's Spenser* (Ithaca, N.Y.: Cornell University Press, 1983), 197.

48. See Louis Adrian Montrose, "'Shaping Fantasies': Figurations of Gender and Power in Elizabethan Culture," in *Representing the English Renaissance*, ed. Stephen Greenblatt (Berkeley and Los Angeles: University of California Press, 1988), 31–64. Speaking of Elizabeth's attitude toward the marriages of her ladies and her wards, Montrose points out that among "the aristocracy, marriage was not merely a legal and affective union between private person but also a political and economic alliance between powerful families; it was an institution over which a careful and insecure monarch might well wish to exercise an absolute control. Behavior which, in the context of Elizabeth's body natural, may have been merely peevish or jealous was, in the context of her body politic, politic indeed" (49).

49. Silberman argues:

> For Britomart, the self is based on figuration; her identity is the product both of self-fashioning and bodily determination. In Book 3 identity is put at risk by the assertion of sexual difference and the re-inclusion of sexuality. Britomart's quest for Artegall involves braving the hermeneutic gap between self and other; Book 3 defines reading as an act of courage, with both moral and sexual connotations of the word "courage" relevant to the hermeneutic enterprise

in "The Hermaphrodite and the Metamorphosis of Spenserian Allegory, 216.

50. Edmund Tilney, *A brief and pleasaunt discourse of duties in Mariage.* Imprinted at London by Henry Denham, dwelling in Paternoster Rowe, at the sign of the Starre. 1568. (no pagination; u/v, f/s modernized here) The book is dedicated to Queen Elizabeth in a series of botanical metaphors that represent marriage as "this fragrant Flower of Friendship."

51. Robert Snawsell, *A Looking Glasse for Maried Folkes.* London: Printed by N.O. for Henry Bell, and are to be sold at his shop on Holburne Hill neere the crosse Keys. 1610. (u/v, f/s, i/j modernized here) No pagination in this edition, but it's 54 in the 1631 edition.

52. Perhaps even more exact than the paradigms and vocabulary of Lacan for a discussion of Britomart's mirror vision and its implications are the theories of Heinz Kohut. Kohut suggest that with "healthy self-assertiveness vis-a-vis the mirroring self-object, [and] healthy admiration for the idealized self-object," an "independent self" will begin "to rise out of the matrix of mirroring and idealized self-objects"; see *The Restoration of the Self* (New York: International Universities Press, 1977), 171 ff. Neither Lacan nor Kohut, I would argue for what I consider to be obvious reasons, should be slavishly applied to Renaissance texts. Nevertheless, their vocabularies can make our discussions more exact, if we take the source of exactness to be the text not the contemporary theories being used to read the text.

53. See Roche on the problem of representing moral beauty by analogy, (*Kindly Flame*, 93–94).

54. Written in Roman numerals, the citation itself is a chiasmus. We cannot place too much weight on this, unfortunately, as some editions have IIII rather than IV.

55. Gross, *Spenserian Poetics*, 179.

56. Luce Irigaray, *Speculum of the Other Woman*, trans. Gillian C. Gill (Ithaca: Cornell University Press, 1985), 138.

57. Bono argues that Britomart's sexuality is not "constrained by her historic mission" (*Literary Transvaluation*, 78). But Bono accepts the priest's version of the Isis Church dream. She further argues: "Britomart then constructively employs her erotic energy as a chaste and faithful wife, rescuing her husband, tempering his justice with equity, securing their succession. Understanding this reciprocity through the dream vision enables her to free Arthegall" (ibid.). I find it very difficult to reconcile this summary with Spenser's poem. Equally unfounded, if at the other end of the spectrum, is Susanne Woods's argument in "Spenser and the Problem of Women's Rule," *Huntington Library Quarterly* 48 (1985): 140–58. Woods argues that: "Spenser's handling of Britomart, including setting her at the core of contradictory statements about women's rule, is genuinely subversive of patriarchal assumptions" (ibid., 156). Both Bono and Woods fail to consider that what is being subverted in book 5 is the patriarchal narrative of the dynastic epic.

58. Gross, *Spenserian Poetics*, 179.

59. The confusion between Britomart and Isis could well be as intentional Frye argues the confusion between Britomart and Amoret to be. Both brief conflations lure the reader into conflating Britomart with Elizabeth.

60. Cavanagh argues that Britomart's errors in the summary of her dream are thus presented because "Britomart will leave the epic shortly after upholding women's inability to govern properly (without special divine dispensation), [therefore] the narrative's presentation of her muddled perceptions helps confirm a female need for male wisdom" (*Wanton Eyes and Chaste Desires*, 160.) While I agree with Cavanagh that these errors are linked to Britomart's departure from the narrative, I do not believe that the need for male wisdom is the only issue here.

61. Irigaray, *Speculum*, 138.

62. Benson, *Invention of the Renaissance Woman*, 294.

63. Although it is not central to this argument, I cannot resist pointing out that by taking Artegall to a bower and causing him to be remade as a proper man, Britomart is mirroring the actions of Venus as figured forth in Malacasta's tapestries.

CHAPTER 4. CLEOPATRA: THE TAIN OF THE MIRROR

1. To say that Cleopatra is Shakespeare's most fully developed representation of a female self is not to say a great deal. Not only do the conventions of Renaissance drama significantly limit the representation of interiority (Hamlet, as I have mentioned, may have that within him "which passes show," and yet we are left in considerable doubt as to exactly what that may be at any given point in the play), but Shakespeare's long-acknowledged preference for complex males

over any sort of female character is also a factor. We may see Lady Macbeth or Ophelia act in madness or Cordelia act with sacrificial love, but we are given access not to their thoughts, only to those of the male title characters.

Thinking along these same lines, but from a metacritical perspective, Linda Woodbridge (then writing under the name L. T. Fitz) makes the very astute observation that the critical habit of comparing women characters to other women characters is both sexist and reductive. Cleopatra and Juliet, she argues, are both women, both in love, and two of the three women who make it into a Shakespeare title, but otherwise, "the two are as apt for comparison as Mae West and St. Cecilia," in "Egyptian Queens and Male Reviewers: Sexist Attitudes in *Antony and Cleopatra* Criticism," *Shakespeare Quarterly* 28 (1977): 298.

2. For other discussions of Elizabeth figures in Shakespeare's plays see Leah S. Marcus, "Shakespeare's Comic Heroines, Elizabeth I, and the Political Uses of Androgyny," in *Women in the Middle Ages and the Renaissance: Literary and Historical Perspectives,* ed. Mary Beth Rose (Syracuse: Syracuse University Press, 1986), 135–54; and Louis Adrian Montrose, "'Shaping Fantasies': Figurations of Gender and Power in Elizabethan Culture," in *Representing the English Renaissance,* ed. Stephen Greenblatt (Berkeley: University of California Press, 1988), 31–64.

3. Catherine Belsey, *The Subject of Tragedy: Identity and difference in Renaissance drama* (London: Methuen, 1985), 184.

4. Janet Adelman, *The Common Liar: An Essay on Antony and Cleopatra* (New Haven: Yale University Press, 1973), 64.

5. Woodbridge/Fitz, "Egyptian Queens and Male Reviewers," 298. Making clear her exasperation with such simple paradigms of female identity, Woodbridge points out that it "is surely questionable whether there is such a thing as a 'typical woman' or even a 'typical Elizabethan woman.' And if there is such a thing as a 'typical Shakespearean woman,' Cleopatra is not the woman" (ibid., 299).

6. Cixous, "Achilles Is Penthesileia Is Achilles," 117.

7. All quotations from the play cite *The Riverside Shakespeare,* eds. G. Blakemore Evans et al. (Boston: Houghton, 1974).

8. Irene G. Dash, *Wooing, Wedding, and Power: Women in Shakespeare's Plays* (New York: Columbia University Press, 1981), 210.

9. Edmund Tilney, *A brief and pleasaunt discourse of duties in Mariage.* Imprinted at London by Henry Denham, dwelling in Paternoster Rowe, at the sign of the Starre. 1568. (u/v, f/s modernized; no pagination, but I counted). The book dedicated to Queen Elizabeth in a series of botanical metaphors that represent marriage as "this fragrant Flower of Friendship."

10. Robert Snawsell. *A Looking Glasse for Maried Folkes.* London: Printed by N.O. for Henry Bell, and are to be sold at his shop on Holburne Hill neere the crosse Keys. 1610. (u/v, f/s, i/j modernized; no pagination in this edition, but this passage is on 54 in the 1631 edition.)

11. Carol Thomas Neely, *Broken Nuptials in Shakespeare's Plays* (New Haven: Yale University Press, 1985), 138.

12. Adelman, *Common Liar,* 69.

13. Ibid., 73.

14. Barbara J. Bono, *Literary Transvaluation: From Vergilian Epic to Shakespearean Tragicomedy* (Berkeley and Los Angeles: University of California Press, 1984), 169.

15. Neely, *Broken Nuptials in Shakespeare's Plays,* 139.

16. In *The Common Liar,* Janet Adelman includes an appendix in which she

compares Marlowe's *Dido, Queen of Carthage* and *Antony and Cleopatra:* "The element of Antony's effeminacy, so crucial in *Antony*, is strongly stated in *Dido:* 'Banish that ticing dame from forth your mouth, / And follow your foreseeing stars in all. / This is no life for men-at-arms to live, / Where dalliance doth consume a soldier's strength, / And wantom motions of alluring eyes / Effeminate our minds, inured to war' (*Dido* 4.3.31–36). / 'That ticing dame' is very like Antony's 'I must from this enchanting queen break off' (*Antony* 1.2.125). Effeminacy is suggested by Octavius (Antony 1.4.5–6), by Canidius (*Antony* 3.7.70), and especially by Scarus' 'We have kiss'd away / Kingdoms and provinces' (*Antony* 3.10.7–8)" 179–80.

17. Lucy Hughes-Hallett, *Cleopatra: Histories, Dreams, and Distortions* (London: Vintage, 1991), 147. This book came to my attention just as I was finishing this study; even on so brief an examination, however, I found its focus curiously blurred. More consistent, if less scholarly, is Mary Harner's relentlessly trendy *Signs of Cleopatra: History, politics, representation* (London: Methuen, 1993).

18. Bono, *Literary Transvaluation*, 175.

19. See Adelman's discussion of the crocodile in *Common Liar*, especially 140.

20. Bono, *Literary Transvaluation*, 218–19.

21. See my forthcoming article, "Reading the Tombs of Elizabeth I," *ELR: English Literary Renaissance* (fall 1996) for a more detailed discussion of this material.

22. Sir Roy Strong, *The Cult of Elizabeth: Elizabethan Portraiture and Pageantry* (Berkeley and Los Angeles: University of California Press, 1977), 14–15.

23. Paul Johnson, *Elizabeth I* (New York: Holt, 1974), 438.

24. Anne Clifford, *Diary*, text from the Women Writer's Project, Brown University.

25. Thomas Millington, *The True Narration of the Entertainment of His Majesty from His Departure from Edinburgh Till His Receiving at London* in *Stuart Tracts 1603–1693*, ed. C. H. Frith (New York: Cooper Square Publishers, 1964), 11–52.

26. Ibid., 40.

27. Ibid.

28. John Manningham, *The Diary of John Manningham of the Middle Temple 1603–1603*, ed. Robert Parker Sorlien (Hanover: University Press of New England, 1976), 210.

29. D. R. Woolf, "Two Elizabeths? James I and the Late Queen's Famous Memory," *Canadian Journal of History* 20 (1985): 173. This is a well-researched study, although Woolf's reading of James's feelings about Elizabeth run counter to most authorities in the field and to the argument of this study. Woolf concludes:

There were, then, two famous memories of the late Queen. Elizabethanism was not always a whip with which to beat the Stuarts. The confusion of the two images results largely from the unwarranted assumption that James I resented respect paid to his predecessor, an assumption which is easy to make when we read back the thoughts of the Cromwellian era into an earlier period. But the ultimate responsibility for this good Queen/bad King dichotomy ... must be laid at the door of the post-1640 memorialists." 190–91

Although Woolf calls it an "unwarranted assumption" that James resented Elizabeth, much of the evidence put forth in Woolf's argument could just as easily bear that interpretation. For example, Woolf argues that "James may not have coined the phrase, 'the late Queen of famous memory,' but he certainly used it with considerable frequency" (176); this phrase, I would suggest, is at worst ambiguous and at best conventional. Woolf also cites the fact that when James ordered a tomb erected for this mother in 1605, he also ordered one for Elizabeth. As I argue here, that simultaneous order can more logically be read as s slight to Elizabeth's memory.

30. Graham Parry, *The Golden Age Restor'd: The Culture of the Stuart Court, 1603–42* (New York: St. Martin's, 1981), 9.

31. Ibid.

32. Ibid., 19.

33. From *The Political Works of James I*, ed. Charles H. McIlwain (Cambridge, 1918) cited by Marie Axton in *The Queen's Two Bodies: Drama and the Elizabethan Succession* (London: Royal Historical Society, 1977), 133.

34. H. Neville Davies, "Jacobean *Antony and Cleopatra*," *Shakespeare Studies* 17 (1985): 124.

35. Ibid., 125–26.

36. Axton, *Queen's Two Bodies*, 133.

37. Sir Roy Strong, *Gloriana: The Portrait of Queen Elizabeth I* (German Democratic Republic: Thames and Hudson, 1987), 164.

38. Ibid.

39. Davies, "Jacobean *Antony and Cleopatra*," 128.

40. Carole Levin, *The Heart and Stomach of a King: Elizabeth I and the Politics of Sex and Power* (Philadelphia: University of Pennsylvania Press, 1994), 169–69.

41. Davies, "Jacobean *Antony and Cleopatra*," 130.

42. Millington, *True Narration*, 15.

43. H. M. Colvin et al., eds. *The History of the King's Works* 1485–1660 (part 1) (London: Her Majesty's Stationery Office, 1975), 3:219.

44. William Camden, *Reges, Reginoe, Nobiles. . . .* (Londoni: Excudebat Melchi Bradwoodus. M.DC.III).

45. WAM 41095. I am deeply grateful to the staff of the Muniments Room in Westminster Abbey for their help in uncovering this crucial bit of evidence. Taken with Camden and Manningham's statements (the former an eyewitness account), this makes a hash of received opinion on the tomb of Elizabeth I. As I argue in my essay on the tombs, the fact that the truth about Elizabeth's burials emerges only in the 1990s is a tribute to the success of James's remaking of Elizabeth's public identity.

46. *Official Guide*, 76.

47. Ibid., 69.

48. Jonathan Goldberg, "Fatherly Authority: The Politics of Stuart Family Images," in *Rewriting the Renaissance: The Discourse of Sexual Difference in Early Modern Europe*, eds. Margaret W. Ferguson, Maureen Quilligan, and Nancy J. Vickers (Chicago: University of Chicago Press, 1986), 5.

49. Ibid., 4–5.

50. I am not suggesting that this burial of his own children's bodies with that of his mother was James's original intention. By the time Prince Henry dies, a large portion of James's available funds was tied up in the wedding of Princess Elizabeth, and at the time of her death, further Stuart building projects—notably the Banqueting Hall—had consumed most of his income.

51. Davies, "Jacobean *Antony and Cleopatra*," 140.

52. Ibid., 139.

53. John Nichols, ed. *The Progresses . . . of James the First. . . .* (New York: Burt Franklin, no date, but first published in London in 1828), 2:52–93.

54. Plutarch, "The Life of Marcus Antonius," trans. Thomas North in *Shakespeare's Plutarch,* ed. C. F. Tucker Brooke (London: Chatto and Windus, 1909) 2:1–136.

55. Woodbridge catalogs the points at which this source is revised by Shakespeare "making numerous small alterations in Plutarch's story, the effect of which is almost always to mitigate Cleopatra's culpability" ("Egyptian Queens and Male Reviewers," 310–13). She does not, however, comment upon the burial as described in either text.

56. Plutarch, "Life of Marcus Antonius," 129.

57. Neely, *Broken Nuptials in Shakespeare's Plays,* 161–62.

58. Ibid., 147.

59. Plutarch, "Life of Marcus Antonius," 128.

60. Ibid., 131–32.

61. Ibid., 133.

62. Ibid., 134–35.

63. I am very grateful to Shelia ffolliott for helping me to see the degree to which tombs can be politicized.

CHAPTER 5. EVE: THE FIRST REFLECTION

1. All quotations from the poem cite the Merritt Y. Hughes edition, *John Milton: Complete Poems and Major Prose* (New York: Odyssey Press, 1957).

2. James Turner, *The Politics of Landscape* (Cambridge: Harvard University Press, 1979), 34.

3. I am grateful to my former research assistant, Anne Clark Bartlett for the excellent work she did on this topic.

4. Milton's gendering of earth, lakes, rivers, and other geographical nouns is not consistent with the grammar of Latin or of Greek or of the most logical source, Hebrew. Although Michael Lieb has said that he plans a study of gendered Hebrew and Milton's poetry, as yet there has been no thorough study of this topic, and I certainly do not propose to undertake one here. I merely wish to point out that Milton's gendering of the creation narrative cannot be explained away on etymological grounds.

5. Turner, *Politics of Landscape,* 25.

6. Uriel's eyewitness account in book 3 is not only radically shortened, but is also remarkable for its insistence upon Earth and paradise as the domain of Adam; Eve is never mentioned and the feminine principle resides only in the moon, which is gendered female.

7. Mary Nyquist, "Gynesis, Genesis, Exegesis, and the Formation of Milton's Eve" [cited hereafter as GGE], in *Cannibals, Witches, and Divorce: Estranging the Renaissance,* ed. Marjorie Garber (Baltimore: Johns Hopkins University Press, 1987), 167. As a result of these attempts to forge a direct link between Genesis and *Paradise Lost,* there also continues to flourish what Nyquist calls "an entire network of misogynistic or idealizing commonplaces and free-floating sexual stereotypes, relating indifferently, to Genesis and to this institutionally privileged text by Milton, English literature's paradigmatic patriarch" (167).

8. See particularly Phyllis Trible, *God and the Rhetoric of Sexuality* (Philadelphia: Fortress Press, 1978) [hereafter cited as GRS] and *Texts of Terror: Literary-Feminist Readings of Biblical Narratives* (Philadelphia: Fortress Press, 1984); Mary

Nyquist, "The Genesis of Gendered Subjectivity in the Divorce Traces and in *Paradise Lost*," in *Re-Membering Milton*, ed. Mary Nyquist and Margaret W. Ferguson (New York: Methuen, 1988), 99–127; Patricia Parker, "Coming Second: Woman's Place" [hereafter cited as CS], in *Literary Fat Ladies: Rhetoric, Gender, Property* (New York: Methuen, 1987), 179–233; and Michael Lieb, *The Dialectics of Creation: Patterns of Birth and Regeneration in "Paradise Lost"* (Amherst: University of Massachusetts Press, 1970).

See also Mieke Bal, "Sexuality, Sin, and Sorrow: The Emergence of the Female Character (A Reading of Genesis 1–3)," *Poetics Today* 6 (1985): 21–42; Phyllis A. Bird, "'Male and Female He Created Them': Gen 1:27b in the Context of the Priestly Account of Creation," *Harvard Theological Review* 74 (1981): 129–59; J. M. Evans, *"Paradise Lost" and The Genesis Tradition* (Oxford: Oxford University Press, 1968); Christine Froula, "When Eve Reads Milton: Undoing the Canonical Economy," *Critical Inquiry* 10 (1983): 321–47; Susan Niditch, *Chaos to Cosmos: Studies in Biblical Patterns of Creation* (Chico, Calif.: Scholars Press, 1985) [201–5 discuss the Christian adaptations of the two narratives]; Regina M. Schwartz, *Remembering and Repeating: Biblical Creation in "Paradise Lost,"* (Cambridge: Cambridge University Press, 1988); and Ilana Pardes, *Countertraditions in the Bible: A Feminist Approach* (Cambridge: Harvard University Press, 1992).

9. Schwartz, *Remembering and Repeating*, 4. In support of her point, Schwartz quotes Milton:

> But it is not known, because there is noting about it in scripture, whether this was ever disclosed to Adam or whether any commandment about the observance of the Sabbath existed before the giving of the Law on Mount Sinai, let along before the fall of man. Probably Moses, who seems to have written the book of Genesis long after the giving of the law, inserted this sentence from the fourth commandment [in Exodus] in what was, as it were, an opportune place [the Priestly creation narrative]. Thus he seized an opportunity of reminding the people about the reason, which was, so to speak, topical at this point in his narrative, but which God had really given many years later to show why he wanted the sabbath to be observed by his people, with whom he had at long last made a solemn covenant" (*CPW*, 6, 353–54, quoted by Schwartz, 4).

10. Unless otherwise acknowledged, all quotations from the Bible cite the Revised Standard Version.

11. Nyquist, GGE, 148–49.

12. Ibid., 150.

13. Ibid.

14. See Michael Lieb's discussion of "womb" in *The Dialectics of Creation*, 22 ff.

15. Nyquist, GGE, 151.

16. Marshall Grossman, *"Authors to Themselves" Milton and the Revelation of History* (New York: Cambridge University Press, 1988), 83. See Grossman's discussion of narcissism on 83–87 and 121–23.

17. James Holly Hanford, *A Milton Handbook*, 4th ed. (New York: Appleton-Century-Crofts, 1961), 203.

18. Stanley Eugene Fish, *Surprised by Sin* (Berkeley: University of California Press, 1971), 360. Tellingly, "Eve at the pool" is an index heading.

19. All quotations from *Metamorphoses*, unless otherwise noted, cite the Loeb Library edition.

20. Richard J. DuRocher, *Milton and Ovid* (Ithaca: Cornell University Press, 1985), 89. I do not see such a great distinction in tonal qualities; if Ovid's is "condescending," I would argue, Milton's is patronizing. DuRocher sees Narcis-

sus as one of a series of Ovidian associations that Milton sets up with Eve, linking her with "in turn, the innocence of Narcissus, the responsiveness of Echo, the chastity of Pomona, the passion of Medea, and the piety of Pyrrha" (109).

21. DuRocher cites Arnold Stein's differentiation between the two passages as a "contrasting [of] Narcissus's ignorance of his predicament with Eve's knowing and clever use of her earlier self-regard to encourage Adam's love" (*The Art of Presence: The Poet and "Paradise Lost"* [Berkeley: University of California Press, 1977], 95 paraphrased by DuRocher, 88) but DuRocher differs slightly with Stein, arguing that "Eve's manner and narrative do compliment Adam, but the allusion to Narcissus further complicates the character of Eve because . . . she would clearly have preferred the self-regarding pose of Narcissus had not Adam . . . pursued and claimed her" (88).

22. Parker (in CS), although also reading "narcissistic" as a pejorative, makes some interesting points about the way in which Eve turns to Adam:

> The actual end of this progression, the final turning point in her conversion from narcissistic self-attachment to "our general mother" (4. 492), is veiled in rhetorical reticentia: we are not told what Eve saw or what Adam finally showed her that made all the difference, that convinced her of the superiority of his "manly grace." But the progression itself is towards a destination whose actual arrival is not immediate but delayed, in contrast to the more straightforward progression of the passage's biblical subtext from Genesis 2. (194)

Michael Lieb, in a discussion paralleling Adam and Eve with Satan and sin, does take into consideration Eve's lack of self-recognition, noting that "Eve inhabits the world of the infant, who loves itself without being guilty of pride because it does not know that it is itself that it loves" (148); and yet he begins his next sentence: "With Eve's becoming enamored of herself. . . ."

23. This is not the only example we find in Milton's poetry of an allusion that can be read only in part. In *Paradise Regained,* as I argue elsewhere, we are forced to limit our reading of allusions to *Orlando Furioso* and to the Oedipus story.

24. And, indeed, subsequent knowledge does embellish memory when she observes that the surface of the lake "seem'd another Sky" (4.159); unlike Adam, she did not look up first.

25. See Marshall Grossman's discussion of Eve's names in "Servile/Sterile/Style: Milton and the Question of Woman," in *Milton and the Idea of Woman,* ed. Julia M. Walker (University of Illinois Press, 1988), especially 151–52.

26. R. D. Laing, *Knots* (New York: Pantheon Books, 1970), 31, 84.

27. Parker, CS, 179–80.

28. Grossman, "Servile/Sterile/Style," 152. Grossman is using "style" here as defined in OED 2.b.18: "A legal, official, or honorific title" (167 n).

29. Of thirty-four feminine pronouns, only six are subject pronouns. Significantly, perhaps, three of these six are widely scattered. That Milton was well aware of these nuances of grammar is apparent in his *Accedence Commenc't Grammar,* where he discusses the way in which the Latin case is applied in English with nouns—"The *Genitive* is Englisht with this Sign *of,* as *Libri* of a book" (88)—and pronouns (95–97), in *Complete Prose Works of John Milton,* vol. 8, eds. Don M. Wolf et al. (New Haven: Yale University Press, 1982).

30. Patricia Parker, "Literary Fat Ladies and the Generation of the Text," [hereafter cited as LFL] in *Literary Fat Ladies: Rhetoric, Gender, Property,* 29.

31. Ibid.

32. We know she thinks about the scene beside the lake, since she begins her book-4 narrative with a reference to "That day I oft remember."

33. See Marshall Grossman's discussion of the narcissistic elements of Adam's gaze in *"Authors to Themselves,"* 121–23.

34. Hazel E. Barnes, "The Look of the Gorgon," in *The Meddling Gods: Four Essays on Classical Themes* (Lincoln: University of Nebraska Press, 1974), 28.

35. Indeed, it is difficult to believe that Virginia Woolf could not have had this passage in mind when she wrote her famous critique of the function of women in the lives of men in *A Room of One's Own:* "Women have served all these centuries as looking-glasses possessing the magic and delicious power of reflecting the figure of man at twice its natural size."

36. A. Bartlett Giamatti, *The Earthly Paradise and the Renaissance Epic* (Princeton, N.J.: Princeton University Press, 1966).

37. John V. Fleming, *The Roman de la Rose: A Study in Allegory and Iconography* (Princeton, N.J.: Princeton University Press, 1969), 50–51, 167.

38. Edward Sichi Jr., "Milton the the *Roman de la Rose:* Adam and Eve at the Fountain of Narcissus," in *Milton and the Middle Ages,* ed. John Mulryan (Bucknell, 1982), 153. See also Albert C. Labriola, "The Aesthetics of Self-Diminution: Christian Iconography and Paradise Lost," in *"Eyes Fast Fixt": Current Perspective in Milton Methodology, Milton Studies* 7 (1975): 267–311.

39. John Freccero, "Medusa: The Letter and the Spirit," *Yearbook of Italian Studies* (1972): 2.

40. Sylvia Huot, "The Medusa Interpolation in the *Romance of the Rose:* Mythographic Program and Ovidian Intertext," *Speculum* 62 (1987): 865–77.

41. Ibid., 870.

42. Ibid.

43. Ibid., 870–71.

44. Ibid., 865.

45. I owe this translation to Anne D. Lutkus, University of Rochester, and Beverly Evans, State University of New York at Geneseo. The original passage is taken from *Le Roman de la Rose* by Guillaume de Lorris and Jean de Meun, publié d'après les manuscrits par Ernest Langlois (Paris: Librairie Ancienne âdouard Champion), 5: 107–9.

46. Huot, "Medusa Interpolation in the *Romance of the Rose,"* 875.

47. John Freccero, "Medusa: The Letter and the Spirit," *Yearbook of Italian Studies* 2 (1972): 7–8. Reading Dante's Medusa is an industry in itself and I will not rehearse the arguments here. I use Freccero not because I find him to be necessarily the most convincing reader of this passage in *Inferno,* but because his scholarly insights in the uses of the Medusa paradigm can enrich and support this study.

48. Huot, "Medusa Interpolation in the *Romance of the Rose,"* 873.

49. Freccero, "Medusa," 13.

50. Petrarch, *Rime sparse,* poem 366, lines 110–11 in *Petrarch's Lyric Poems,* trans. and ed. Robert M. Durling (Cambridge: Harvard University Press, 1976), 582–83.

51. Freccero, "Medusa," 14–15.

CHAPTER 6. THE MIRRORS OF MEDUSA

1. Susanne Kappeler, *The Pornography of Representation* (Minneapolis: University of Minnesota Press, 1986), 90.

2. Andrea Dworkin, *Pornography: Men Possessing Women* (New York: Putnam, 1981), 136.

3. Susan Griffin, *Pornography and Silence: Culture's Revenge Against Nature.* (New York: Harper, 1981), 3.

4. I do, however, in a limited way make that suggestion about Milton's Ludlow mask. See my forthcoming essay "Milton's Mask, Pornography, and the Revocation of Chronological Absolution."

5. Dworkin, *Pornography,* 23.

6. Can this not be said of murder or robbery or nonsexual assault? Yes, but those crimes are not as gender specific as rape. I do not mean to diminish the pain felt by male rape victims; but statistically and culturally, this is a crime that men enact against women and I will discuss it as such.

7. Stephen Greenblatt, *Renaissance Self-Fashioning: From More to Shakespeare* (Chicago: University of Chicago Press, 1980), 2.

8. Ibid., 7.

9. Ibid.

10. Ibid., 167.

11. Carol Thomas Neely, "Constructing the Subject: Feminist Practice and the New Renaissance Discourses," *English Literary Renaissance* 18 (1988): 5–18.

12. Luce Irigaray, *Speculum of the Other Woman,* trans. Gillian C. Gill (Ithaca: Cornell University Press, 1985), 362–63.

Bibliography

PRIMARY SOURCES

Alcibiades in *The Dialogues of Plato.* Vol. 1, translated by B. Jowett. Oxford: Oxford University Press, 1964.

Ariosto, Ludovico. *Orlando Furioso.* Translated by Barbara Reynolds. New York: Penguin, 1987.

Boccaccio, Giovanni. *Concerning Famous Women.* Translated by Guido A. Guarino. New Brunswick: Rutgers University Press, 1963.

Calendar of State Papers 1603–1610. Edited by Mary Anne Everett Green. Her Majesty's Stationery Office. 1858. Reprint, 1967.

Camden, William. *Reges, Reginæ, Nobiles.* . . . Londini: Excudebat Melchi Bradwoodus. M.DC. III.

Clifford, Anne. *Diary,* text from the Women Writer's Project, Brown University.

de Lorris, Guillaume, and Jean de Meun. *The Romance of the Rose.* Translated by Charles Dahlberg. Hanover: University Press of New England, 1983.

——— and Jean de Meun. *Le Roman de la Rose,* publié d'après les manuscrits par Ernest Langlois. Paris: Librairie Ancienne âdouard Champion.

Donne, John. *Catalogus Librorum,* 14, cited by Charles Monroe Coffin in *John Donne and the New Philosophy.* New York: Humanities Press, 1958.

———. *The Complete Poetry of John Donne.* Edited by John T. Shawcross. Garden City, N.Y: Anchor, 1967.

Fulgentius. *Fulgentius the Mythographer.* Translated by Leslie George Whitbread. Columbus: Ohio University Press, 1971.

Gascoigne, George. *The Steel Glass in The Renaissance in England.* Edited by Hyder E. Rollins and Herschell Baker. Lexington, Mass.: D.C. Heath, 1954.

Lucan. *The Civil War.* Translated by J. D. Duff for the Loeb Classical Library. Cambridge: Harvard University Press, 1962.

Manningham, John. *Diary of John Manningham of the Middle Temple, and of Braddbourne, Kent, Barrister-at-Law, 1603–1608.* Edited from the original manuscript by John Bruce, Esq., and presented to the Camden Society by William Tite, Esq., MP, FRS, FSA, President of the Society (Westminster: Printed by J. B. Nichols and Sons, 1868.

———. *The Diary of John Manningham of the Middle Temple 1603–1603.* Edited by Robert Parker Sorlien (Hanover: University Press of New England, 1976.

Millington, Thomas. *The True Narration of the Entertainment of his Majesty from his departure from Edinburgh till his receiving at London.* In *Stuart Tracts 1603–1693,* edited by C. H. Frith. New York: Cooper Square Publishers, 1964.

Milton, John. *Accedence Commenc't Grammar.* In *Complete Prose Works of John Milton.* Vol. 8, edited by Don M. Wolf et al. (New Haven: Yale University Press, 1982.

————. *Paradise Lost.* In *John Milton: Complete Poems and Major Prose,* edited by Merritt Y. Hughes. New York: Odyssey Press, 1957.

Molin, Nicolas. *Venetian State Papers 1603–1607,* 509–14. In *James I by His Contemporaries: And account of his career and character as seen by some of his contemporaries,* edited by Robert Ashton (London: Hutchinson, 1969.

Ovid. *Metamorphoses.* Edited and translated by Frank Justice Miller for the Loeb Classical Library. Cambridge: Harvard University Press, 1984.

Petrarch. *Rime sparse,* poem 366, lines 110–11. In *Petrarch's Lyric Poems,* translated and edited by Robert M. Durling. Cambridge: Harvard University Press: 1976.

————. "The Life of Marcus Antonius." Translated by Thomas North. In *Shakespeare's Plutarch.* Vol. 2, edited by C. F. Tucker Brooke. London: Chatto and Windus, 1909.

Quarles, Francis. *Emblemes* (London, 1635). In *An Index of Icons in English Emblem Books 1500–1700,* by Huston Diehl. Oklahoma: Oklahoma University Press, 1986.

Shakespeare, William. *Antony and Cleopatra.* In *The Riverside Shakespeare,* edited by G. Blakemore Evans et al. (Boston: Houghton, 1974.

Skelton, John. *Poems.* Edited by Richard Hughes London: William Heinemann,1924.

Snawsell, Robert. *A Looking Glasse for Maried Folkes.* London: Printed by N.O. for Henry Bell, and are to be sold at his shop on Holburne Hill neere the crosse Keys, 1610.

Spenser, Edmund. *Poetical Works.* Edited by J. C. Smith and E. de Selincourt. Oxford: Oxford University Press, 1975.

————. *The Faerie Queene.* Edited by A. C. Hamilton. New York: Longman, 1977.

Tilney, Edmund. *A brief and pleasaunt discourse of duties in Mariage.* Imprinted at London by Henry Denham, dwelling in Paternoster Rowe, at the sign of the Starre. 1568.

Virgil. *The Aeneid of Virgil.* Translated by Allen Mandelbaum. New York: Bantam, 1985.

————. *The Aeneid.* Edited by J. B. Greenough and G. L. Kittredge. Boston: Ginn, 1895.

Walton, Izaak. *The Lives of John Donne, Sir Henry Wotton, Richard Hooker, George Herbert, & Robert Sanderson.* New York: Oxford University Press, 1956.

Westminster Abbey Muniments (WAM) 41095.

Secondary Sources

Adelman, Janet. *The Common Liar: An Essay on Antony and Cleopatra.* New Haven: Yale University Press, 1973.

Axton, Marie. *The Queen's Two Bodies: Drama and the Elizabethan Succession.* London: Royal Historical Society, 1977.

Bal, Mieke. "Sexuality, Sin, and Sorrow: The Emergence of the Female Character (Reading of Genesis 1–3)" *Poetics Today* 6 (1985).

Bald, R. C. *John Donne: A Life.* New York: Oxford University Press, 1970.

Barnes, Hazel E. "The Look of the Gorgon." In *The Meddling Gods: Four Essays on Classical Themes*. Lincoln: University of Nebraska Press, 1974.

Bell, Susan Groag. "Medieval Women Book Owners: Arbiters of Lay Piety and Ambassadors of Culture." In *Women and Power in the Middle Ages,* edited by Mary Erler and Maryanne Kowaleski. Athens: University of Georgia Press, 1988.

Bellamy, Elizabeth J. "The Vocative and the Vocational: The Unreadability of Elizabeth in *The Faerie Queene.*" *ELH* 54 (1987).

———. *Translations of Power: Narcissism and the Unconscious in Epic History.* Ithaca: Cornell University Press, 1992.

Belsey, Andrew, and Catherine Belsey: "Icons of Divinity: Portraits of Elizabeth I." In *Renaissance Bodies: The Human Figure in English Culture c. 1540–1660,* edited by Lucy Gent and Nigel Llewellyn. London: Reaktion Books, 1990.

Belsey, Catherine. "A Future for Materialist Feminist Criticism?" In *The Matter of Difference: Materialist Feminist Criticism of Shakespeare,* edited by Valerie Wayne. Ithaca: Cornell University Press, 1991.

———. "Richard Levin and In-different Reading." *New Literary History* 21 (spring 1990).

———. *The Subject of Tragedy: Identity and difference in Renaissance Drama.* London: Methuen, 1985.

Bender, John B. *Spenser and Literary Pictorialism* (Princeton: Princeton University Press, 1972.

Benson, Pamela Joseph. *The Invention of the Renaissance Woman: The Challenge of Female Independence in the Literature and Thought of Italy and England.* University Park: Pennsylvania State University Press, 1992.

Berry, Philippa. *Of Chastity and Power: Elizabethan Literature and the Unmarried Queen.* London: Routledge, 1989.

Bird, Phyllis A. "'Male and Female He Created Them': Gen 1 : 27b in the Context of the Priestly Account of Creation." *Harvard Theological Review* 74 (1981).

Bono, Barbara J. *Literary Transvaluation: From Vergilian Epic to Shakespearean Tragicomedy.* Berkeley: University of California Press, 1984.

Bradley, Ritamary. "Backgrounds of the Title *Speculum* in Medieaval Literature." *Speculum* 29 (1954).

Broaddus, James W. "Renaissance Psychology and Britomart's Adventures in *Faerie Queene* III." *English Literary Renaissance* 17 (1987).

Carey, John. *John Donne: Life, Mind and Art.* New York: Oxford University Press, 1981.

Cavanagh, Sheila T. *Wanton Eyes and Chaste Desires: Female Sexuality in The Faerie Queene.* Bloomington: Indiana University Press, 1994.

Cixous, Hélène. "Achilles is Penthesileia is Achilles." In *The Newly Born Woman,* edited by Cixous and Catherine Clément, translated by Betsy Wing. Minneapolis: University of Minnesota Press, 1988.

———. "The Laugh of the Medusa," *Signs* 1 (1976).

Colvin, H. M. et al, eds. *The History of the King's Works.* Vol. 3. 1485–1660 (part 1). London: Her Majesty's Stationery Office, 1975.

Dash, Irene G. *Wooing, Wedding, and Power: Women in Shakespeare's Plays.* New York: Columbia University Press, 1981.

Davies, H. Neville. "Jacobean *Antony and Cleopatra.*" *Shakespeare Studies* 17 (1985).

Dollimore, Jonathan. "Shakespeare, Cultural Materialism, Feminism, and Marxist Humanism." *New Literary History* 21 (spring 1990).

DuRocher, Richard J. *Milton and Ovid* (Ithaca: Cornell University Press, 1985.

Dworkin, Andrea. *Pornography: Men Possessing Women.* New York: Putnam, 1981.

Evans, J. M. *"Paradise Lost" and The Genesis Tradition.* Oxford: Oxford University Press, 1968.

Feldman, Thalia. "Gorgon and the Origins of Fear." *Arion* 4, no. 3 (autumn 1965).

Fineman, Joel. "More about 'Medusa's Head'." *Representations* 4 (fall 1983).

Fish, Stanley Eugene. *Surprised by Sin.* Berkeley: University of California Press, 1971.

Fitz, L. T. [Linda Woodbridge]. "Egyptian Queens and Male Reviewers: Sexist Attitudes in *Antony and Cleopatra* Criticism." *Shakespeare Quarterly* 28 (1977) .

Fleming, John V. *The Roman de la Rose: A Study in Allegory and Iconography.* Princeton: Princeton University Press, 1969.

Flynn, Dennis. "Donne and a Female Coterie." *LIT: Literature and Interpretation Theory* 1 (1989).

Fowler, Alastair. *Triumphal Forms.* Cambridge: Cambridge University Press, 1970.

Freccero, John. "Medusa: The Letter and the Spirit," *Yearbook of Italian Studies* 2 (1972).

Freud, Sigmund. "The Medusa's Head." In *The Standard Edition of the Complete Psychological Works of Sigmund Freud.* Vol. 18, edited and translated by James Strachey et al. London: Hogarth Press, 1955.

Froula, Christine. "When Eve Reads Milton: Undoing the Canonical Economy." *Critical Inquiry* 10 (1983).

Frye, Susan. *Elizabeth I: The Competition for Representation.* Oxford: Oxford University Press, 1993.

Gallagher, Lowell. *Medusa's Gaze: Casuistry and Conscience in the Renaissance.* Stanford: Stanford University Press, 1991.

Genette, Gerard. *Narrative Discourse.* Ithaca: Cornell University Press, 1980.

Gent, Lucy. *Picture and Poetry, 1560–1620: Relations between Literature and the Visual Arts in the English Renaissance.* Leamington Spa: James Hall, 1981.

Giamatti, A. Bartlett. *The Earthly Paradise and the Renaissance Epic.* Princeton, N.J., Princeton University Press, 1966.

Gohlke, Madelon. "'I wooed the with my sword': Shakespeare's Tragic Paradigms." In *Representing Shakespeare: New Psychoanalytic Essays,* edited by Murray M. Schwartz and Coppélia Kahn. Baltimore: Johns Hopkins University Press, 1980.

Goldberg, Benjamin. *The Mirror and Man.* Charlottesville: University Press of Virginia, 1985.

Goldberg, Jonathan. "Fatherly Authority: The Politics of Stuart Family Images." In *Rewriting the Renaissance: The Discourse of Sexual Difference in Early Modern Europe,* edited by Margaret W. Ferguson, Maureen Quilligan, and Nancy J. Vickers. Chicago: University of Chicago Press, 1986.

———. "Making Sense." *New Literary History* 21 (spring 1990).

———. *Endlesse Worke: Spenser and the Structures of Discourse.* Baltimore: Johns Hopkins University Press, 1981.

Goodenough, Erwin R. *Jewish Symbols in the Greco-Roman Period.* Vol. 8. Bollingen Foundation, 1958.

Grabes, Herbert. *The Mutable Glass.* Cambridge University Press, 1982.

Grafton, Antony, and Lisa Jardine. *From Humanism to the Humanities* (Cambridge: Harvard University Press, 1986.

Graves, Robert. *The Greek Myths.* New York: Penguin, 1957.

Greenblatt, Stephen. "Psychoanalysis and Renaissance Culture." In *Literary Theory/Renaissance Texts,* edited by Patricia Parker and David Quint. Baltimore: Johns Hopkins University Press, 1986.

———. *Renaissance Self-Fashioning: From More to Shakespeare* .Chicago: University of Chicago Press, 1980.

Greene, Thomas *The Light in Troy.* New Haven: Yale University Press, 1983.

Gregerson, Linda. "Narcissus Interrupted: Specularity and the Subject of the Tudor State." *Criticism* 35 (1993).

Griffin, Susan. *Pornography and Silence: Culture's Revenge Against Nature.* New York: Harper, 1981.

Gross, Kenneth. *Spenserian Poetics: Idolatry, Iconoclasm, and Magic.* Ithaca: Cornell University Press, 1985.

Grossman, Marshall. *"Authors to Themselves": Milton and the Revelation of History.* New York: Cambridge University Press, 1988.

———. "Servile/Sterile/Style: Milton and the Question of Woman." In *Milton and the Idea of Woman,* edited by Julia M. Walker. University of Illinois Press, 1988.

Hackett, Helen. *Virgin Mother, Maiden Queen: Elizabeth I and the Cult of the Virgin Mary.* New York: St. Martin's, 1995.

Halley, Janet E. "Textual Intercourse: Anne Donne, John Donne, and the Sexual Poetics of Textual Exchange." In *Seeking the Woman in Late Medieval and Renaissance Writings: Essays in Feminist Contextual Criticism,* edited by Sheila Fisher and Janet E. Halley. Knoxville: University of Tennessee Press, 1989.

Hanford, James Holly. *A Milton Handbook,* 4th ed. New York: Appleton, 1961.

Harrison, Jane. *Prolegomena to the Study of Greek Religion.* New York: Meridian Books, 1955.

Hertz, Neil. "Medusa's Head: Male Hysteria under Political Pressure." *Representations* 4 (fall 1983).

Hieatt, A. Kent. *Short Time's Endless Monument.* New York: Columbia University Press, 1960.

Hopper, Vincent F. *Medieval Number Symbolism.* New York: Columbia University Press, 1938.

Hughes-Hallett, Lucy. *Cleopatra: Histories, Dreams, and Distortions.* London: Vintage, 1991.

Hulse, Clark. *The Rule of Art: Literature and Painting in the Renaissance.* Chicago: University of Chicago Press, 1990.

Huot, Sylvia. "The Medusa Interpolation in the *Romance of the Rose:* Mythographic Program and Ovidian Intertext" *Speculum* 62 (1987).

Irigaray, Luce. *Speculum of the Other Woman.* Translated by Gillian C. Gill. Ithaca: Cornell University Press, 1985.

———. *This Sex Which Is Not One.* Translated by Catherine Porter and Carolyn Burke. Ithaca: Cornell University Press, 1985.

Johnson, Paul. *Elizabeth I.* New York: Holt, 1974.

Jordan, Constance. "Representing Political Androgyny: More on the Siena Portrait of Queen Elizabeth I." In *The Renaissance Englishwoman in Print: Counterbalancing the Canon,* edited by Anne M. Haselkorn and Betty S. Travitsky. Amherst: University of Massachusetts Press, 1990.

Kappeler, Susanne. *The Pornography of Representation.* Minneapolis: University of Minnesota Press, 1986.

Kelly, Joan. "Early Feminist Theory and the *Querelle des femmes,* 1400–1789." *Signs* 8 (1982).

Kohut, Heinz. *The Restoration of the Self.* New York: International Universities Press, 1977.

LaBelle, Jenijoy. *Herself Beheld: The Literature of the Looking Glass.* Ithaca: Cornell University Press, 1988.

Labriola, Albert C. "The Aesthetics of Self-Diminution: Christian Iconography and Paradise Lost." In *"Eyes Fast Fixt": Current Perspective in Milton Methodology,* a special edition of *Milton Studies* 7 (1975).

Laing, R. D. *Knots.* New York: Pantheon, 1970.

Levin, Carole. *The Heart and Stomach of a King: Elizabeth I and the Politics of Sex and Power.* Philadelphia: University of Pennsylvania Press, 1994.

Levin, Richard. "Unthinkable Thoughts in the New Historicizing of English Renaissance Drama." *New Literary History* 21 (spring 1990).

Lieb, Michael. *The Dialectics of Creation: Patterns of Birth and Regeneration in "Paradise Lost."* Amherst: University of Massachusetts Press, 1970.

Marcus, Leah S. "Shakespeare's Comic Heroines, Elizabeth I, and the Political Uses of Androgyny." In *Women in the Middle Ages and the Renaissance: Literary and Historical Perspectives,* edited by Mary Beth Rose. Syracuse: Syracuse University Press, 1986.

Marotti, Arthur. *John Donne, Coterie Poet.* Madison: University of Wisconsin Press, 1986.

Maus, Katharine Eisaman. "Proof and Consequences: Inwardness and Its Exposure in the English Renaissance." *Representations* 34 (1991): 29–52.

———. "A Womb of His Own: Male Renaissance Poets in the Female Body." In *Sexuality and Gender in Early Modern Europe: Institutions, Texts, Images,* edited by James Grantham Turner. Cambridge: Cambridge University Press, 1993, 266–88.

———. *Inwardness and Theatre in the English Renaissance.* Chicago: University of Chicago Press, 1995.

McIlwain, Charles H., ed. *The Political Works of James I.* Cambridge: Harvard University Press, 1918.

Michaels, Walter Benn. "The Victims of the New Historicism." *Modern Language Quarterly* 54 (March 1993).

Miller, David Lee. *The Poem's Two Bodies: The Poetics of the 1590 Faerie Queene.* Princeton: Princeton University Press, 1988.

Montrose, Louis Adrian. "'Shaping Fantasies': Figurations of Gender and Power in Elizabethan Culture." In *Representing the English Renaissance,* edited by Stephen Greenblatt. Berkeley: University of California Press, 1988.

————. "The Elizabethan Subject and the Spenserian Text." In *Literary Theory/ Renaissance Texts,* edited by Patricia Parker and David Quint. Baltimore: Johns Hopkins University Press, 1986.

Mulvey, Laura. "You Don't Know What Is Happening, Do You, Mr. Jones." In *Framing Feminism: Art and the Women's Movement 1970–1985,* edited by Roziska Parker and Griselda Pollock. London: Pandora Press, 1987.

Neely, Carol Thomas. "Constructing the Subject: Feminist Practice and the New Renaissance Discourses." *English Literary Renaissance,* 18 (1988).

————. *Broken Nuptials in Shakespeare's Plays.* New Haven: Yale University Press, 1985.

Nichols, John, ed. *The Progresses . . . of James the First. . . .* Vol. 2. New York: Burt Franklin, n.d., but first published in London in 1828).

Niditch, Susan. *Chaos to Cosmos: Studies in Biblical Patterns of Creation.* Chico, Calif.: Scholars Press, 1985.

Nightingale, Jeanne A. "From Mirror to Metamorphosis: Echos of Ovid's Narcissus in Chrétien's *Erec et Enide.*" In *The Mythographic Art: Classical Fable and the Rise of the Vernacular in Early France and England,* edited by Jane Chance. Gainesville: University of Florida Press, 1990.

Nohrnberg, James. *The Analogy of the Faerie Queene.* Princeton: Princeton University Press, 1976.

Nyquist, Mary. "The Genesis of Gendered Subjectivity in the Divorce Tracts and in *Paradise Lost.*" In *Re-Membering Milton,* edited by Mary Nyquist and Margaret W. Ferguson. New York: Methuen, 1987.

————. "Gynesis, Genesis, Exegesis, and the Formation of Milton's Eve." In *Cannibals, Witches, and Divorce: Estranging the Renaissance,* edited by Marjorie Garber. Baltimore: Johns Hopkins University Press, 1987.

Pardes, Ilana *Countertraditions in the Bible: A Feminist Approach.* Cambridge: Harvard University Press, 1992.

Parker, Patricia. "Coming Second: Woman's Place." In *Literary Fat Ladies: Rhetoric, Gender, Property.* New York: Methuen, 1987.

————. "Literary Fat Ladies and the Generation of the Text." In *Literary Fat Ladies: Rhetoric, Gender, Property.* New York: Methuen, 1987.

Parry, Graham. *The Golden Age Restor'd: The Culture of the Stuart Court, 1603–42.* New York: St. Martin's, 1981.

Patterson, Lee. *Chaucer and the Subject of History.* Madison: University of Wisconsin Press, 1991.

Petrarch. *Rime Sparse,* poem 366, lines 110–11. In *Petrarch's Lyric Poems,* translated and edited by Robert M. Durling. Cambridge: Harvard University Press, 1976, 582–83.

Quilligan, Maureen. *Milton's Spenser.* Ithaca: Cornell University Press, 1983.

Reynolds, William D. "Sources, Nature, and Influence of the *Ovidius Moralizatus* of Pierre Bersuire." In *The Mythographic Art: Classical Fable and the Rise of the Vernacular in Early France and England,* edited by Jane Chance. Gainesville: University of Florida Press, 1990.

Roche, Thomas P. Jr. *Petrarch and the English Sonnet Sequences* (New York: AMS Press, 1989).

————. *The Kindly Flame.* Princeton: Princeton University Press, 1964.

Schwartz, Regina M. *Remembering and Repeating: Biblical Creation in "Paradise Lost."* Cambridge: Cambridge University Press, 1988.

The Scottish Queen's Burial at Peterborough (1589) Printed by AJ for Edward Venge. In *An English Garner.* Vol. 8, edited by Edward Arber Archibald Constable, 1896.

Sichi, Edward Jr. "Milton the the *Roman de la Rose:* Adam and Eve at the Fountain of Narcissus." In *Milton and the Middle Ages,* edited by John Mulryan. Pa.: Bucknell University Press, 1982.

Siebers, Tobin. *The Mirror of Medusa.* Berkeley: University of California Press, 1983.

Silberman, Lauren. "The Hermaphrodite and the Metamorphosis of Spenserian Allegory." *English Literary Renaissance* 17 (1987).

———. *Transforming Desire: Erotic Knowledge in Books II and IV of The Faerie Queene.* Berkeley: University of California Press, 1995.

Skura, Meredith Anne. "Understanding the Living and Talking to the Dead: The Historicity of Psychoanalysis." *Modern Language Quarterly* 54 (March 1993).

———. "Discourse and the Individual: The Case of Colonialism in *The Tempest.*" *Shakespeare Quarterly* 40 (1989).

Spitzer, Leo. "Notes on the Empirical and Poetic 'I' in Medieval Authors." *Traditio* 4 (1946).

Stallybrass, Peter. "Editing as Cultural Formation: The Sexing of Shakespeare's Sonnets." *Modern Language Quarterly* 54 (March 1993).

Stein, Arnold. *The Art of Presence: The Poet and "Paradise Lost."* Berkeley: University of California Press, 1977.

Strong, Roy Sir. *The Cult of Elizabeth: Elizabethan Portraiture and Pageantry.* Berkeley: University of California Press, 1977.

———. *Gloriana: The Portraits of Queen Elizabeth I.* German Democratic Republic: Thames and Hudson, 1987.

Suzuki, Mihoko. "'Unfitly yokt together in one term': Vergil and Ovid in *Faerie Queene,* III.ix." *ELR* 17 (1987).

Three Ovidian Tales of Love, translated and edited by Raymond Cormier, Volume 26, Series A, Garland Library of Medieval Literature. New York: Garland Publishing, Inc., 1986.

Trevor-Roper, H. R. *Queen Elizabeth's first Historian: William Camden and the Beginnings of English "Civil" History* (1971).

Trible, Phyllis. *God and the Rhetoric of Sexuality.* Philadelphia: Fortress Press, 1978.

———. *Texts of Terror: Literary-Feminist Readings of Biblical Narratives.* Philadelphia: Fortress Press, 1984.

Turner, James. *The Politics of Landscape.* Cambridge: Harvard University Press, 1979.

Walker, Julia M. "'Here You See Me'": Donne's Autographed Valediction," *John Donne Journal* 4 (1985).

———. "Spenser's Elizabeth Portrait and the Fiction of Dynastic Epic," *Modern Philology* 90, no. 2 (1992): 172–99.

———. "Reading the Tombs of Elizabeth I," *ELR: English Literary Renaissance* (fall 1996) (Forthcoming).

————, ed. *Milton and the Idea of Woman*. Illinois: University of Illinois Press, 1988.

Warner, Marina. *Monuments and Maidens: The Allegory of the Female Form*. New York: Atheneum, 1985.

Woods, Susanne. "Spenser and the Problem of Women's Rule." *Huntington Library Quarterly* 48 (1985).

Woolf, D. R. "Two Elizabeths? James I and the Late Queen's Famous Memory." *Canadian Journal of History* 20 (1985).

Yates, Frances. *Astraea: The Imperial Theme in the Sixteenth Century*. London: Routledge and Kegan Paul, 1975.

Ziolkowski, Theodore. *Disenchanted Images: A Literary Iconology*. Princeton: Princeton University Press, 1977.

Zocca, Louis R. *Elizabethan Narrative Poetry*. New Brunswick: Rutgers University Press, 1950.

Index

Adam: creation narrative of, 180–81; as Narcissus, 174–87; and sense of self, 171–87

Adelman, Janet, 120, 125, 216 n. 16

Alcibiades (pseudo-Platonic dialogue), 66

Antony: and Medusa, 137; and mirrors, 134–37; as Mars, 130; Narcissus, 137; and sense of self, 137–42

Ariosto, Ludovico, 47, 52, 74, 87–88, 97

Aristotle, 12

Bald, R. C., 31

Barnes, Hazel E., 174, 201 n. 1

Beaufort, Lady Margaret, 149–50

Bell, Susan Groag, 30

Bellamy, Elizabeth, 21, 22, 74, 81, 210 n. 13, 211 n. 17

Belsey, Catherine, 24, 119

Benson, Pamela Joseph, 91, 108, 212 n. 27

Berry, Philippa, 59

Boccaccio, 182

Bono, Barbara J., 127, 131, 138, 212 nn. 28, 30, and 32, 215 n. 57

Britomart, 14–15, 19, 26, 52, 54, 61, 67–68, 188–89; and Aeneas, 87–88, 96, 109, 114, 211 n. 24; as Amazon, 77–81, 88–89, 92; and Amoret, 94–96, 107, 215 n. 59; and Bradamante, 87; and Camilla, 79, 91; childbirth, 81; and Clorinda, 79; and Dante the Pilgrim, 87; and Deborah, 91; and Dido, 83, 86–88, 92, 96, 109, 114; and Queen Elizabeth, 69–116, 210; and the Faire Hermaphrodite, 95, 115; fictive childhood of, 76–81; and Gloriana, 85, 111, 115; and House of Busirane, 93–96, 104–5, 107, 112–13, 115, 213 n. 41; illness of, 83–89; and Isis, 103–8, 190,

215 n. 57; in Isis Church, 112–13; in Malacasta's Castle, 77–79; and Marinell, 92; as Medusa figure, 114; and Mercilla, 103, 108, 113–16; and Mercilla/Elizabeth, 74; and Merlin's mirror, 70; and Merlin's prophecy, 88–89, 103, 113–14; mirror vision of, 77–113, 99, 169; as mirroring Arthegall, 98–101; as mother, 99, 106–7; and motherhood, 79–80; and Narcissus, 85; as object of Arthegall's courtship, 101–3; outlawing of female rule, 111–13; and Ovid, 85; and Penelope, 109, 114; and Pentheselia, 91; and Radigund, 101, 109–10, 113, 115, 190; and rape, 80–81, 106; and rescue of Arthegall, 109–13; and role of Glauce, 86–88, 92–93, 100–2; and sense of self, 156, 190–92; sexual identity of, 78–116; subsconscious of, 82–88; and Venus, 103, 12–13, 115; and Venus and Adonis tapestries, 77–79; 211 n. 17; and Venus statue, 215 n. 63

Carey, John, 29

Carravaggio, 52

Cavanagh, Sheila T., 89, 209 n. 10, 215 n. 60

Cecil, Robert, 145

Charles I, 67

Chaucer, Geoffrey, 93, 178, 189

Chrétien de Troyes: *Erec et Enide*, 58

Christian IV, King of Denmark, 150–51

Cixous, Hélène, 117, 118, 123, 204 n. 16

Cleopatra, 14–15, 25, 52, 54, 62–65, 67, 68; and Antony as Venus and Mars, 130; and Dido, 122, 125–26, 156; and Queen Elizabeth, 142–57;